ia

hands-on
science
An Inquiry Approach

Properties of Energy
for Grades K–2

Senior Author

Jennifer Lawson

PORTAGE &
MAIN PRESS

Winnipeg • Manitoba • Canada

Portage & Main Press gratefully acknowledges the financial support of the Province of Manitoba through the Department of Sport, Culture, and Heritage and the Manitoba Book Publishing Tax Credit, and the Government of Canada through the Canada Book Fund (CBF), for our publishing activities.

Hands-On Science for British Columbia
Properties of Energy for Grades K–2
An Inquiry Approach

ISBN: 978-1-55379-798-2
Printed and bound in Canada by Prolific Group

2 3 4 5 6 7 8 9 10 11 12

Download the image banks and reproducibles that accompany this book by going to the Portage & Main Press website at <www.portageandmainpress.com/product/HOSENERGYK2/>. Use the password **LIGHTANDSOUND** to access this free download. For step-by-step instructions to access this download, see the Appendix on page 177.

The publisher has made every effort to acknowledge all sources of photographs used in the image banks and to ensure the authenticity of all Indigenous resources. The publisher would be grateful if any errors or omissions were pointed out, so that they may be corrected.

A special thank-you to the following people for their generous contributions to this project:

Project Consultants:
Faye Brownlie
Kathleen Gregory

Science Consultant:
Rosalind Poon

Early Years Consultants:
Lisa Schwartz
Deidre Sagert

Indigenous Consultant:
Melanie Nelson, Stó:lō and In-SHUCK-ch

Makerspace Contributors:
Joan Badger
Todd Johnson

Curriculum Correlation Consultant:
Susan Atcheson

Book and Cover Design:
Relish New Brand Experience Inc.

Cover Photo:
Adobestock

Illustrations:
ArtPlus Ltd.
26 Projects
Jess Dixon

PORTAGE & MAIN PRESS

www.portageandmainpress.com
Winnipeg, Manitoba
Treaty 1 Territory and homeland of the Métis Nation

FSC
MIX
Paper from responsible sources
FSC® C006215

Contents

Portage & Main Press, 2019 · Hands-On Science for British Columbia · Properties of Energy for Grades K–2 · ISBN: 978-1-55379-798-2

Introduction to *Hands-On Science*

About *Hands-On Science*

Hands-On Science helps develop students' scientific literacy through active inquiry, problem solving, and decision making. With each activity in *Hands-On Science*, students are encouraged to explore, investigate, and ask questions as a means of heightening their own curiosity about the world around them. Students solve problems through firsthand experiences and by observing and examining objects within their environment. In order for young students to develop scientific literacy, concrete experience is of utmost importance—in fact, it is essential.

Format of *Hands-On Science*

The redesigned Science Curriculum for British Columbia (<https://curriculum.gov.bc.ca/>) is based on a **"Know-Do-Understand"** model. The three elements—Content (Know), Curricular Competencies (Do), and Big Ideas (Understand) all work together to support deeper learning. *Hands-On Science* promotes this model through its inquiry-based, student-centred approach. As such, it is structured around the following elements.

The **Big Ideas** are broad concepts introduced in kindergarten and expanded upon in subsequent grades, fostering a deep understanding of science. The Big Ideas form the basis of the *Hands-On Science* modules to address important concepts in biology, chemistry, physics, and earth/space science.

The **Core Competencies** are embedded throughout the curriculum and throughout *Hands-On Science*. These competencies enable students to engage in deeper lifelong learning.

Core Competencies

Thinking	■ knowledge, skills, and processes that enable students to explore problems, weigh alternatives, and arrive at solutions ■ problem solving and making effective decisions, and applying them to real-world contexts
Communication	■ effectively reading, writing, speaking, listening, viewing, and representing ■ using a variety of information sources and digital tools
Personal and Social	■ relates to a student's identity as an individual and as a member of a group or community ■ contributing to the care of themselves, others, and the larger community

The **Learning Standards** are made up of **Curricular Competencies** and **Content**. **Curricular Competencies** are skills, strategies, and processes students develop as they explore science through hands-on activities. Curricular Competencies are addressed further on page 33.

The **Content** of the Science Curriculum for British Columbia and *Hands-On Science* is concept-based and relates directly to the Big Ideas. The Content relies on cross-cutting concepts developed throughout the grade levels, including:

- cause and effect
- change
- cycles
- evolution
- form and function
- interactions
- matter and energy
- order
- patterns
- systems

▶

Portage & Main Press, 2019 · *Hands-On Science for British Columbia · Properties of Energy for Grades K–2* · ISBN: 978-1-55379-798-2

The Multi-Age Approach

Hands-On Science is designed with a multi-age approach to meet the needs of students in kindergarten to grade two (K–2). Each module explores the Big Ideas, Core Competencies, and Learning Standards for K–2. This approach provides teachers and students with flexible, personalized learning opportunities.

Inquiry and Science

Throughout *Hands-On Science*, as students explore science concepts, they are encouraged to ask questions to guide their own learning. The inquiry model is based on five components:

1. formulating questions
2. gathering and organizing information, evidence, or data
3. interpreting and analyzing information, evidence, or data
4. evaluating information, evidence, or data, and drawing conclusions
5. communicating findings

Using this model, teachers facilitate the learning, and students drive the process through inquiry. As such, the approach focuses on students' self-reflections as they ask questions, discover answers, and communicate their understanding. An inquiry approach begins with structured inquiry, moves to guided inquiry and, finally, results in open inquiry.

Structured Inquiry	■ The teacher provides the initial question and structures the procedures to answer it. ■ Students follow the given procedures and draw conclusions to answer the given question.
Guided Inquiry	■ The teacher provides the initial question. ■ Students are involved in designing ways to answer the question and communicate their findings.
Open Inquiry	■ Students formulate their own question(s), design and follow through with a developed procedure, and communicate their findings and results.

Inquiry takes time to foster and requires scaffolding from a structured approach to more open inquiry as students gain skills and experience.

In *Hands-On Science*, the focus of most activities is on guided inquiry, as teachers pose the main question for the lesson, based on the Learning Standards. Students are involved in generating further inquiry questions to personalize learning, but will continue to benefit from guidance and support from the teacher.

> Open inquiry activities are only successful if students are motivated by intrinsic interests and if they are equipped with the skills to conduct their own research study. (Banchi and Bell, 2008)

The Goals of Science Education in British Columbia

Science plays a fundamental role in the lives of Canadians. The Science Curriculum for British Columbia (<https://curriculum.gov.bc.ca/>) states:

> Science provides opportunities for us to better understand our natural world. Through science, we ask questions and seek answers to grow our collective scientific knowledge. We continually revise and refine our knowledge as we acquire new evidence. While maintaining our respect for evidence, we are aware that our scientific knowledge is provisional and is influenced by our culture, values, and ethics. Linking traditional and contemporary First Peoples understandings and current scientific knowledge enables us to make meaningful connections to our everyday lives and the world beyond.

> The Science curriculum takes a place-based approach to science learning. Students will develop place-based knowledge about the area in which they live, learning about and building on First Peoples knowledge and other traditional knowledge of the area. This provides a basis for an intuitive relationship with and respect for the natural world; connections to their ecosystem

▶

Portage & Main Press, 2019 · Hands-On Science for British Columbia · Properties of Energy for Grades K–2 · ISBN: 978-1-55379-798-2

and community; and a sense of relatedness that encourages lifelong harmony with nature.

The Science Curriculum for British Columbia identifies five goals that form the foundation of science education. In keeping with this focus on scientific literacy, these goals are the bases for the lessons in *Hands-On Science*. The Science Curriculum for British Columbia contributes to students' development as educated citizens through the achievement of the following goals. Students are expected to develop:

1. an understanding and appreciation of the nature of science as an evidence-based way of knowing the natural world that yields descriptions and explanations that are continually being improved within the context of our cultural values and ethics

2. place-based knowledge of the natural world and experience in the local area in which they live by accessing and building on existing understandings, including those of First Peoples

3. a solid foundation of conceptual and procedural knowledge in science that they can use to interpret the natural world and apply to new problems, issues, and events; to further learning; and to their lives

4. the habits of mind associated with science—a sustained curiosity; an appreciation for questions; an openness to new ideas and consideration of alternatives; an appreciation of evidence; an awareness of assumptions and a questioning of given information; a healthy, informed skepticism; a seeking of patterns, connections, and understanding; and a consideration of social, ethical, and environmental implications

5. a lifelong interest in science and the attitudes that will make them scientifically literate citizens who bring a scientific perspective, as appropriate, to social, moral, and ethical

decisions and actions in their own lives, culture, and the environment

Hands-On Science Principles

- Effective science education involves hands-on inquiry, problem solving, and decision making.
- The development of Big Ideas, Core Competencies, Curricular Competencies, and Content form the foundation of science education.
- Children have a natural curiosity about science and the world around them. This curiosity must be maintained, fostered, and enhanced through active learning.
- Science activities must be meaningful, worthwhile, and related to real-life experiences.
- The teacher's role is to facilitate activities and encourage critical thinking and reflection. Children learn best by doing, rather than by just listening. Instead of simply telling, the teacher, therefore, should focus on formulating and asking questions, setting the conditions for students to ask their own questions, and helping students to make sense of the events and phenomena they have experienced.
- Science should be taught in conjunction with other school subjects. Themes and topics of study should integrate ideas and skills from several core areas whenever possible.
- Science education should encompass, and draw on, a wide range of educational resources, including literature, nonfiction research material, audio-visual resources, and technology, as well as people and places in the local community.
- Science education should be infused with knowledge and worldviews of Indigenous peoples, as well as other diverse multicultural perspectives.

▶

Portage & Main Press, 2019 · *Hands-On Science for British Columbia · Properties of Energy for Grades K–2* · ISBN: 978-1-55379-798-2

- Science education should emphasize personalized learning. Personalized learning also focuses on enhancing student engagement and providing them with choices to explore and investigate ideas. Personalized learning also encompasses place-based learning, where learning focuses on the local environment.
- Science education is inclusive in nature. Learning opportunities should meet the diverse needs of all students through differentiated instruction and individualized learning experiences.
- Self-assessment is an integral part of science education. Students should be involved in reflecting on their work and setting new goals based on their reflections which, in turn, enables them to take control of their learning.
- Teacher assessment of student learning in science should be designed to focus on performance and understanding, and should be conducted through meaningful assessment techniques implemented throughout each module.

Cultural Connections

To acknowledge and celebrate the cultural diversity represented in Canadian classrooms, it is important to infuse cultural connections into classroom learning experiences. It is essential for teachers to be aware of the cultural makeup of their class and to celebrate these diverse cultures by making connections to curricular outcomes. In the same way, it is important to explore other cultures represented in the community and beyond, to encourage intercultural understanding and harmony. For example, teachers in British Columbia should make connections to the local cultural communities to highlight their contributions to the province. Throughout *Hands-On Science*, suggestions are made for connecting science topics to cultural explorations and activities.

Portage & Main Press, 2019 · Hands-On Science for British Columbia · Properties of Energy for Grades K–2 · ISBN: 978-1-55379-798-2

Indigenous Perspectives and Knowledge

Indigenous peoples are central to the Canadian context, and it is important to infuse Indigenous knowledge into the learning experiences of all students. The intentional integration of Indigenous knowledge in **Hands-On Science** helps to address the Calls to Action of the Truth and Reconciliation Commission of Canada, particularly the call to "integrate Indigenous knowledge and teaching methods into classrooms" (Action 62) and "build student capacity for intercultural understanding, empathy and mutual respect" (Action 63).

Indigenous peoples have depended on the land since time immemorial. The environment shapes the way of life: geography, vegetation, climate, and natural resources of the land determine the methods used to survive. Because they observe the land and its inhabitants, the environment teaches Indigenous peoples to survive. The land continues to shape Indigenous peoples' way of life today because of their ongoing, deep connection with the land. Cultural practices, stories, languages, and knowledge originate from the land.

The traditional territories of the First Peoples cover the entirety of what is now British Columbia. The worldviews of Indigenous peoples and their approaches and contributions to science are now being acknowledged and incorporated into science education. It is also important to recognize the diversity of Indigenous peoples in British Columbia and to focus on both the traditions and contemporary lives of the Indigenous communities in your area. Contact personnel in your school district—Indigenous consultants and/or those responsible for Indigenous education—to find out what resources (e.g., people, books, videos) are available. Many such resources are also featured in **Hands-On Science**.

NOTE: When implementing place-based learning, many opportunities abound to consider Indigenous perspectives and knowledge. Outdoor learning provides an excellent opportunity to identify the importance of place. For example, use a map of the local area to have students identify where the location is in relation to the school. This will help students develop a stronger image of their community and surrounding area.

It is also important to identify on whose traditional territory the school is located, the traditional territory of the location for the place-based learning, as well as the traditional names for both locations. The following map, "First Nations in British Columbia," from Indigenous Services Canada can be used for this purpose: <https://www.aadnc-aandc.gc.ca/DAM/DAM-INTER-BC/STAGING/texte-text/fnmp_1100100021018_eng.pdf>.

Incorporate land acknowledgment once students have learned on whose territory the school and place-based learning location are located. The following example can be used for guidance:
- We would like to acknowledge that we are gathered today on the traditional, ancestral, and unceded territory of the _____ people, in the place traditionally known as _____.

When incorporating Indigenous perspectives, it is important to value Traditional Ecological Knowledge (TEK):

> Traditional Ecological Knowledge, or TEK, is the most popular term to denote the vast local knowledge First Peoples have about the natural world found in their traditional environment… TEK is, above all, local knowledge based in people's relationship to place. It is also holistic, not subject to the segmentation of contemporary science. Knowledge about a specific plant may include understanding its life cycle, its spiritual connections, its relationship to the seasons and with other plants and animals in its ecosystem, as well as its uses and its stories. (*Science First Peoples Teacher Resource Guide*)

Indigenous peoples developed technologies and survived on this land for millennia because of

▶

Portage & Main Press, 2019 · Hands-On Science for British Columbia · Properties of Energy for Grades K–2 · ISBN: 978-1-55379-798-2

their knowledge of the land. Indigenous peoples used observation and experimentation to refine technologies, such as building canoes and longhouses and discovering food-preservation techniques. As such, TEK serves as an invaluable resource for students and teachers of science.

Indigenous peoples do not view their knowledges as "science" but, rather, from a more holistic perspective, as is reflected in this quote from Dr. Jolly, Cherokee, and President of the Science Museum of Minnesota:

> When I weave a basket, I talk about the different dyes and how you make them and how the Oklahoma clay that we put on our baskets doesn't permeate the cell walls, it deposits on the outside. It makes a very nice dye but if you cut through the reed you'll see white still on the inside of the reed, whereas if I make a walnut dye and if I use as my mordent, alum and I use as my acid cider, that walnut dye will permeate the cell walls. You cut through the reed and it's brown through and through. Now what I've just described is the difference between osmosis and dialysis. That Western science calls those scientific terms is really wonderful, but it's not scientific terms if you are a basket weaver. Our culture incorporates so much of what people would call scientific knowledge and ways of thinking so naturally that we haven't parsed it out and put it in a book and said this is our science knowledge versus our weaver's knowledge. When I weave a basket I also tell the stories of the spirituality and not just the ways of which I dyed it. A basket weaver is as much a scientist, as an artist, and a spiritual teacher. We'd never think that you'd separate out just the science part, but you can't weave a basket without knowing the science. (*Science First Peoples Teacher Resource Guide*)

Throughout **Hands-On Science**, there are many opportunities to incorporate culturally appropriate teaching methodologies from an Indigenous worldview. First Peoples Pedagogy indicates that making connections to the local community is central to learning (*Science First Peoples Teacher Resource Guide*). As one example, Elders and Knowledge Keepers offer a wealth of knowledge that can be shared with students. Consider inviting a local Elder or Knowledge Keeper as a guest into the classroom in connection with specific topics being studied (as identified within the given lessons throughout the module). An Elder or Knowledge Keeper can guide a nature walk, share stories and experiences, share traditional technologies, and help students understand Indigenous peoples' perspectives of the natural world. Elders and Knowledge Keepers will provide guidance for learners and opportunities to build bridges between the school and the community.

Here are a few suggestions about working with Elders and Knowledge Keepers:

- Elders and Knowledge Keepers have a deep spirituality that influences every aspect of their lives and teachings. They are recognized because they have earned the respect of their community through wisdom, harmony, and balance in their actions and teachings. (see "Aboriginal Elder Definition" at <https://www.ictinc.ca/blog/aboriginal-elder-definition>).

- Some Indigenous keepers of knowledge are more comfortable being called "Knowledge Keepers" than "Elders." Be sensitive to their preference. In many communities, there are also "Junior Elders" who may also be invited to share their knowledge with students and school staff.

- Elders and Knowledge Keepers may wish to speak about what seems appropriate to them, instead of being directed to talk about something specific. It is important to respect this choice and not be directive about what an Elder or Knowledge Keeper will talk about during their visit.

▶

Portage & Main Press, 2019 · Hands-On Science for British Columbia · Properties of Energy for Grades K–2 · ISBN: 978-1-55379-798-2

- It is important to properly acknowledge any visiting Elders or Knowledge Keepers and their knowledge, as they have traditionally been and are recognized within Indigenous communities as highly esteemed individuals. There are certain protocols that should be followed when inviting an Elder or Knowledge Keeper to support student learning in the classroom or on the land. The *Science First Peoples Teacher Resource Guide* offers guidelines and considerations for this.

It is especially important to connect with Indigenous communities, Elders, and Knowledge Keepers in your local area, and to study local issues related to Indigenous peoples in British Columbia. Consider contacting Indigenous education consultants within your local school district or with the British Columbia Ministry of Education to access referrals. The following link provides a province-wide list of Indigenous contacts: <www.bced.gov.bc.ca/apps/imcl/imclWeb/AB.do>. Also, consider contacting local Indigenous organizations for referrals to Elders and Knowledge Keepers. Such organizations may also be able to offer resources and opportunities for field trips and place-based learning.

NOTE: It is important for educators to understand the significant contribution that Elders, Knowledge Keepers, and Indigenous communities make when they share their traditional knowledge. In their culture of reciprocity, this understanding should extend past giving a gift or honorarium to an Elder or Knowledge Keeper for sharing sacred knowledge. As such, educators should think deeply about reciprocity and what they can do beyond inviting Indigenous guests to their classrooms. Educators can expand their own learning and become connected to Indigenous people by, for example, engaging in Indigenous community events, working with the Education Department of the local Nations, or exploring ways to continue developing the relationship between the local Nations and educators in the district.

The First Nations Education Steering Committee of British Columbia has articulated the following **First Peoples Principles of Learning**:

- Learning ultimately supports the well-being of the self, the family, the community, the land, the spirits, and the ancestors.
- Learning is holistic, reflexive, reflective, experiential, and relational (focused on connectedness, on reciprocal relationships, and a sense of place).
- Learning involves recognizing the consequences of one's actions.
- Learning involves generational roles and responsibilities.
- Learning recognizes the role of Indigenous knowledge.
- Learning is embedded in memory, history, and story.
- Learning involves patience and time.
- Learning requires exploration of one's identity.
- Learning involves recognizing that some knowledge is sacred and only shared with permission and/or in certain situations.

These principles generally reflect First Peoples pedagogy, and have been considered in the development of **Hands-On Science**.

The First People Principles of Learning (FPPL) is a framework for approaching learning, or a worldview on what learning is and how it happens. Teachers are encouraged to find their own meaning in them, explore them with their class, and take them up in a way that is meaningful to them. They are embedded in the new curriculum—the new curriculum was created based on these principles. Teachers can make their own connections to the FPPL through the **Hands-On Science** resource. (Melanie Nelson, February 12, 2018)

▶

Portage & Main Press, 2019 · Hands-On Science for British Columbia · Properties of Energy for Grades K–2 · ISBN: 978-1-55379-798-2

It is also important to note that the *Science First Peoples Teacher Resource Guide* recommends a 7E model for guiding experiential learning activities in science. This model suggests that the following elements are essential to the learning experience:

The 7E Model

Environment	▪ using the local land (place-based learning)
Engage	▪ inspiring curiosity and activating knowledge
Explore	▪ investigating science concepts through hands-on experiences
Elders	▪ connecting local Knowledge Keepers to learning
Explain	▪ describing observations and sharing new knowledge
Elaborate	▪ extending and enhancing learning
Evaluation	▪ providing opportunities for students to demonstrate understanding and skills

These seven elements are strongly evident in the approach used in **Hands-On Science**, as is explained in the following sections.

For more information on First Peoples Pedagogy and First Peoples Principles of Learning, please see the *Science First Peoples Teacher Resource Guide*.

NOTE: Indigenous resources recommended in **Hands-On Science** are considered to be authentic resources, meaning that they reference the Indigenous community they came from, they state the individual who shared the story and gave permission for the story to be used publicly, and the person who originally shared the story is Indigenous. Stories that are works of fiction were written by an Indigenous author. For more information, please see *Authentic First Peoples Resources* at: <www.fnesc.ca/learningfirstpeoples/>.

References

"Aboriginal Contacts—Basic Information." British Columbia Ministry of Education. <www.bced.gov.bc.ca/apps/imcl/imclWeb/AB.do>

Banchi, Heather, and Randi Bell. "The Many Levels of Inquiry." *Science and Children*, 46.2 (2008): 26–29.

British Columbia Ministry of Education. *BC's New Curriculum*. 2016. <https://curriculum.gov.bc.ca/>

"First Nations in British Columbia." Indigenous Services Canada. <https://www.aadnc-aandc.gc.ca/DAM/DAM-INTER-BC/STAGING/texte-text/fnmp_1100100021018_eng.pdf>

"Aboriginal Elder Definition." Indigenous Corporate Training, Inc., 2012. <https://www.ictinc.ca/blog/aboriginal-elder-definition>

"Learning First Peoples Classroom Resources." First Nations Education Steering Committee. <http://www.fnesc.ca/learningfirstpeoples/> (includes *First Peoples Principles of Learning* and *Authentic First Peoples Resources*)

Mack, E., H. Augare, L. Different Cloud-Jones, D. David, H. Quiver Gaddie, R. Honey, & R. Wippert. "Effective practices for creating transformative informal science education programs grounded in Native ways of knowing." *Cultural Studies of Science Education*, 7, 49-70. 2012.

Truth and Reconciliation Commission of Canada: Calls to Action. Truth and Reconciliation Commission of Canada, 2015. <http://www.trc.ca/websites/trcinstitution/File/2015/Findings/Calls_to_Action_English2.pdf>

Science First Peoples Teacher Resource Guide. First Nations Education Steering Committee and First Nations Schools Association, 2016.

Portage & Main Press, 2019 · Hands-On Science for British Columbia · Properties of Energy for Grades K–2 · ISBN: 978-1-55379-798-2

How to Use *Hands-On Science* in Your Classroom

Hands-On Science is organized in a format that makes it easy for teachers to plan and implement. Four modules address the selected topics of study for kindergarten to grade-two classrooms. The modules relate directly to the Big Ideas, Core Competencies, Curricular Competencies, and Content outlined in the Science Curriculum for British Columbia.

Multi-Age Teaching and Learning

Whether working with students in a single-grade classroom from kindergarten to grade two, or working with multi-age classes, teachers will find appropriate learning opportunities in ***Hands-On Science***. The lessons meet the diverse needs of all students through the implementation of differentiated instruction and personalized learning.

The Science Curriculum for British Columbia establishes specific Big Ideas, Curricular Competencies, and Content for each grade level. ***Hands-On Science*** has worked within themes to infuse these Big Ideas, Curricular Competencies, and Content into multi-age modules (see the Curriculum Learning Framework at the beginning of each module). It is therefore important for teachers to work collaboratively with their colleagues across grade levels to determine how best to implement lessons. The Curriculum Learning Frameworks will also be helpful, as each one includes a grade-level focus for specific lessons. This will assist teachers in both single-grade classrooms or multi-age classrooms to identify lessons and topics appropriate to their class.

Differentiated instruction and personalized learning will also ensure the needs of all students are met during science lessons. For example, in any classroom, whether multi-age or single-grade, students will be working at varying levels of literacy. As such, some students may be communicating their learning through drawing, while others may use single words, and yet others write several sentences. The lessons in ***Hands-On Science*** are developed to foster growth and learning at all literacy levels.

The same situation may be evident in terms of numeracy. For example, some students may be using comparative nonstandard measurement, while other students may be capable of working with standard metric measurement units and devices. There is plenty of flexibility in ***Hands-On Science*** to ensure that all students' learning needs can be met through active, student-centred learning.

Module Overview

Each module features an overarching question that fosters inquiry related to the Big Ideas. The module also has its own introduction, which summarizes the general concepts and goals for the module. This introduction provides background information for teachers, planning tips, and lists of vocabulary related to the module, as well as other pertinent information (e.g., how to embed Indigenous perspectives).

Also included at the beginning of each module is a Curriculum Learning Framework, which is based on the Big Ideas and Learning Standards (Curricular Competencies and Content) from the Science Curriculum for British Columbia (https://curriculum.gov.bc.ca/).

The Curriculum Learning Framework identifies the Big Ideas, Sample Guided Inquiry Questions, and Content for each grade level. As well, Content is connected to specific lessons, which are listed below each Content concept. Although specific lessons were intentionally written for grade-level content, much of this content is interconnected. As such, the overarching theme of the module provides a variety of connections to all three grade levels and, therefore, offers many springboards to learning.

▶

Portage & Main Press, 2019 · Hands-On Science for British Columbia · Properties of Energy for Grades K–2 · ISBN: 978-1-55379-798-2

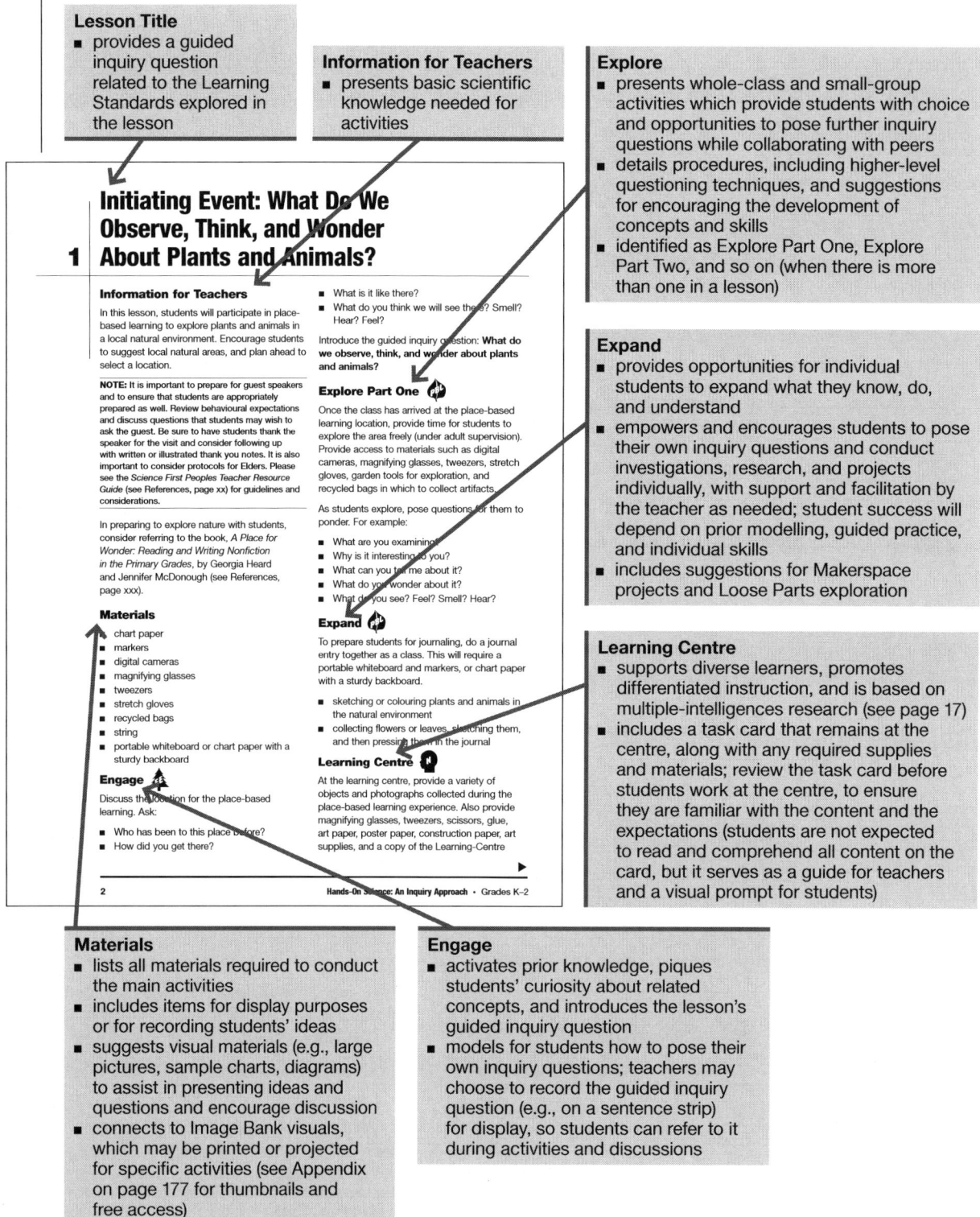

Lesson Title
- provides a guided inquiry question related to the Learning Standards explored in the lesson

Information for Teachers
- presents basic scientific knowledge needed for activities

Explore
- presents whole-class and small-group activities which provide students with choice and opportunities to pose further inquiry questions while collaborating with peers
- details procedures, including higher-level questioning techniques, and suggestions for encouraging the development of concepts and skills
- identified as Explore Part One, Explore Part Two, and so on (when there is more than one in a lesson)

Expand
- provides opportunities for individual students to expand what they know, do, and understand
- empowers and encourages students to pose their own inquiry questions and conduct investigations, research, and projects individually, with support and facilitation by the teacher as needed; student success will depend on prior modelling, guided practice, and individual skills
- includes suggestions for Makerspace projects and Loose Parts exploration

Learning Centre
- supports diverse learners, promotes differentiated instruction, and is based on multiple-intelligences research (see page 17)
- includes a task card that remains at the centre, along with any required supplies and materials; review the task card before students work at the centre, to ensure they are familiar with the content and the expectations (students are not expected to read and comprehend all content on the card, but it serves as a guide for teachers and a visual prompt for students)

---

1 Initiating Event: What Do We Observe, Think, and Wonder About Plants and Animals?

Information for Teachers

In this lesson, students will participate in place-based learning to explore plants and animals in a local natural environment. Encourage students to suggest local natural areas, and plan ahead to select a location.

NOTE: It is important to prepare for guest speakers and to ensure that students are appropriately prepared as well. Review behavioural expectations and discuss questions that students may wish to ask the guest. Be sure to have students thank the speaker for the visit and consider following up with written or illustrated thank you notes. It is also important to consider protocols for Elders. Please see the *Science First Peoples Teacher Resource Guide* (see References, page xx) for guidelines and considerations.

In preparing to explore nature with students, consider referring to the book, *A Place for Wonder: Reading and Writing Nonfiction in the Primary Grades*, by Georgia Heard and Jennifer McDonough (see References, page xxx).

Materials
- chart paper
- markers
- digital cameras
- magnifying glasses
- tweezers
- stretch gloves
- recycled bags
- string
- portable whiteboard or chart paper with a sturdy backboard

Engage

Discuss the location for the place-based learning. Ask:
- Who has been to this place before?
- How did you get there?

- What is it like there?
- What do you think we will see there? Smell? Hear? Feel?

Introduce the guided inquiry question: **What do we observe, think, and wonder about plants and animals?**

Explore Part One

Once the class has arrived at the place-based learning location, provide time for students to explore the area freely (under adult supervision). Provide access to materials such as digital cameras, magnifying glasses, tweezers, stretch gloves, garden tools for exploration, and recycled bags in which to collect artifacts.

As students explore, pose questions for them to ponder. For example:
- What are you examining?
- Why is it interesting to you?
- What can you tell me about it?
- What do you wonder about it?
- What do you see? Feel? Smell? Hear?

Expand

To prepare students for journaling, do a journal entry together as a class. This will require a portable whiteboard and markers, or chart paper with a sturdy backboard.

- sketching or colouring plants and animals in the natural environment
- collecting flowers or leaves, sketching them, and then pressing them in the journal

Learning Centre

At the learning centre, provide a variety of objects and photographs collected during the place-based learning experience. Also provide magnifying glasses, tweezers, scissors, glue, art paper, poster paper, construction paper, art supplies, and a copy of the Learning-Centre

▶

Materials
- lists all materials required to conduct the main activities
- includes items for display purposes or for recording students' ideas
- suggests visual materials (e.g., large pictures, sample charts, diagrams) to assist in presenting ideas and questions and encourage discussion
- connects to Image Bank visuals, which may be printed or projected for specific activities (see Appendix on page 177 for thumbnails and free access)

Engage
- activates prior knowledge, piques students' curiosity about related concepts, and introduces the lesson's guided inquiry question
- models for students how to pose their own inquiry questions; teachers may choose to record the guided inquiry question (e.g., on a sentence strip) for display, so students can refer to it during activities and discussions

Portage & Main Press, 2019 · Hands-On Science for British Columbia · Properties of Energy for Grades K–2 · ISBN: 978-1-55379-798-2

Reproducibles
- may be used to guide activities or record data
- may also serve as a template for designing and constructing graphic organizers
- included as thumbnails in the lessons
- provided as full-sized, printable version on the Portage & Main website (see Appendix for URL and password)

Enhance
- enriches and elaborates on the Big Idea, Core Competencies, and Learning Standards with optional activities
- encourages active participation and learning through Family Connections

Embed Part One
- provides students with opportunities to participate in a Talking Circle (see page 16) to demonstrate their learning through consolidation and reflection
- allows for synthesis and application of inquiry and new ideas
- reviews main ideas of the lesson, focusing on the Big Idea, Core Competencies, and Learning Standards
- reviews guided inquiry question so students can share their knowledge, provide examples, and ask further inquiry questions

Embed Part Two
- embeds learning by adding to graphic organizers; having students record, describe, and illustrate new vocabulary; and adding new vocabulary to the word wall throughout the module or even all year
- provides opportunity to reflect the cultural diversity of the classroom and the community by including new terminology in languages other than English, including Indigenous languages
- explores Core Competencies with students to foster student self-assessment of how these skills were used throughout the lesson

Assessment
- provides suggestions for authentic assessment
- includes student self-assessment, formative assessment, and summative assessment (see pages 29–34)

1

Learning Centre

How Can I Sort Objects From Nature?

1. Look at each object from our nature walk.
2. Describe how it looks, feels, smells, and sounds. (Do not taste it!)
3. Sort the objects into the bins.
4. Describe your sorting rules to others.

Embed Part One: Talking Circle

Revisit the guided inquiry question: **What do we observe, think, and wonder about plants and animals?** Have students share their experiences and knowledge, provide examples, and ask further inquiry questions.

Embed Part Two

- Focus on students' use of the Core Competencies. Have students reflect on how they used one of the Core Competencies (Thinking, Communicating, or Personal and Social skills) during the various lesson activities. Project one of the CORE COMPETENCY DISCUSSION PROMPTS templates (page xx–xx), and use it to inspire group reflection. Referring to the template, choose one or two "I Can" statements on which to focus. Then, have students use the "I Can" statements to provide evidence for how

they demonstrated that competency. Ask questions directly related to that competency to inspire discussion. For example:

- Where did you get your ideas for your place-based journal entry today? (Creative Thinking)

Have students reflect orally, encouraging participation, questions, and the sharing of evidence (See page xx in the introduction for more information on these templates).

As part of this process, students can also set goals. Ask:

- What would you do differently next time and why?
- How will you know if you are successful in meeting your goal?

NOTE: Use the same prompts from these templates over time to see how thinking changes with different activities.

Enhance

- **Family Connection:** Provide students with the following sentence starter:
  - A favourite place for us to visit outside is_____.

  Have students take home the sentence starter to complete. Family members can help the student draw and write about this topic.

Student Self-Assessment (E)
Have students complete the COOPERATIVE SKILLS SELF-ASSESSMENT template, on page xx, to reflect on their success working with others, as they share and compare ideas.

Living Things   3

Portage & Main Press, 2019 · Hands-On Science for British Columbia · Properties of Energy for Grades K–2 · ISBN: 978-1-55379-798-2

The Curricular Competencies Correlation Chart at the beginning of each module provides details on how students' Curricular Competencies are developed through scientific inquiry. The chart outlines the skills, strategies, and processes that students use in the module and identifies the specific lessons in which these Curricular Competencies are the focus. The Curricular Competencies are developed in various ways over time, and therefore are addressed in multiple lessons throughout **Hands-On Science** modules.

Each module includes a list of related resources for students (books, websites, and online videos).

Each module is organized into lessons based on the Learning Standards. The first lesson in each module provides an initiating event, using an Observe-Think-Wonder strategy. Real-life explorations, often within the local environment, provide opportunity for place-based learning, which is discussed in more detail on page 18.

The second lesson in each module explores storytelling as it relates to the inquiry topics. This lesson includes an emphasis on Indigenous stories, children's literature, and nonfiction texts, while providing opportunities for students to engage in activities that focus on literacy and creative storytelling.

The last lesson in each module provides an opportunity for personalized learning through individualized inquiry, as students explore what more they would like to know, do, and understand about the module's Big Ideas.

Talking Circles

Talking Circles originated with First Nations leaders as a process to encourage dialogue, respect, and the co-construction of ideas. The following process is generally used in a Talking Circle:

- the group forms a complete circle
- one person holds an object such as a stick, feather, shell, or stone
- only the person holding the stick talks, while the rest listen
- the stick is passed around in a clockwise direction
- each person talks until they are finished, being respectful of time
- the Talking Circle is complete when everyone has had a chance to speak
- a person may pass the stick without speaking, if they choose

See <www.firstnationspedagogy.ca/circletalks. html> for more information. Also consider inviting a local Elder or Knowledge Keeper to share with the class the process of a Talking Circle.

Portage & Main Press, 2019 · Hands-On Science for British Columbia · Properties of Energy for Grades K–2 · ISBN: 978-1-55379-798-2

▶

Multiple Intelligences Learning Centres

Learning centres in **Hands-On Science** focus on a different multiple intelligence to provide opportunities for students to use areas of strength and also to expose them to new ways of learning.

Teachers are encouraged to explore the topic of multiple intelligences with their students and to have students self-reflect to identify ways they learn best, and ways that are challenging for them. Guidelines for this process are included in *Teaching to Diversity* by Jennifer Katz (see References, page 21).

Multiple Intelligence		These learners…
Verbal-Linguistic		…think in words and enjoy reading, writing, word puzzles, and oral storytelling.
Logical-Mathematical		…think by reasoning and enjoy problem solving, puzzles, and working with data.
Visual-Spatial		…think in visual pictures and enjoy drawing and creating visual designs.
Bodily-Kinesthetic		…think by using their physical bodies and enjoy movement, sports, dance, and hands-on activities.
Musical-Rhythmic		…think in melodies and rhythms and enjoy singing, listening to music, and creating music.
Interpersonal		…think by talking to others about their ideas and enjoy group work, planning social events, and taking a leadership role with friends or classmates.
Intrapersonal		…think within themselves and enjoy quietly thinking, reflecting, and working individually.
Naturalistic		…learn by classifying objects and events and enjoy anything to do with nature and scientific exploration of natural phenomena.
Existential		…learn by probing deep philosophical questions and enjoy examining the bigger picture as to why ideas are important.

Portage & Main Press, 2019 · Hands-On Science for British Columbia · Properties of Energy for Grades K–2 · ISBN: 978-1-55379-798-2

▶

Icons

To provide a clear indication of important features of **Hands-On Science**, the following icons are used throughout lessons:

Place-Based Learning	Place-based learning focuses on the local environment and community. It is important for students to explore the local area in order to build personalized and contextual knowledge.
	Place-based learning:
	■ emphasizes exploring the natural environment, replacing classroom walls with the natural land
	■ offers firsthand opportunities to observe, explore, and investigate the land, waters, organisms, and atmosphere of the local region
	■ promotes a healthy interplay between society and nature
	■ helps students envision a world where there is meaningful appreciation and respect for our natural environment—an environment that sustains all life
	Many lessons in **Hands-On Science** incorporate place-based learning activities, whether it be a casual walk around the neighbourhood to examine trees or a more involved exploration of local waterways.
Applied Design, Skills, and Technologies	Throughout **Hands-On Science**, students have opportunities to use applied design, skills, and technologies to plan and construct objects. For example, in *Living Things for Grades K–2*, students design and construct models of an animal's environment to show how the animal meets its basic needs.
	Using applied design skills and technology, students seek solutions to practical problems through research and experimentation. There are specific steps:
	1. Identify a need. Recognize practical problems and the need to solve them.
	2. Create a plan. Seek alternate solutions to a given problem, create a plan based on a chosen solution, and record the plan through writing and labelled diagrams.
	3. Develop a product or prototype. Construct an object that solves the given problem, and use predetermined criteria to test the product.
	4. Communicate the results. Identify and make improvements to the product, and explain the changes.
Ecology and the Environment	**Hands-On Science** provides numerous opportunities for students to investigate issues related to ecology, the environment, and sustainable development. The meaning of sustainability can be clarified by asking students: "Is there enough for everyone, forever?" These topics also connect to Indigenous worldviews about respecting and caring for the Earth.
Technology	Digital learning, or information and communication technology (ICT), is an important component of any classroom. As such, technological supports available in schools—digital cameras, computers/tablets, interactive whiteboards (IWB), projectors, document cameras, audio-recording devices, calculators—can be used with and by students to enhance their learning experiences.
Classroom Safety	When there are safety concerns, teachers may decide to demonstrate an activity, while still encouraging as much student interaction as possible. The nature of science and scientific experimentation means that safety concerns do arise from time to time.

▶

Portage & Main Press, 2019 · *Hands-On Science for British Columbia* · *Properties of Energy for Grades K–2* · ISBN: 978-1-55379-798-2

Makerspaces

To foster open inquiry and promote personalized learning, each module of **Hands-On Science** suggests a Makerspace as part of the Expand section. A Makerspace is a creative do-it-yourself environment, where participants pose questions, share ideas, and explore hands-on projects. In the school setting, a Makerspace is usually cross-curricular and should allow for inquiry, discovery, and innovation. Sometimes, the Makerspace is housed in a common area, such as the library, which means it is a space used by the whole school community. A classroom Makerspace is usually designed as a centre where students create do-it-yourself projects, emphasizing personalized learning, while collaborating with others on cross-curricular ideas. It is important to remember learning is not directed here. Rather, simply create conditions for learning to happen.

There is no list of required equipment that defines a Makerspace; however, the centre may evolve to foster inquiry within a specific topic. Students are given the opportunity to work with a variety of age-appropriate tools, as well as with everyday, arts-and-crafts, and recycled materials. Materials to consider at Makerspaces include:

- general supplies (e.g., graph or grid paper for planning and designing, pencils, markers, paper, cardstock, cardboard, scissors, masking tape, duct tape, glue, rulers, metre sticks, tape measures, elastic bands, string, Plasticine, modelling clay, fabric/cloth, straws, pipe cleaners, aluminum foil)
- recycled materials (e.g., various sizes of boxes, cardboard rolls, milk cartons, plastic bottles, spools, plastic lids)
- art supplies (e.g., paper, paint, markers, chalk, pastels, crayons, pencil crayons, beads, sequins, foam shapes, yarn, glass beads)
- building materials (e.g., sticks, wooden blocks, wooden dowels, toothpicks, craft sticks, balsa wood)
- age-appropriate tools (e.g., hammers, nails, screwdrivers, screws)
- natural objects (e.g., rocks, shells, feathers, seeds, wood slices, sticks)
- commercial products (e.g., LEGO, LEGO Story Starter, WeDo, MakeDo, Meccano, Plus-Plus, K'Nex, KEVA Planks, Dominoes, Wedgits)
- technology (e.g., Green Screen, iPads, coding/programming [Beebots, Code-a Pillar], apps such as Hopscotch, Tynker, Scratch Jr., Tickle)
- topic-based literature to inspire projects
- reference materials (e.g., books, videos, websites, visual images)

Work with students to develop a collaborative culture in which they tinker, invent, and improve on their creations. Ask students for ideas on how to stock the Makerspace, based on their project ideas, and then work collaboratively to acquire these supplies. The internet may also provide ideas for projects and materials.

Set up a recycling box/bin at the Makerspace for paper, cardboard, clean plastics, and other materials students can use for their creations. Stress to students that Makerspaces can help reuse many items destined for a landfill. Discuss which items can/should be placed in this bin.

Some things to consider when planning and developing a Makerspace are:

- Always address safety concerns, ensuring materials, equipment, and tools are safe for student use. Include safety gloves and goggles, as appropriate. Engage students in a discussion about safety and respect at the Makerspace before beginning each module. Consider sharp objects, small parts, and other potential hazards for students of

▶

Portage & Main Press, 2019 · Hands-On Science for British Columbia · Properties of Energy for Grades K–2 · ISBN: 978-1-55379-798-2

all ages and abilities who will have access to the Makerspace. At this age, this exploration needs to be supervised.

- Consider space and storage needs. Mobile carts and/or bins are handy for storing raw materials and tools.

- Work with students to write a letter to parents/guardians, explaining the purpose of the Makerspace, and asking for donations of materials.

In **Hands-On Science**, each module includes a variety of suggestions for Makerspace materials, equipment, possible challenges, and literature links related to the Big Ideas being explored.

The Makerspace process is intended for solving design problems, so it is helpful to have visuals at the Makerspace to encourage innovation, creativity, and the use of Applied Design, Skills, and Technologies (see page 18). In addition, although individual inquiry is encouraged, the Makerspace process is often collaborative in nature. Therefore, it is important to focus on skills related to working with others (see the Cooperative Skills Assessment templates on pages 49 and 51).

Before students begin working at a Makerspace, review Applied Design, Skills, and Technologies and collaborative skills with students. As a class, co-construct criteria for each skill, record on chart paper, and display at the Makerspace. Or, challenge students to create posters for the Makerspace that convey what Applied Design, Skills, and Technologies and collaboration look like. Refer to these visual prompts before, during, and after students work at the centre, as a means of guiding and assessing the process.

As students create, photograph their creations to share with the class, and discuss the unique properties of their designs. Model appropriate digital citizenship with students by asking their permission to photograph and share

their creations. Facilitate regular debriefing sessions as a class, after students have spent time at the Makerspace. Consider focusing this discussion on the Core Competencies (Thinking, Communication, and Personal and Social Skills) as an anchor for reflective practice.

The nature of a Makerspace is such that it provides an excellent venue for personalized learning. As students pose their own inquiry questions, they may choose to use the Makerspace to explore that question further.

Loose Parts

Closely related to the open inquiry fostered by the Makerspace, the theory of Loose Parts was first proposed back in the 1970s by architect Simon Nicholson. He believed it is the Loose Parts in our environment that empower our creativity. The theory has begun to influence early years educators intent on offering students opportunities to play freely with objects and materials, and to pose their own questions and investigations. Loose Parts include anything natural or synthetic (e.g., beads, buttons, fabric, washers and nuts, cardboard rolls, pom poms, acorns, leaves) that students can move, control, and manipulate. Loose Parts promote open-ended thinking that leads to problem solving, curiosity, and creativity. Play and learning possibilities are endless, as there is no single outcome that is achieved. Instead, Loose Parts offer opportunities for students to consider a wide range of possibilities and ideas.

When appropriate, provide provocations (questions to inspire play) that offer an entry point for a Loose Parts activity. As an example, while studying living things, teachers may provide bins of stones, twigs, bark, shells, and seed pods with the provocation, "How many different ways can you sort the objects?" Students may begin with such a sorting task, but expand to build structures, compare and

▶

Portage & Main Press, 2019 · Hands-On Science for British Columbia · Properties of Energy for Grades K–2 · ISBN: 978-1-55379-798-2

measure, or examine patterns on the various objects.

Throughout **Hands-On Science**, Loose Parts are used to engage students and as an opportunity to expand investigations, generate their own inquiry questions, and personalize learning. Suggestions for Loose Parts exploration are included in the Expand section of lessons. For more information about Loose Parts, see *Loose Parts: Inspiring Play in Young Children* by Lisa Daly and Miriam Beloglovsky and *Loose Parts: A Start-Up Guide* by Sally Haughey and Nicole Hill.

References

British Columbia Ministry of Education. *BC's New Curriculum.* 2016. <https://curriculum.gov.bc.ca/>

Daly, Lisa, and Miriam Beloglovsky. *Loose Parts: Inspiring Play in Young Children*. Redleaf Press, 2014.

Haughey, Sally, and Nicole Hill. *Loose Parts: A Start-Up Guide*. Fairy Dust Teaching, 2017.

Katz, Jennifer. *Teaching to Diversity*. Winnipeg, MB: Portage & Main Press, 2012.

"Talking Circles." *First Nations Pedagogy Online.* <www.firstnationspedagogy.ca/circletalks.html>

Portage & Main Press, 2019 · Hands-On Science for British Columbia · Properties of Energy for Grades K–2 · ISBN: 978-1-55379-798-2

Curricular Competencies: How to Infuse Scientific Inquiry Skills and Processes Into Lessons

Hands-On Science is based on a scientific inquiry approach. While participating in the activities of *Hands-On Science*, students use a variety of scientific inquiry skills and processes as they answer questions, solve problems, and make decisions. These skills and processes are not unique to science, but they are integral to students' acquisition of scientific literacy. At the kindergarten to grade-two level, these include:

QP	questioning and predicting
PC	planning and conducting
PA	processing and analyzing data and information
AI	applying and innovating
C	communicating
E	evaluating

The icons above are used to link assessment suggestions to Curricular Competencies (see page 33 for more information).

Use the following guidelines to encourage the development of students' skills and processes in specific areas.

Observing

Students learn to perceive characteristics and changes through the use of all five senses. Encourage students to safely use sight, smell, touch, hearing, and taste to gain information about objects and events. Observations may be qualitative (e.g., texture, colour), quantitative (e.g., size, number), or both.

Observing includes:

- gaining information through the senses
- identifying similarities and differences, and making comparisons

Encourage students to communicate their observations in a variety of ways, including orally, in writing, by sketching labelled diagrams, and by capturing evidence digitally (e.g., with a digital camera).

Questioning

Generating thoughtful inquiry questions is an essential skill for students when participating in inquiry-based learning. Encourage students to be curious and to extend their questions beyond those posed to them.

Students should learn to formulate a specific question to investigate, one that can be answered through experimentation. This skill takes time to develop with young learners. Be patient, and provide the appropriate scaffolds as needed. Then students can create, from a variety of possible methods, a plan to find answers to the questions they pose.

Exploring

Students need ample opportunity to manipulate materials and equipment in order to discover and learn new ideas and concepts. During exploration, encourage students to use all of their senses and observation skills.

Oral discussion is an integral component of exploration; it allows students to communicate their discoveries. At a deeper level, discussion also allows students to make meaning by discussing inconsistencies and by comparing/contrasting their observations with others. This

▶

Portage & Main Press, 2019 · Hands-On Science for British Columbia · Properties of Energy for Grades K–2 · ISBN: 978-1-55379-798-2

is the constructivist model of learning, which is essential in inquiry-based learning. It is also essential to document the learning that is taking place for each child. This can be done through anecdotal observation records, photographs, videos, and interviews.

Classifying

Classification is used to group or sort objects and events, and is based on observable properties. For example, objects can be classified into groups according to colour, shape, or size. Two strategies for sorting include sorting mats and Venn diagrams. Sorting mats show distinct groups, while Venn diagrams intersect to show similar characteristics among sets.

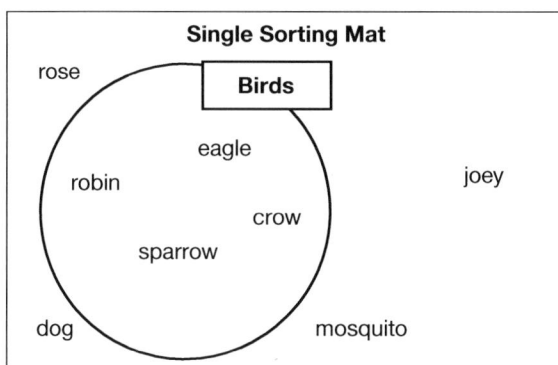

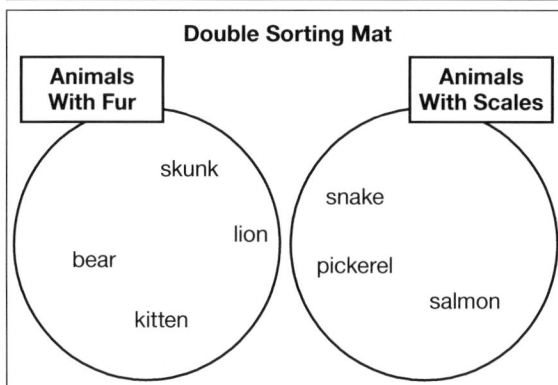

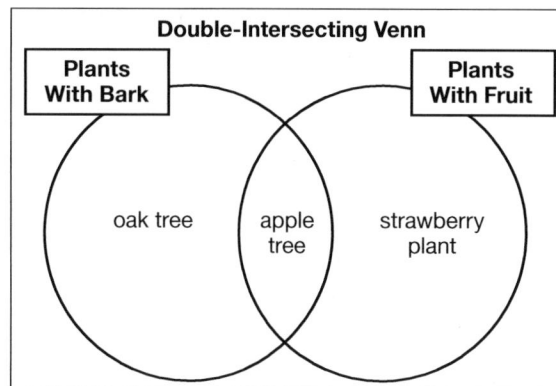

Single Sorting Mat

rose

Birds

eagle

robin

joey

crow

sparrow

dog

mosquito

Double Sorting Mat

Animals With Fur

skunk

lion

bear

Animals With Scales

snake

pickerel

salmon

kitten

Double-Intersecting Venn

Plants With Bark

Plants With Fruit

oak tree

apple tree

strawberry plant

Measuring

Measuring is the process of discovering the dimensions or the quantity of objects or events and, at the kindergarten to grade-one level, usually involves comparing and ordering objects by length, area, volume, and mass. Measuring activities first involve the use of nonstandard units of measure (e.g., interlocking cubes, paper clips) to determine length. At the kindergarten to grade-one level, students generally use only nonstandard units to make simple measurements, as they build understanding of how to observe, compare, and communicate dimensions and quantity. This is a critical preface to measuring with standard units. By grade two, and/or in cases where students have demonstrated competence with nonstandard measurement, students may be introduced to standard units (e.g., centimetres, metres, grams, kilograms) and the use of measuring devices (e.g., metre sticks, tape measures, spring scales, calibrated beakers).

An essential skill of measurement is estimating. Encourage students to estimate before they measure, whether in nonstandard or standard units. Estimation gives students opportunities to take risks, use background knowledge, and enhance their measuring skills by comparing estimates and actual results.

▶

Portage & Main Press, 2019 · Hands-On Science for British Columbia · Properties of Energy for Grades K–2 · ISBN: 978-1-55379-798-2

Communicating, Analyzing, and Interpreting

In science, communication is achieved through diagrams, graphs, charts, maps, models, and symbols, as well as with written and spoken languages. At the kindergarten to grade-two level, communicating includes:

- viewing images
- making labelled diagrams*
- journaling
- reading and interpreting data from simple tables and charts
- making tables and charts
- reading and interpreting data from pictographs
- making pictographs
- making models
- using oral languages
- sequencing and grouping events, objects, and data according to attributes

*NOTE: Depending on students' literacy skills, they may label diagrams with letters and words. Model this to show that a scientific diagram includes accurate illustrations, labels, and sometimes measurements.

Journaling is an important strategy that offers students an opportunity to communicate their ideas, understandings, and questions through emergent writing and illustrating. A journal can be used to summarize activities, share new knowledge, or record observations.

A journal is especially useful during place-based learning experiences. Scientists, such as Charles Darwin, a naturalist, and Rachel Carson, a marine biologist and conservationist, used this strategy for recording observations. The **place-based journal** encourages students to slow down, pay attention to the world around them, heighten their senses, observe more accurately, and reflect on experiences (Bell,

2017). See About This Module, page 60, for more information.

Other forms of communication in science include reading and interpreting charts and graphs. When presenting students with charts and graphs, or when students make their own as part of a specific activity, there are guidelines that should be followed:

- A **pictograph** has a title and information on one axis that denotes the items being compared (note that the first letter of each word on both the title and the axis text is capitalized). There is generally no graduated scale or heading for the axis representing numerical values.

Favourite Dessert				
		Ice Cream		
		Ice Cream		
	Pie	Ice Cream		
Cake	Pie	Ice Cream		
Cake	Pie	Ice Cream		

- A **tally chart** is a means of recording data as an organized count. The count is grouped in fives for ease of determining the total by counting by fives.

Favourite Sport		
Sport	**Tally**	**Total**
baseball	⊞		6
hockey	⊞ ⊞	10
soccer	⊞ ⊞ ||	12

▶

Portage & Main Press, 2019 · Hands-On Science for British Columbia · Properties of Energy for Grades K–2 · ISBN: 978-1-55379-798-2

- A **chart (table)** requires an appropriate title, and both columns and rows need specific headings. Again, all titles and headings require capitalization of the first letter of each word, as in the title of a story. In some cases, pictures can be used to make the chart easier for young students to understand. Charts can be made in the form of checklists or can include room for additional written information and data.

Checklist Chart

Which Substances Dissolve in Water?		
Substance	Dissolves in Water	Does Not Dissolve in Water
Beads		√
Sugar	√	
Drink Mix	√	
Rice		√
Pepper		√

Data Chart

Local Snowfall		
Month	2016/2017 Snowfall (cm)	Average Snowfall (cm)
October	7	5
November	9	8
December	23	20
January	29	25
February	16	18
March	11	10

Communicating also involves using the language and terminology of science. Encourage students to use the appropriate vocabulary related to their investigations (e.g., *object, metal, heavy, strong, movement*). The language of science also includes terms such as *predict, infer, estimate, measure, experiment*, and *hypothesize*. Use this vocabulary regularly throughout all activities and encourage students to do the same. In each module, work with students to develop a word wall on which to record terms students have learned. Have students provide visuals, and define the terms in their own words.

Predicting

Predicting refers to the question, "What do you think will happen?" For example, ask students to predict what they think will happen to an inflated balloon that is placed in a basin of water. It is important to provide opportunities for students to make predictions and to feel safe doing so.

Inferring

In a scientific context, inferring refers to deducing why something occurs. For example, ask students to infer why an inflated balloon floats when placed into a basin of water. Again, it is important to encourage students to take risks when making inferences. Instead of explaining scientific phenomena to them, give students opportunities to infer for themselves, using a variety of perspectives, and then build their knowledge base through inquiry and investigation.

Inquiry Through Investigation and Experimentation

When investigations and experiments are conducted in the classroom, planning and recording both the process and the results are essential. The traditional scientific method uses the following format:

- **purpose:** what we want to find out, or a testable question we want to answer
- **hypothesis:** a prediction; what we think will happen, and why
- **materials:** what we used to conduct the experiment or investigation
- **method:** what we did
- **results:** what we observed and measured
- **conclusion:** what we found out
- **application:** how we can use what we learned

▶

Portage & Main Press, 2019 · Hands-On Science for British Columbia · Properties of Energy for Grades K–2 · ISBN: 978-1-55379-798-2

This method of recording investigations may be used in later school years. However, in the early grades, it may be more appropriate to focus on a narrative style of reporting such as:

- what we want to know
- what we think might happen
- what we used
- what we did
- what we observed
- what we found out

A simpler four-question narrative may also be used with any age group. The structure includes the following questions:

- What was I looking for? (Describe the question you were trying to answer, or the hypothesis/prediction you were testing.)
- How did I look for it? (Tell what you did. Include materials and method.)
- What did I find? (Describe observations and data.)
- What does this mean? (Draw conclusions, and consider applications to real life.)

This narrative may be done in a variety of ways: oral discussion as a class, recording findings as a class, having students use drawings, or a combination of these.

Throughout *Hands-On Science*, a variety of methods are used to encourage students to communicate the inquiry process, including those above. Other formats such as concept maps and other graphic organizers are also used.

Inquiry Through Research

In addition to hands-on inquiry, research is another aspect of inquiry that involves finding, organizing, and presenting information related to a specific topic or question. Scientific inquiry involves making observations, exploring, asking questions, and looking for answers to those questions. Even at a young age, students can begin to research topics studied in class if they are provided with support and guidelines.

Accordingly, guided research is a teaching and learning strategy encouraged throughout *Hands-On Science*. Guided research provides an opportunity for students to seek further information about subjects of inquiry, personal interests, or topics of their choice. As such, students are empowered and engaged in the process.

Guided research encourages students and teachers to do the following:

Students	Teachers
<ul><li>ask questions of interest related to a topic being studied by the class</li><li>choose resources</li><li>collect information</li><li>make a plan to present findings</li><li>present research in a variety of ways</li></ul>	<ul><li>provide opportunities for students to ask questions of personal interest</li><li>provide access to resources</li><li>model and support the research process</li><li>offer opportunities for students to present their findings in a variety of ways and to a variety of audiences</li></ul>

In *Hands-On Science*, the approach to inquiry and research is one of gradual release. In order to provide more opportunity for success and independence in conducting research, it is important to scaffold the process. Consider using gradual release of responsibility (Regie Routman, 2008) as a learning model for research:

▶

Portage & Main Press, 2019 · Hands-On Science for British Columbia · Properties of Energy for Grades K–2 · ISBN: 978-1-55379-798-2

I Do It	■ Begin by modeling the process. Select an inquiry question and demonstrate how to choose resources. ■ Use the resources available in the class science library. Also use selected websites appropriate for your students (see Resources for Students at the beginning of each module). ■ Next, demonstrate how to collect information through note taking (jot notes), labelled diagrams, pictures, or photographs. ■ Finally, make a plan to present and display findings for the class.
We Do It	■ Next, have the class choose another inquiry question. ■ Together, choose resources and collect information. ■ Together, make a plan to present findings and display findings for another class or for family/community members.
You Do It	■ Students now choose their own inquiry questions, conduct research, and present findings.

Throughout this gradual release process, the teacher provides substantial support in initial inquiry experiences and, over time, presents students with more and more opportunities for directing their own research.

NOTE: Given that this module of *Hands-On Science* was developed for students in kindergarten to grade two, research needs to be age-appropriate. Collect a variety of resources at early reading levels, including visuals, books, and websites. Students can then access information and record their ideas using pictures, labelled diagrams, and simple texts, such as jot notes. If, for example, a student is researching how an eagle builds a nest, they may examine a variety of pictures, books, websites, and videos, and then create a series of labelled drawings to present their findings.

As students build research skills and progress through the grades, research will increase in sophistication. The guided approach and the

I Do, We Do, You Do model will support students with independent inquiry as they continue to do scientific research in higher grades. For more information about this model (also known as the Optimal Learning Model), see *Teaching Essentials: Expecting the Most and Getting the Best from Every Learner, K-8* by Regie Routman, "Gradual Release of Responsibility: I do, We do, You do" by E. Levy, and "Teaching New Concepts: 'I Do It, We Do It, You Do It' Method" by A. McCoy.

Addressing Students' Early Literacy Needs

The inquiry process involves having students ask questions and conduct investigations and research to answer these questions. At the kindergarten to grade-two level, students will benefit from literacy support while conducting research. Consider having volunteers, student mentors, or educational assistants provide support during these processes to help young students conduct appropriate research and communicate their findings orally or visually. Also consider conducting brief lessons on how to read and glean information from pictures when investigating questions through the inquiry process. As well, students can show their learning through labelled pictures, invented/ temporary spelling, or the use of technology that allows them to record their research orally.

Online Considerations

As our technological world continues to expand at an accelerating rate, and information is increasingly available online, students will turn to the internet more and more to expand their learning. Accordingly, *Hands-On Science* is replete with opportunities for students to use online resources for research and investigation. Discuss online safety protocols with students. Be vigilant in supervising student use of the internet. Similarly, review websites and bookmark those appropriate for student use. ▶

Portage & Main Press, 2019 · Hands-On Science for British Columbia · Properties of Energy for Grades K-2 · ISBN: 978-1-55379-798-2

Portage & Main Press, 2019 · Hands-On Science for British Columbia · Properties of Energy for Grades K–2 · ISBN: 978-1-55379-798-2

Also discuss plagiarism with students: copying information word for word—whether from a book, the internet, or another resource—is wrong. Such information should always be paraphrased in the student's own words, and the source of the information cited. Photographs, drawings, figures, and other images found online should also only be used with permission and citation of the source. Alternatively, students can source images for which permission has already been granted, such as through Creative Commons. Creative Commons is a non-profit organization that "promotes and enables the sharing of knowledge and creativity…[and which] produces and maintains a free suite of licensing tools to allow anyone to easily share, reuse, and remix materials with a fair 'some rights reserved' approach to copyright." See <creativecommons.org>.

References

Banchi, Heather, and Randi Bell. "The Many Levels of Inquiry," *Science and Children* 46.2 (2008): 26–29.

Bell, Antonella. *Nature Journaling*. University of Alberta, 2017.

British Columbia Ministry of Education. *BC's New Curriculum.* 2016. <https://curriculum.gov.bc.ca/>

Creative Commons. <creativecommons.org>

Davies, Anne. *Making Classroom Assessment Work* (3rd ed.). Courtenay, BC: Connections Publishing, 2011.

First Nations Schools Association. *Science First Peoples Teacher Resource Guide* (2016).

Fullan, Michael. *Great to Excellent: Launching the Next Stage of Ontario's Education Agenda* (2013).

Levy, E. (2007). Gradual Release of Responsibility: I do, We do, You do. <www.sjboces.org/doc/Gifted/GradualReleaseResponsibilityJan08.pdf>

Katz, Jennifer. *Teaching to Diversity: The Three-Block Model of Universal Design for Learning.* Winnipeg: Portage & Main Press, 2012.

Manitoba Education and Training. *Kindergarten to Grade 4 Science: Manitoba Curriculum Framework of Outcomes*, 1999. (See: <www.edu.gov.mb.ca/>)

McCoy, Antoine (2011, March 4). Teaching New Concepts: "I Do It, We Do It, You Do It" Method. <antoinemccoy.com/teaching-new-concepts>

Ontario Literacy and Numeracy Secretariat. "Inquiry-based Learning," Capacity Building series 32, p. 4 (May 2013).

Routman, Regie. *Teaching Essentials: Expecting the Most and Getting the Best from Every Learner, K–8.* Portsmouth, NH: Heinemann, 2008.

Toulouse, Pamela. *Achieving Aboriginal Student Success.* Winnipeg: Portage & Main Press, 2011.

Truth and Reconciliation Commission of Canada: *Calls to Action*, 2015. <www.trc.ca>

The *Hands-On Science* Assessment Plan

Hands-On Science provides a variety of assessment tools that enable teachers to build a comprehensive and authentic daily assessment plan for students. Based on current research about the value of quality classroom assessment (Davies, 2011), suggestions are provided for authentic assessment, which includes student self-assessment and reporting of Core Competencies.

British Columbia's K–12 Assessment System (see <https://curriculum.gov.bc.ca/assessment-system> and <https://curriculum.gov.bc.ca/classroom-assessment-and-reporting>) states:

> Assessment and curriculum are interconnected. Curriculum sets the learning standards that give focus to classroom instruction and assessment. Assessment involves the wide variety of methods or tools that educators use to identify student learning needs, measure competency acquisition, and evaluate students' progress toward meeting provincial learning standards.

> [British Columbia's] assessment system is being redesigned to align with the new curriculum. Assessment of all forms will support a more flexible, personalized approach to learning and measure deeper, complex thinking. [British Columbia's] educational assessment system strives to support student learning by providing timely, meaningful information on student learning through multiple forms of assessment. The assessment system has three programs:

> 1. Classroom Assessment and Reporting
> 2. Provincial Assessment
> 3. National and International Assessment

> Classroom assessment is an integral part of the instructional process and can serve as a meaningful source of information about student learning. Feedback from ongoing assessment in the classroom can be immediate and personal for a learner and guide the learner to understand their [strengths and challenges] and use the information to set new learning goals.

The primary purpose of assessment is to improve student learning. *Hands-On Science* provides assessment suggestions, rubrics, and templates for use during the teaching/learning process. These assessment suggestions include tasks related to *student self-assessment* of the Core Competencies, as well as *formative assessment* and *summative assessment* by the teacher.

Student self-assessment helps students develop their capacity to set their own goals, monitor their own progress, determine their next steps in learning, and reflect on their learning in relation to the three Core Competencies—Thinking, Communication, and Social and Personal.

Formative assessment requires that teachers provide students with descriptive feedback and coaching for improvement in relation to the Learning Standards (Curricular Competencies and Content).

Summative Assessment is comprehensive in nature, and is intended to identify student progress in relation to the Learning Standards (Curricular Competencies and Content).

Both summative and formative assessments are an integral part of a balanced classroom assessment plan. Then, when student self-assessment is infused in this assessment plan, a clearer picture emerges of where a student is in relation to the Core Competencies and Learning Standards.

Student Self-Assessment

It is important for students to reflect on their own learning. For this purpose, a variety of assessment templates are provided in *Hands-On Science*. Depending on their literacy levels, students may complete self-assessments in various ways. For example, the templates may be used as guides for oral conferences between teacher and student, or an adult may act as a

▶

Portage & Main Press, 2019 · Hands-On Science for British Columbia · Properties of Energy for Grades K–2 · ISBN: 978-1-55379-798-2

scribe for the student, recording their responses. As well, students can show their learning through labelled pictures, invented/temporary spelling, and writing, with guidance and support as needed.

For the purpose of self-assessment, find a STUDENT SELF-ASSESSMENT template, on page 35, as well as a STUDENT REFLECTIONS template on page 36.

The SCIENCE JOURNAL, on page 37, will encourage students to reflect on their own learning. Print several copies for each student, cut the pages in half, add a cover, and bind the pages together. Students can then create their own title pages for their journals. For variety, have students use the blank reverse side of each page for other reflections, such as drawing or writing about:

- new challenges
- favourite activities
- real-life experiences
- new terminology
- new places explored during investigations

Students may also journal in other ways, such as by adding notes to their portfolios, or by keeping online science blogs or journals to record successes, challenges, and next steps related to learning goals.

NOTE: This SCIENCE JOURNAL template is provided as a suggestion, but journals can also be made from simple notebooks or recycled paper.

Another component of student self-assessment involves opportunities for students to reflect on their use of the Core Competencies. During each lesson, spend time discussing and reflecting on one of the Core Competencies. The intent here is to enhance students' ability to recognize how and when they use the competencies during the inquiry process. Reflection on Core Competencies is ongoing, since students' strengths and challenges in using the Core

Competencies may differ in various contexts and activities.

For the purpose of this assessment process, project a copy of one of the five CORE COMPETENCY DISCUSSION PROMPTS templates on page 38–42 (one each on Communication, Creative Thinking, Critical Thinking, Positive Personal and Cultural Identity, and Personal Awareness and Responsibility). Choose one or two "I Can" statements on which to focus discussion. Students then use the "I Can" statements to provide evidence of how they demonstrated that competency (model this process for the class). For example, a student might say:

- I can ask and answer questions. I know this because I asked lots of questions about the Sun. I also answered questions about how to stay safe by wearing sunscreen, sunglasses, and hats.

The intent is to provide an opportunity for group discussion and modelling, while encouraging individual students to reflect on their use of the Core Competencies. Choose the Core Competencies and facets that are most appropriate for each lesson. There is lots of room for differentiating based on the strengths and needs of the class.

NOTE: Although the facets are identified on these templates, they are featured only for teacher reference. Students are not expected to refer to the facets during reflective discussion.

To inspire students to further reflect on each Core Competency, use a variety of self-reflection prompts. For this purpose, use the CORE COMPETENCY SELF-REFLECTION FRAMES on pages 43–47 throughout the learning process. There are five frames provided to address the Core Competencies, one each on Communication, Creative Thinking, Critical Thinking, Positive Personal and Cultural Identity, and Personal Awareness and Responsibility. Conference

▶

Portage & Main Press, 2019 · Hands-On Science for British Columbia · Properties of Energy for Grades K–2 · ISBN: 978-1-55379-798-2

individually with students to support self-reflection, or students may complete prompts using words and pictures.

> **NOTE:** Use the same prompts from these templates over time, to see how thinking changes with different activities.

Another component of student self-assessment utilizes the CORE COMPETENCY STUDENT REFLECTIONS: MODULE SUMMARY template, on page 48. This is completed by students at the end of a module, in order to encourage them to reflect on how their Core Competencies have developed over time. Students' reflections are recorded in the rectangle on the template. Then, the student considers next steps in learning as related to that particular Core Competency. These reflections are recorded on the arrow on the template, again, using words and drawings.

> **NOTE:** It is important to keep in mind that the Core Competencies will only be self-assessed by students, and not directly assessed by teachers. However, teachers may conference with students in order to encourage them to think about and discuss their learning over time.

Students should also be encouraged to reflect on their cooperative group work skills, since these are directly related to Core Competencies, as well as to the skills scientists use as they collaborate in team settings. For this purpose, a COOPERATIVE SKILLS SELF-ASSESSMENT template is on page 49.

Student reflections can also be done in many other ways. For example, students can:

- interview one another
- write an outline or script and make a video
- create a slide show with an audio recording

Formative Assessment

It is important to assess students' understanding before, during, and after a lesson. The information gathered helps determine students' needs in order to plan the next steps in instruction. Students may come into class with misconceptions about science concepts. By identifying what they already know, teachers can help students make connections and address any challenges.

Formative assessment provides opportunities for teachers to document evidence of each student's learning. Along with utilizing evidence gathered from photographs, videos, and digital portfolios, document evidence of learning by using the formative assessment templates provided in *Hands-On Science*.

To assess students as they work, use the formative assessment suggestions provided with many of the activities. While observing and conversing with students, use the ANECDOTAL RECORD template and/or the INDIVIDUAL STUDENT OBSERVATIONS template to record assessment data.

- **Anecdotal Record**: To gain an authentic view of a student's progress, it is critical to record observations during lessons. The ANECDOTAL RECORD template, on page 50, provides a format for recording individual or group observations.
- **Individual Student Observations**: To focus on individual students for a longer period of time, consider using the INDIVIDUAL STUDENT OBSERVATIONS template, on page 51. This template provides more space for comments and is especially useful during conferences, interviews, or individual student performance tasks. It is important to note that not every student has to be observed during the same lesson. Observations can take place over time in order to focus on each student's learning.

Formative assessment also involves the consideration of students' collaborative skills. Always assess a student's individual

▶

Portage & Main Press, 2019 · *Hands-On Science for British Columbia · Properties of Energy for Grades K–2* · ISBN: 978-1-55379-798-2

performance, not the work of a group. Assess how an individual student works within a group. Such skill development includes the ability to use words and actions to encourage other students, contribute to group work, and use strengths and skills to complete a given task (British Columbia Ministry of Education, 2016). For this purpose, use the COOPERATIVE SKILLS TEACHER ASSESSMENT template on page 52. Use this template as a checklist or for anecdotal comments.

Both formative assessment and summative assessment include *performance assessment*. Performance assessment is planned, systematic observation and assessment based on students actually doing a specific science activity. A SAMPLE RUBRIC and a RUBRIC template for teacher use are on pages 54 and 53. For any specific activity, before the work begins, discuss and co-construct with students success criteria for completing the task. This will ensure the success criteria relate to the lesson's learning goals. Record these criteria on the rubric. Use the rubric criteria to assess student performance, using the proficiency scale from the British Columbia Ministry of Education Framework for Classroom Assessment (see References, page 34):

Emerging	The student demonstrates an initial understanding of the concepts and competencies relevant to the expected learning.
Developing	The student demonstrates a partial understanding of the concepts and competencies relevant to the expected learning.
Proficient	The student demonstrates a complete understanding of the concepts and competencies relevant to the expected learning.
Extending	The student demonstrates a sophisticated understanding of the concepts and competencies relevant to the expected learning.

Observe student during the performance task being assessed to determine their level of proficiency on each criterion (see SAMPLE RUBRIC, page 54). Share this data with students to provide descriptive feedback, and to encourage student reflection related to performance task criteria and the level of proficiency.

Summative Assessment

Summative assessment provides a summary of student progress related to the Learning Standards at a particular point in time. It is important to gather a variety of assessment data to draw conclusions about what a student knows, can do, and understands. As such, consider collecting student products, observing processes, and having conversations with students. Only the most recent and consistent evidence should be used.

Summative assessment suggestions are provided with the culminating lesson of each module of **Hands-On Science**. Use the ANECDOTAL RECORD template, found on page 50, the INDIVIDUAL STUDENT OBSERVATIONS template, found on page 51, and the RUBRIC, found on page 53, to record student results.

A student portfolio is another format that can be used for summative assessment. A portfolio is a collection of work that shows evidence of a student's learning. There are many types of portfolios—the showcase portfolio and the progress portfolio are two popular formats. *Showcase portfolios* highlight the best of students' work, with students involved in the selection of pieces and justification for choices. *Progress portfolios* reflect students' progress as their work improves and aim to demonstrate in-depth understanding of the materials over time. Select, with student input, work to include in a science portfolio or in a science section of a multi-subject portfolio. Selections should include

▶

Portage & Main Press, 2019 · Hands-On Science for British Columbia · Properties of Energy for Grades K–2 · ISBN: 978-1-55379-798-2

representative samples of student work in all types of science activities.

Templates are included to organize the portfolio (PORTFOLIO TABLE OF CONTENTS, page 55, and PORTFOLIO ENTRY RECORD, page 56).

Indigenous Perspectives on Assessment

From an Indigenous perspective, assessment is community-based, qualitative, and holistic, and includes input from all the people who influence an individual student's learning—parents, caregivers, Elders, Knowledge Keepers, community members, and educators. An assessment that includes all these perspectives provides a balanced understanding of what represents success for Indigenous students and their families/community. A strong partnership between parents/guardians/communities and school improves student achievement. Be aware that some Indigenous students may feel apprehensive about a formal process of assessment; others may find that Western achievement goals do not fit their worldview.

In *Hands-On Science*, consideration has been given to assessment from an Indigenous perspective. The following suggestions will assist in supporting this perspective:

- Consider learning and assessment in a holistic way, acknowledging that each student will find identity, meaning, and purpose through connections to the community, to the natural world, and to values such as respect and gratitude.

- Incorporate family and community in learning and assessment. Include parents/caregivers, siblings, grandparents, aunts and uncles, and cousins. Also include community members, such as Elders, Knowledge Keepers, daycare staff, babysitters, and coaches. For this purpose, a template is included for FAMILY

AND COMMUNITY CONNECTIONS: ASSESSING TOGETHER, which is found on page 57. After any lesson or module, students can take home a copy of this template to complete with family or community members (with permission). This template can also be completed by students in pairs, to enhance the sense of community in the classroom.

- Have students take home one of their self-assessment templates (STUDENT SELF-ASSESSMENT, STUDENT REFLECTIONS, SCIENCE JOURNAL, CORE COMPETENCY SELF-REFLECTION FRAMES, CORE COMPETENCY STUDENT REFLECTIONS: MODULE SUMMARY, or COOPERATIVE SKILLS SELF-ASSESSMENT) to explain it to a family or community member. These templates can also be shared with a peer to enhance the sense of community within the school.

Connecting Assessment to Curricular Competencies

Throughout *Hands-On Science*, suggestions are provided for student self-assessment, formative assessment, and summative assessment. Many of these suggestions are linked to the Curricular Competencies, as in the following example that focuses on Communication:

Formative Assessment Ⓒ

- Photograph students as they journal, to collect evidence of learning activities. Be sure to document student thinking after journaling. For example, meet with them individually to have them share their thoughts about the journaling experience and what they recorded in their journal. Use photographs taken as they journal to inspire reflection. Focus on students' ability to express and reflect on personal experiences of place. Use the INDIVIDUAL STUDENT OBSERVATIONS template on page 51 to record interview highlights.

▶

Portage & Main Press, 2019 · *Hands-On Science for British Columbia · Properties of Energy for Grades K–2* · ISBN: 978-1-55379-798-2

This feature of the *Hands-On Science* Assessment Plan supports teachers in making connections between assessment strategies and the Curricular Connections focused upon at the kindergarten to grade-two levels.

Module Assessment Summary

At the end of each module, suggestions are provided for a summary of assessment. This includes:

- Collecting student work in a portfolio, so students can examine and discuss these artifacts of learning during a conference.
- Having students take home a copy of the FAMILY AND COMMUNITY CONNECTIONS: ASSESSING TOGETHER template on page 57 to complete with a family or community member.
- Having students complete the CORE COMPETENCY STUDENT REFLECTIONS: MODULE SUMMARY template, on page 48, to reflect on their use of the Core Competencies throughout the module and to determine next steps in their learning.
- Reviewing assessment templates completed by students and teachers throughout the module.

Important Note to Teachers

It is important to keep in mind that the ideas provided in *Hands-On Science* for student self-assessment, formative assessment, and summative assessment are merely suggestions. Teachers are encouraged to use the assessment strategies presented in a wide variety of ways, and to ensure that they build an effective assessment plan using these assessment ideas, as well as their own valuable experiences as educators.

References

British Columbia Ministry of Education. *A Framework for Classroom Assessment.* <https://curriculum.gov.bc.ca/sites/curriculum.gov.bc.ca/files/pdf/assessment/a-framework-for-classroom-assessment.pdf>

British Columbia Ministry of Education. *B.C. Performance Standards.* <https://www2.gov.bc.ca/gov/content/education-training/k-12/teach/bc-performance-standards>

British Columbia Ministry of Education. *BC's New Curriculum.* 2016. <https://curriculum.gov.bc.ca/>

British Columbia Ministry of Education. *Supporting the Self-Assessment and Reporting of Core Competencies*, 2016 <https://curriculum.gov.bc.ca/sites/curriculum.gov.bc.ca/files/pdf/supporting-self-assessment.pdf>.

Cameron, Caren, and Kathleen Gregory. *Rethinking Letter Grades: A Five-Step Approach for Aligning Letter Grades to Learning Standards.* Winnipeg: Portage & Main Press, 2014.

Davies, Anne. *Making Classroom Assessment Work* (3rd ed.). Courtenay, BC: Connections Publishing, 2011.

Manitoba Education. *Rethinking Classroom Assessment with Purpose in Mind: Assessment for Learning, Assessment as Learning, Assessment of Learning*, 2006.

Ontario Ministry of Education. *Growing Success: Assessment, Evaluation, and Reporting in Ontario Schools*, 2010. <www.edu.gov.on.ca/>.

Toulouse, Pamela. *Achieving Aboriginal Student Success.* Winnipeg: Portage & Main Press, 2011.

Portage & Main Press, 2019 · Hands-On Science for British Columbia · Properties of Energy for Grades K–2 · ISBN: 978-1-55379-798-2

Student Self-Assessment

Looking at My Science Learning

1. **Today in science, I** _____

_____

_____

2. **In science, I learned** _____

_____

_____

3. **I did very well at** _____

_____

_____

4. **One science skill that I am working on is** _____

_____

_____

5. **I would like to learn more about** _____

_____

_____

6. **One thing I like about science is** _____

_____

_____

Note: The student may complete this self-assessment or the teacher can scribe for the student.

Portage & Main Press, 2019 · Hands-On Science for British Columbia · Properties of Energy for Grades K–2 · ISBN: 978-1-55379-798-2

Date: _____   **Name:** _____

Student Reflections

| What I Did | What I Learned |

| Next Steps in My Learning | My Strengths and Challenges |

Portage & Main Press, 2019 · Hands-On Science for British Columbia · Properties of Energy for Grades K–2 · ISBN: 978-1-55379-798-2

Science Journal

Date: _____

Name: _____

Today, I _____
_____
_____

I learned _____
_____
_____

I would like to learn more about _____
_____

Science Journal

Date: _____

Name: _____

Today, I _____
_____
_____

I learned _____
_____
_____

I would like to learn more about _____
_____

Portage & Main Press, 2019 · Hands-On Science for British Columbia · Properties of Energy for Grades K–2 · ISBN: 978-1-55379-798-2

Core Competency Discussion Prompts
Communication

Facet	I Can...
A. **Connect and engage with others (to share and develop ideas)**	■ ask questions ■ answer questions ■ be an active listener (My eyes are on the speaker. I show that I am interested in what they are saying.) ■ see that my classmates and I can sometimes have different ways to do things, see things, and understand things ■ use a calm voice when I disagree with others
B. **Acquire, interpret, and present information (includes inquiries)**	■ understand and share information about a topic that is important to me ■ present information clearly and in an organized way ■ present information and ideas to an audience I may not know
C. **Collaborate to plan, carry out, and review constructions and activities**	■ work with others; I do my share of my group's job ■ take on roles and responsibilities in a group ■ describe ideas ■ explain the ways my group agrees with our ideas
D. **Explain/recount and reflect on experiences and accomplishments**	■ give feedback to my classmates ■ listen to feedback from my classmates ■ use feedback from my classmates to make changes to my ideas ■ share simple experiences and activities and tell something I learned ■ show my learning ■ tell how my learning is connected to my experiences and hard work

Portage & Main Press, 2019 · Hands-On Science for British Columbia · Properties of Energy for Grades K–2 · ISBN: 978-1-55379-798-2

Core Competency Discussion Prompts
Thinking: Critical Thinking

Facet	I Can...
A. **Analyze and critique**	■ show if I like something or not ■ use criteria ■ look at results from different points of view ■ reflect on and evaluate my thinking, products, and actions ■ think about my own beliefs and consider views that do not fit with them
B. **Question and investigate**	■ explore materials and actions ■ ask questions that have more than one answer ■ gather information ■ carefully think about different ways to solve a problem ■ decide if my sources of information are dependable ■ tell the difference between facts and opinions
C. **Develop and design**	■ experiment with different ways of doing things ■ help create criteria for design projects ■ keep track of my progress ■ change my actions to make sure I reach my goal ■ make choices that will help me meet my goals

Portage & Main Press, 2019 · Hands-On Science for British Columbia · Properties of Energy for Grades K–2 · ISBN: 978-1-55379-798-2

Core Competency Discussion Prompts
Thinking: Creative Thinking

Facet	I Can...
A. **Novelty and value**	■ get ideas when I play (My ideas are fun for me and make me happy.) ■ get new ideas or build on other people's ideas, to create new things ■ think of new ideas as I follow my interests ■ think of ideas that are new to my classmates ■ make creative projects in an area that interests me
B. **Generating ideas**	■ get ideas when I use my senses to explore ■ build on others' ideas ■ add new ideas of my own to create new things ■ add new ideas of my own to solve problems ■ learn a lot about something (e.g., by doing research, talking to others, practising), so I can create new ideas ■ calm my mind (e.g., walking away for a while, doing something relaxing, being playful), so I can be more creative ■ have interests that I continue for a long time
C. **Developing ideas**	■ make my ideas work or I change what I am doing ■ usually make my ideas work with materials if I keep playing with them ■ learn and use the skills I need to make my ideas work, and usually succeed, even if it takes a few tries ■ use my experiences for future learning ■ try to develop my ideas over a long period of time

Portage & Main Press, 2019 · Hands-On Science for British Columbia · Properties of Energy for Grades K–2 · ISBN: 978-1-55379-798-2

Core Competency Discussion Prompts
Personal and Social: Positive Personal & Cultural Identity

Facet	I Can...
A. **Relationships and cultural contexts**	■ describe my family ■ describe my community ■ tell about the different groups that I belong to ■ understand that my identity is made up of life experiences, family history, heritage, and peer groups ■ understand that learning is forever, and I will continue to grow as a person
B. **Personal values and choices**	■ tell what is important to me ■ explain my values and how they affect choices I make ■ tell how some important parts of my life have influenced my values ■ understand how my values affect my choices
C. **Personal strengths and abilities**	■ describe my characteristics ■ describe my talents and the things I do well ■ think about the things I do well ■ describe how I am a leader in my community ■ understand that I will continue to develop new strengths and skills to help me meet new challenges

Portage & Main Press, 2019 · Hands-On Science for British Columbia · Properties of Energy for Grades K–2 · ISBN: 978-1-55379-798-2

Core Competency Discussion Prompts
Personal and Social: Personal Awareness and Responsibility

Facet	I Can...
A. **Self-determination**	■ be happy and proud of how well I did ■ celebrate my hard work and success ■ believe in myself ■ believe in my ideas ■ imagine and work toward change in myself and the world ■ learn about things in which people have different opinions
B. **Self-regulation**	■ sometimes name different emotions ■ use strategies that help me manage my feelings and emotions ■ work through hard tasks ■ make a plan and evaluate the results ■ take responsibility for my goals ■ take responsibility for my own learning ■ take responsibility for my own behaviour
C. **Well-being**	■ participate in activities that are healthy for my mind and body ■ tell/show how these healthy activities help me ■ take some responsibility for caring for my own body and mind ■ make choices that are good for my mind and body and keep me safe in my community, including my online conversations with others ■ use strategies to find peace when I am feeling stress ■ live a healthy life that includes both work and play

Portage & Main Press, 2019 · Hands-On Science for British Columbia · Properties of Energy for Grades K–2 · ISBN: 978-1-55379-798-2

Core Competency Self-Reflection Frame
Communication

I Can...	Examples	Next Steps
I can answer questions.		
I can listen to others when they speak.		
I can share my learning.		
I can work in a group.		

Portage & Main Press, 2019 · Hands-On Science for British Columbia · Properties of Energy for Grades K–2 · ISBN: 978-1-55379-798-2

Portage & Main Press, 2019 · Hands-On Science for British Columbia · Properties of Energy for Grades K–2 · ISBN: 978-1-55379-798-2

Name: _____

Date: _____

Core Competency Self-Reflection Frame
Creative Thinking

I can get new
ideas as I learn.

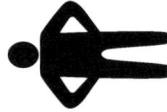

I can make
my ideas work.

I can learn
a lot through play.

I can learn
new skills as I try out my ideas.

One thing that I would like to work on is _____

Date: _____

Core Competency Self-Reflection Frame
Critical Thinking

I can explore materials.

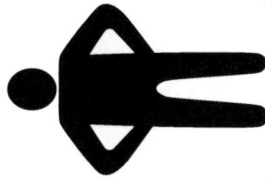

I can experiment with different ways of doing things.

I can show if I like something or not.

I can ask questions and gather information.

One goal that I have is _____

Portage & Main Press, 2019 · Hands-On Science for British Columbia · Properties of Energy for Grades K–2 · ISBN: 978-1-55379-798-2

Portage & Main Press, 2019 · *Hands-On Science for British Columbia · Properties of Energy for Grades K–2* · ISBN: 978-1-55379-798-2

Name: _____

Date: _____

Core Competency Self-Reflection Frame
Positive Personal and Cultural Identity

I can describe my family and community.

I can tell what is important to me.

I can show that I am growing as a learner.

Examples

I can describe my strengths.

Core Competency Self-Reflection Frame Personal Awareness and Responsibility

I can be proud when I have done well.

I can describe my feelings.

I can work hard to finish a job.

I can make choices that make me feel good and stay safe.

Portage & Main Press, 2019 · Hands-On Science for British Columbia · Properties of Energy for Grades K–2 · ISBN: 978-1-55379-798-2

Portage & Main Press, 2019 · Hands-On Science for British Columbia · Properties of Energy for Grades K–2 · ISBN: 978-1-55379-798-2

Date: _____

Name: _____

Core Competency Student Reflections

Module Summary

Core Competency: _____

What I Did

Next Steps

Date: _____   Name: _____

Cooperative Skills Self-Assessment

Students in my group:

_____   _____

_____   _____

Group Work—How Did I Do Today?

Group Work	How I Did (✔)		
	🌰	🌱	🌻
I shared ideas.			
I listened to others.			
I asked questions.			
I encouraged others.			
I helped with the work.			
I stayed on task.			

I did very well at _____

_____

Next time, I would like to do better at _____

_____

Portage & Main Press, 2019 · Hands-On Science for British Columbia · Properties of Energy for Grades K–2 · ISBN: 978-1-55379-798-2

Anecdotal Record

Purpose of Observation: _____

Student/Group	Date	Student/Group	Date
Comments		**Comments**	
Student/Group	**Date**	**Student/Group**	**Date**
Comments		**Comments**	
Student/Group	**Date**	**Student/Group**	**Date**
Comments		**Comments**	

Portage & Main Press, 2019 · Hands-On Science for British Columbia · Properties of Energy for Grades K–2 · ISBN: 978-1-55379-798-2

Individual Student Observations

Purpose of Observation: _____

Student:	Date:
Observations:	

Student:	Date:
Observations:	

Student:	Date:
Observations:	

Portage & Main Press, 2019 · Hands-On Science for British Columbia · Properties of Energy for Grades K–2 · ISBN: 978-1-55379-798-2

Cooperative Skills Teacher Assessment

Date: _____

Task: _____

Group Member	Cooperative Skills				
	Contributes ideas and questions	Respects and accepts contributions of others	Negotiates roles and responsibilities of each group member	Remains focused and encourages others to stay on task	Completes individual commitment to the group

Portage & Main Press, 2019 · Hands-On Science for British Columbia · Properties of Energy for Grades K–2 · ISBN: 978-1-55379-798-2

Rubric

Activity: _____

Module: _____

Date: _____

E – Emerging
D – Developing
P – Proficient
EX – Extending

Criteria

Student										

Portage & Main Press, 2019 · Hands-On Science for British Columbia · Properties of Energy for Grades K–2 · ISBN: 978-1-55379-798-2

Sample Rubric

Activity: Looking at Seeds

Module: Living Things

Date: _____

| E – Emerging |
| D – Developing |
| P – Proficient |
| EX – Extending |

Criteria

Student	Observes Seeds Carefully	Asks Questions About the Seeds	Sorts Seeds and Gives Sorting Rules	Describes Seeds in Detail						
Jarod	P	P	D	P						
Aisha	P	D	P	D						

SAMPLE

Name: _____

Portfolio Table of Contents

Entry	Date	Selection
1.	_____	_____
2.	_____	_____
3.	_____	_____
4.	_____	_____
5.	_____	_____
6.	_____	_____
7.	_____	_____
8.	_____	_____
9.	_____	_____
10.	_____	_____
11.	_____	_____
12.	_____	_____
13.	_____	_____
14.	_____	_____
15.	_____	_____
16.	_____	_____
17.	_____	_____
18.	_____	_____
19.	_____	_____
20.	_____	_____

Portage & Main Press, 2019 · Hands-On Science for British Columbia · Properties of Energy for Grades K–2 · ISBN: 978-1-55379-798-2

Portfolio Entry Record

This work was chosen by _____

This work is _____

_____

I chose this work because _____

_____

_____

_____

_____

Note: The student may complete this form or the teacher can scribe for the student.

✂ -

Date: _____   Name: _____

Portfolio Entry Record

This work was chosen by _____

This work is _____

_____

I chose this work because _____

_____

_____

_____

_____

Note: The student may complete this form or the teacher can scribe for the student.

Portage & Main Press, 2019 · Hands-On Science for British Columbia · Properties of Energy for Grades K–2 · ISBN: 978-1-55379-798-2

Family and Community Connections: Assessing Together

Family/Community Member's Name: _____

Draw a picture that shows what you have been learning in science. Work together to label your picture and describe your learning in words.

```
┌────────────────────────────────────────────┐
│                                            │
│                                            │
│                                            │
│                                            │
│  _____  │
│                                            │
│  _____  │
│                                            │
│  _____  │
└────────────────────────────────────────────┘
```

What do you like best about what you have been learning in science?

_____

_____

_____

What does your family/community member like best about what you have been learning in science?

_____

_____

_____

_____

Portage & Main Press, 2019 · Hands-On Science for British Columbia · Properties of Energy for Grades K–2 · ISBN: 978-1-55379-798-2

What Are the
Properties of Energy?

About This Module

This module of **Hands-On Science** focuses on the properties of energy. Students will conduct investigations that explore the following Big Ideas:

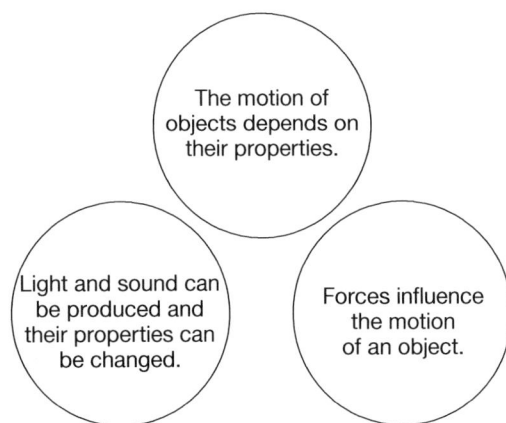

The motion of objects depends on their properties.

Light and sound can be produced and their properties can be changed.

Forces influence the motion of an object.

While investigating these Big Ideas, the Curricular Competencies will be addressed, as students use the following skills, strategies, and processes:

QP	questioning and predicting
PC	planning and conducting investigations
PA	processing and analyzing data and information
AI	applying and innovating
C	communicating
E	evaluating

Energy is the ability to make things move. Forms of energy include gravitational, chemical, nuclear, mechanical, muscular, heat, light, electrical, sound, and radiation.

Energy can come in many different forms, but there are two main forms: kinetic energy and potential energy. These two forms of energy are found in all objects. If an object is in motion (i.e., moving), it has *kinetic energy*. Energy stored within a motionless object is known as *potential energy*.

The Sun is the source of all energy for our planet. It gives off several different forms of energy, including light, heat, and radiation. All living things rely on the Sun's energy for survival.

Until about 300 years ago, humans had few sources of energy. We relied on muscular energy from human and animal labour; heat and light energy from fire (e.g., wood, candles, torches); and mechanical energy from wind (e.g., ships, windmills) and water (e.g., water mills).

During the Industrial Revolution, technologies were developed to access the energy from fossil fuels: coal, oil, and natural gas. When demands for energy exceeded known energy supplies, alternative sources were developed. Today, the two main sources of energy are hydroelectric power and nuclear power.

In this module, students will explore kinetic energy as it relates to objects in motion, as well as forces that affect motion (e.g., static electricity, magnetism). Students will also be introduced to light and sound as forms of energy.

Incorporate Indigenous perspectives and worldviews into lessons whenever possible, including the following:

■ Energy flows through every object in the universe, and that energy needs to be kept in balance and harmony. We, as humans, are part of that balance and harmony. We should not over-consume resources, and we need to be respectful whenever we harvest resources. We also need to monitor our own harmony and balance in the physical, mental, emotional, and spiritual realms.

▶

Portage & Main Press, 2018 · Hands-On Science for British Columbia · Properties of Energy for Grades K–2 · ISBN: 978-1-55379-798-2

- The medicine wheel reminds us of the cyclical nature of life, the need for balance and harmony, and the fact that everything is interconnected.

- This module also includes Indigenous understandings of motion through observation of animal movement (e.g., a rabbit hopping, an eagle flying, a salmon swimming).

  This might also include movement of objects (e.g., canoe, sled pulled by dogs) for travel, as well as the knowledge that the Sun, moon, and stars are in motion and affect daily activities.

- Forces that cause movement are infused into Indigenous perspectives as part of daily life, such as the Earth/Sun relationship or the phenomenon of the Northern Lights (aurora borealis) being more brilliant during the winter season.

- The Sun is important in determining the time of day as well as how much daylight is available to complete daily tasks. The available daylight changes with the four seasons. Sundials placed in strategic locations can tell time; placement varies, depending on the location of the community (longitude/latitude) in relation to the Sun.

- The moon also has very important cultural significance. Nations such as the Gitxsan recognize a 13-month calendar based on the lunar cycle of 28 days. Each lunar month has a name that corresponds to natural events, often associated with food or spiritual occasions.

- This module also provides an opportunity to explore Indigenous perspectives on sound. Sound is important to Indigenous peoples' survival: for hunters, fishers, and gatherers, understanding what certain sounds mean (e.g., an animal of prey is nearby; a threatening animal is approaching; a storm or other challenging weather is imminent), as well as how sound is produced and transmitted, is vital to both their subsistence and existence.

- A variety of instruments (e.g., drums, whistles, rattles, bells, voice) are used during various religious and cultural events. As well, some of these instruments are used for communication—the whistle or the drum, for example, might be used to alert a community of impending danger.

- When implementing place-based learning, there are many opportunities to consider Indigenous perspectives and knowledge. Outdoor learning provides an excellent opportunity to identify the importance of place. For example, use a map of the local area to have students identify the location in relation to the school. This will help students develop a stronger image of their community and surrounding area and meets the First Peoples Principle of Learning that says "learning is holistic, reflexive, reflective, experiential, and relational (focused on connectedness, on reciprocal relationships, and a sense of place)."

  Also identify on whose traditional territory the school is located, the traditional territory of the location for the place-based learning, as well as the traditional names for both. The following map, "First Nations in British Columbia," from Indigenous Services Canada can be used for this purpose: <www.aadnc-aandc.gc.ca/DAM/DAM-INTER-BC/STAGING/texte-text/inacmp_1100100021016_eng.pdf>

  Incorporate land acknowledgment once students have learned on whose territory the school and place-based learning location are located. The following example can be used for guidance:

▶

Portage & Main Press, 2018 · *Hands-On Science for British Columbia · Properties of Energy for Grades K-2* · ISBN: 978-1-55379-798-2

- We would like to acknowledge that we are gathered today on the traditional, ancestral, and unceded territory of the _____ people, in the place traditionally known as _____.

NOTE: Many school districts have established protocols for land acknowledgement. Check with colleagues who support Indigenous education to see if there are specific protocols to follow.

Planning Tips for Teachers

- Collect reading materials related to the properties of energy. Include a range of reading levels to allow students to engage with the materials more frequently and to help them build their knowledge base.

- Preview websites, and bookmark those appropriate for student use as well as those for teacher reference.

- Collect specific materials and science equipment required for lessons. Include a variety of everyday devices that use electrical energy from outlets (e.g., hair dryer, blender, toaster), everyday devices that use batteries (e.g., flashlights, radio), light sources (e.g., lanterns, lamps), tuning forks, musical instruments, and a variety of magnets.

NOTE: The materials needed to complete some activities are extensive. Review the materials list for each lesson ahead of time and make a note of items students may be able to bring from home (e.g., plastic containers, paper plates and/or cups, spoons, pie plates, fabric samples, balls of wool). Then, prior to beginning the lesson, send a letter home with students asking parents/guardians to donate some of these materials.

- In lesson 11, teachers are asked to make a mystery box. Consider collecting supplies and making the mystery box ahead of time. Take a large cardboard box, and cut a small peephole (about 5 cm^2) in the top. Push a pencil through the side of the box to create a hole for a light source. Fill the box with an assortment of objects that have varying abilities to reflect light (e.g., black socks, aluminum foil, plastic ball, book, bicycle reflector, hockey puck, pocket mirror). For added excitement, consider including a class treat inside the box.

- Have students make place-based journals for use throughout the module. These can be made from notebooks with sturdy covers or made simply from drawing paper and clipboards. Use a zipper-lock plastic bag to carry journal supplies such as pencils, sharpeners, pencil crayons (rather than markers, which will bleed if wet), and stretch gloves for journaling on cooler days.

- Keep all charts and displays created throughout the module, as well as completed student work. Often, these are referred to again in subsequent lessons and are used in the concluding lesson, which is a final inquiry project.

- Record the guided inquiry question for each lesson (e.g., on a sentence strip) for display throughout related investigations.

Loose Parts

Create Loose Parts bins for students to explore energy. Fill bins with various objects and materials (e.g., objects that roll, bounce, and slide [balls, bolts, coins, ball bearings, beads]; elastic bands; recycled batteries; magnets and objects attracted to magnets; candle ends; toy cars and other vehicles; Slinkies and springs).

Also include a variety of standard Loose Parts bins that can be used to challenge students to explore similarities and differences on their own. For example, this collection could also include objects that do not roll, so students are encouraged to sort and identify that attribute on their own. These Loose Parts bins can encourage personalized learning, as students can select bins to expand their inquiry.

▶

Portage & Main Press, 2018 · Hands-On Science for British Columbia · Properties of Energy for Grades K–2 · ISBN: 978-1-55379-798-2

Makerspace

Develop a Makerspace. Classroom Makerspaces are usually designed as centres where students learn together and collaborate on do-it-yourself projects. Students are given the opportunity to work with a variety of age-appropriate tools, as well as with everyday, arts-and-crafts, and recycled materials.

For this module, set up a Makerspace in your classroom that encourages informal learning about the properties of energy. Collect a variety of materials and equipment that reflect the challenges students might take on at the centre. Include general materials, such as those listed in the Introduction (page 19), as well as module-specific materials. For example, provide materials for "take-apart" exploration (e.g., battery-operated toys, windup toys) and other devices (e.g., old clocks, radios, cellphones), along with tools (e.g., screwdrivers, pliers, magnifying glasses). Also provide items that students can use to explore motion and energy (e.g., toy cars, elastics, Slinkies, springs, magnets, devices that use magnets in their design), as well as items for students to explore light and sound (e.g., bulbs, batteries, LEDs, glow-in-the-dark tape and paint, small glass and mirror pieces).

Do-it-yourself projects may include anything related to the concepts of this module. Projects students might initiate include (but are not limited to):

- creating a device that uses pushes and pulls to move
- designing a device that uses solar energy to do something
- designing and constructing a sinker to pull fishing nets down using gravity (see <staff.royalbcmuseum.bc.ca/2016/12/21/the-archaeology-and-history-of-macaulay-point/>)

- designing and constructing a reef net for salmon (see <staff.royalbcmuseum.bc.ca/2016/12/21/the-archaeology-and-history-of-macaulay-point/>)
- building a model of a plant that shows how it gets its energy
- building a model of an elevator or another device that moves people from one place to another
- exploring how things move using spheres, such as marbles, and participating in the Fluor Engineering challenge (see <www.sciencebuddies.org/fluor-challenge>)
- designing and building a model catapult
- designing and building a hoist or crane to lift blocks
- investigating the use of magnets in a specific device
- using an elastic to create something that moves using tension
- creating a stage and using magnets to move characters from underneath
- creating a device that launches a paper airplane
- creating a model flashlight/lamp
- using a LEGO wall to create a rainbow
- making paper bag lanterns to light up your favourite books and characters
- making a bookmark or other useful object that glows in the dark
- designing a night-light
- making a disco ball
- making a homemade megaphone

Literacy connections that might inspire projects include:

- *The Boy Who Harnessed the Wind* by William Kamkwamba and Bryan Mealer
- *Energy Island: How One Community Harnessed the Wind and Changed Their World* by Allan Drummond
- *How Do You Lift a Lion?* by Robert E. Wells

▶

Portage & Main Press, 2018 · Hands-On Science for British Columbia · Properties of Energy for Grades K-2 · ISBN: 978-1-55379-798-2

- *And Everyone Shouted, "Pull!": A First Look at Forces and Motion* by Claire Llewellyn
- *Toy Stories: Photos of Children From Around the World and Their Favorite Things* by Gabriele Galimberti
- *The Light* by Jo Oliver
- *Oscar and the Moth: A Book About Light and Dark* by Geoff Waring
- *Polar Bear, Polar Bear, What Do You Hear?* by Bill Martin, Jr. and Eric Carle
- *The Sound of Silence* by Katrina Goldsaito
- *It Looked Like Spilt Milk* by Charles G. Shaw

As inquiry questions are posed with each lesson, you will find these questions inspire other do-it-yourself projects related to the module. Students may determine solutions to these questions through the creating they do at the Makerspace. Remember to not direct the learning here; simply create the conditions for learning to happen.

Science Vocabulary

Throughout this module, use, and encourage students to use, vocabulary such as:

- *absorb, artificial light, attract, bounce, brightness, colour, energy, force, friction, gravity, light, loudness, magnet, motion, movement, natural light, pitch, prism, pull, push, reflect, roll, shadow, slide, sound, spin, static charge, static electricity, swing, vibration, wave(s), wheel and axle, wind energy*

Infuse vocabulary related to scientific inquiry skills into daily lessons. This vocabulary could be displayed in the classroom throughout the year, as it relates to all science Big Ideas. Have students brainstorm which skills they are being asked to use as they work on particular lessons. Discuss with students how the skill looks and sounds as they explore and investigate.

Vocabulary related to scientific inquiry skills includes:

- *ask, brainstorm, collect, compare, connect, consider, construct, cooperate, create, describe, estimate, explain, explore, find, follow, graph, identify, improve, investigate, match, measure, observe, order, plan, predict, recognize, record, repeat, research, respond, select, sequence, test*

Early in the module, create a word wall. The word wall can be created on a bulletin board or simply on poster or chart paper. Record new vocabulary on the bulletin board or poster as it is introduced during the module. Ensure the word wall is placed in a location in the classroom where all students can see and refer to the words during activities and discussion. Have students work with the terms on a regular basis by creating their own definitions, giving examples, linking terms in sentences, and using terms in context.

NOTE: Include terminology in languages other than English on the word wall. This is a way of acknowledging and respecting students' cultural backgrounds, while enhancing learning for all students.

Use online dictionaries as a source for translations. For example:

- <www.freelang.net/online/haida.php>
- <www.firstvoices.com/en/Halqemeylem>

Online dictionaries are also available for languages other than English that may be reflective of the class cultural makeup.

Portage & Main Press, 2018 · Hands-On Science for British Columbia · Properties of Energy for Grades K–2 · ISBN: 978-1-55379-798-2

Curriculum Learning Framework

	K	1	2
Big Idea	The motion of objects depends on their properties.	Light and sound can be produced, and their properties can be changed.	Forces influence the motion of an object.
Sample Guiding Inquiry Questions	■ How can you make objects move? ■ How does the shape or size of an object affect the object's movement? ■ How does the material the object is made of affect the object's movement?	■ How can you explore the properties of light and sound? ■ What discoveries did you make?	■ What are different ways objects can be moved? ■ How do different materials influence the motion of an object?

Content	■ effects of pushes/pulls on movement [lesson 1, 2, 3, 4, 6, 7, 8, 19]
	■ how things move (e.g., bounce, roll, slide) [lesson 1, 2, 3, 4, 5, 6, 7, 8, 19]
	■ effects of size, shape, and materials on movement [lesson 1, 2, 3, 4, 5, 6, 7, 8, 19]
		■ natural light sources include the Sun; artificial sources include light bulbs [lesson 2, 9, 10, 19]
		■ natural sound sources include crickets; artificial sources include car horns [lesson 2, 13, 14, 15, 16, 19]
		■ properties of light (e.g., brightness, colour) [lesson 2, 9, 10, 11, 12, 19]
		■ properties of sound [lesson 2, 13, 14, 15, 16, 19]
		■ objects are made visible by radiating their own light or being illuminated by reflected light [lesson 2, 9, 11, 19]
		■ interactions of light with different objects create images and shadows [lesson 2, 9, 11, 12, 19]
		■ light interactions can make plants grow, make shadows, or cause sunburn, depending on the source and location (seasons depend on light from the Sun and how spread out the Sun's rays are) [lesson 2, 9, 10, 12, 19]
		■ plants grow toward light [lesson 2, 9, 10, 19]
			■ types of forces [lesson 1, 2, 3, 4, 5, 6, 7, 8, 17, 18, 19]
			■ contact forces and at-a-distance forces
			  ■ different types of magnets
			  ■ static electricity [lesson 17, 18, 19]
			■ balanced and unbalanced forces
			  ■ the way different objects fall depending on their shape (air resistance)
			  ■ the way objects move over/in different materials (water, air, ice, snow)
			  ■ the motion caused by different strengths of forces [lesson 1, 2, 3, 4, 5, 6, 7, 8, 17, 18, 19]

Core Competencies	*Thinking* *Communicating* *Social and Personal*		

Portage & Main Press, 2018 · Hands-On Science for British Columbia · Properties of Energy for Grades K–2 · ISBN: 978-1-55379-798-2

Curricular Competencies Correlation Chart

Throughout this module, students will develop Curricular Competencies by participating in rich learning experiences that focus on specific skills, strategies, and processes. The chart below suggests ways in which students explore Curricular Competencies in specific lessons.

Curricular Competencies	Lesson																		
	1	2	3	4	5	6	7	8	9	10	11	12	13	14	15	16	17	18	19
QP Questioning and Predicting																			
Demonstrate curiosity and a sense of wonder about energy.	√	√	√	√	√	√	√	√	√	√	√	√	√	√	√	√	√	√	√
Observe objects and events in familiar contexts.	√	√	√	√	√	√	√	√	√	√	√	√	√	√	√	√	√	√	√
Ask simple questions about energy.	√	√	√	√	√	√	√	√	√	√	√	√	√	√	√	√	√	√	√
Make simple predictions about energy.	√		√	√	√	√	√	√		√	√			√			√		
PC Planning and Conducting Investigations																			
Make exploratory observations using their senses.	√	√	√	√	√	√	√	√	√	√	√	√	√	√	√	√	√	√	√
Record observations.	√	√	√	√	√	√	√	√	√	√			√			√			√
Safely manipulate materials.	√	√	√	√	√	√	√	√	√	√	√	√	√	√	√	√	√	√	√
Make simple measurements using nonstandard units.			√		√		√	√		√								√	
PA Processing and Analyzing Data and Information																			
Experience and interpret the local environment.	√		√	√						√			√						
Recognize First Peoples stories (including oral and written narratives), songs, and art, as ways to share knowledge.	√	√	√	√	√	√	√	√	√	√	√	√	√	√	√	√	√	√	√
Discuss observations about energy.	√	√	√	√	√	√	√	√	√	√	√	√	√	√	√	√	√	√	√
Represent observations and ideas by drawing charts and simple pictographs.	√		√	√	√	√			√	√			√				√	√	
Sort and classify data and information using drawings, pictographs, and provided tables.	√		√	√					√	√			√		√		√		√

▶

Portage & Main Press, 2018 · Hands-On Science for British Columbia · Properties of Energy for Grades K–2 · ISBN: 978-1-55379-798-2

Curricular Competencies	Lesson																		
	1	2	3	4	5	6	7	8	9	10	11	12	13	14	15	16	17	18	19
Compare observations with predictions through discussion.	√		√	√	√	√	√	√		√	√			√			√	√	
Identify simple patterns and connections related to energy.									√	√		√		√					
(AI) Applying and Innovating																			
Take part in caring for self, family, classroom, and school through personal approaches.						√	√	√		√	√							√	
Transfer and apply learning to new situations.		√			√	√	√	√	√	√	√	√	√	√	√	√	√	√	√
Generate and introduce new or refined ideas when problem solving.	√	√	√	√	√	√	√	√	√	√	√	√	√	√		√	√	√	√
(C) Communicating																			
Share observations and ideas orally, or through written language, drawing, or role-play.	√	√	√	√	√	√	√	√	√	√	√	√	√	√	√	√	√	√	√
Express and reflect on personal experiences of place.	√		√	√				√		√			√						
(E) Evaluating																			
Compare observations of energy with those of others.	√	√	√		√	√	√	√	√	√			√			√	√	√	√
Consider some environmental consequences of their actions as related to energy.	√		√		√			√			√		√						

Portage & Main Press, 2018 · Hands-On Science for British Columbia · Properties of Energy for Grades K-2 · ISBN: 978-1-55379-798-2

Resources for Students

Portage & Main Press, 2018 · Hands-On Science for British Columbia · Properties of Energy for Grades K–2 · ISBN: 978-1-55379-798-2

NOTE: Resources marked with an asterisk are considered to be authentic resources. This means that traditional stories reference the Indigenous community they came from, they state the individual who shared the story and gave permission for the story to be used publicly, and the person who originally shared the story is Indigenous. Stories that are works of fiction were written by an Indigenous author. For more information, please see *Authentic First Peoples Resources* at: <http://www.fnesc.ca/learningfirstpeoples/>.

Motion

Books

Drummond, Allan. *Energy Island: How One Community Harnessed the Wind and Changed Their World*. New York: Square Fish, 2015.

*Eyvindson, Peter. *The Wish Wind*. Winnipeg, MB: Pemmican Publications, 1987.

Kamkwamba, William, and Bryan Mealer. *The Boy Who Harnessed the Wind*. New York: Puffin Books, 2016.

*Miller, Bruce. *Our Original Games: A Look at Aboriginal Sport in Canada*. Owen Sound, ON: Ningwakwe Learning Press, 2002.

Steig, William. *Brave Irene*. New York: Square Fish, 2011.

*Taylor, C. J. *How We Saw the World*. Toronto: Tundra Books, 1999.

Wells, Robert E. *How Do You Lift a Lion?* Park Ridge, IL: Albert Whitman & Company, 1996.

Williamson, Sarah. *Where Are You?* New York: Knopf Books For Young Readers, 2017.

Websites

- **www.happalmer.com**
  Hap Palmer: The website of children's musician Hap Palmer includes song lyrics, links to videos, and other information related to his music.

- **aboriginalperspectives.uregina.ca/games**
  Games From the Aboriginal People of North America: Compilation of games played by different Indigenous peoples.

- **http://natgeotv.com/me/monster-moves**
  National Geographic UK—Monster Moves: Find photos and videos of large structures being moved from the show Monster Moves.

- **www.sciencebuddies.org/fluor-challenge**
  Take the Fluor Engineering Challenge!: Each year, a new challenge is presented for students around the world to solve.

- **https://studio.code.org/s/mc/stage/1/puzzle/1**
  Minecraft Hour of Code: Teach students some basics of coding with Minecraft.

Videos

- **https://youtu.be/iSoR9oGGpOc**
  "THE STICKMAKER – Alf Jaques "UNSTRUNG" Handmakes Wood Lacrosse Sticks." Stylin Strings (3:32).

- **https://www.youtube.com/watch?v=Bhfw5R2U5mE**
  "Physics of a Lacrosse Shot." jennthoomas (6:30).

- **https://www.youtube.com/watch?v=loOFL_Gz_C4**
  "Brave Irene read by Al Gore." StorylineOnline (14:01).

- **https://www.youtube.com/watch?v=xSsDbneWFJ8**
  "The Elephant – by Hap Palmer." Hap Palmer (2:33).

- **https://www.youtube.com/watch?v=zpfo55a6YPk**
  "Dropping a Ping Pong Ball with a Golf Ball." Mr. Mangiacapre (0:42).

▶

- **https://www.youtube.com/ watch?v=RezOCzxcvmM**
  "Comanche Archery 101: Aiming and Shooting." Comanche Museum (3:02).

- **https://www.youtube.com/ watch?v=5mgivuYJ_TM**
  "Native American Bow Hunting." Historic Westville (0:26).

- **https://www.youtube.com/watch?v=dhp_ MFa6o6c**
  "TRIBAL CANOE JOURNEY – NW COAST FIRST NATION CULTURES." Executive Productions (7:45).

Light

Books

Andersen, H. C. *The Ugly Duckling*. New York: Alfred A. Knopf, 2001

Bardoe, Cheryl. *The Ugly Duckling Dinosaur: A Prehistoric Tale*. New York: Abrams Books for Young Readers, 2011

*Bouchard, David. *Rainbow Crow: Nagweyaabi-Aandeg*. English/Cree Edition. Markham, ON: Red Deer Press, 2012.

Brown, Marcia. *Walk With Your Eyes*. London, UK: Franklin Watts, 1979.

Bushey, Jeanne. *Orphans in the Sky*. Markham, ON: Red Deer Press, 2004.

Carle, Eric. *Hello, Red Fox*. Toronto: Simon & Schuster Canada, 2001.

*Confederated Salish and Kootenai Tribes. *Beaver Steals Fire: A Salish Coyote Story*. Lincoln, NE: University of Nebraska Press, 2005.

Dwyer, Mindy. *Aurora: A Tale of the Northern Lights*. Berkeley, CA: Graphic Arts Books, 2001.

Higgins, Nadia. *Busy, Busy Leaves*. North Mankoto, MN: Capstone Publishing, 2017.

*Ipellie, Alootook, with David MacDonald. *The Inuit Thought of It: Amazing Arctic Innovations*. Toronto: Annick Press, 2007.

Isadora, Rachel. *The Ugly Duckling*. New York: G. P. Putnam's Sons, 2009

Oliver, Jo. *The Light*. Forest Lodge, AU: New Frontier Publishing, 2013.

Llewellyn, Claire. *And Everyone Shouted, "Pull!": A First Look at Forces and Motion*. Minneapolis, MN: Picture Window Books, 2005.

Mallory, Carolyn. *Painted Skies*. Iqaluit, NU: Inhabit Media, 2015.

Meeks, Arone Raymond. *Enora and the Black Crane*. Nanaimo, BC: Strong Nations, 2010.

Ortiz, Simon J. *The Good Rainbow Road*. Tucson, AZ: University of Arizona Press, 2010.

*Robertson, David Alexander. *Warren Whistles at the Sky*. Winnipeg, MB: Manitoba First Nations Education Resource Centre, 2016.

Rockwell, Anne. *Four Seasons Make a Year*. New York: Walker Books, 2004.

Sabuda, Robert. *The Blizzard's Robe*. New York: Atheneum, 1999.

Shaw, Charles G. *It Looked Like Spilt Milk*. New York: HarperCollins, 1988.

*Waboose, Jan Bourdeau. *SkySisters*. Toronto: Kids Can Press, 2002.

Waring, Geoff. *Oscar and the Moth: A Book About Light and Dark*. Cambridge, MA: Candlewick, 2007.

▶

Portage & Main Press, 2018 · Hands-On Science for British Columbia · Properties of Energy for Grades K-2 · ISBN: 978-1-55379-798-2

Websites

- **astro-canada.ca/l_univers-universe-eng**
Universe—Canada Under the Stars—Virtual Museum of Canada: Use the sidebar links to explore Indigenous astronomy.

- **https://www.enchantedlearning.com/inventors/edison/lightbulb.shtml**
The Invention of the Light Bulb: Davy, Swan and Edison—Enchanted Learning.

- **https://www.optics4kids.org/home/content/classroom-activities/easy**
Optics 4 Kids—OSA The Optical Society: Activities about how light travels, how colour and light interact, and how the human eye perceives colour and illusions.

- **https://www.historymuseum.ca/cmc/exhibitions/aborig/reid/reid14e.shtml**
"The Raven Steals the Light," by Bill Reid, storyteller—Canadian Museum of History.

- **www.virtualmuseum.ca/edu/**
Snaring the Sun—The Anishinabe of Central North America—Sky Stories: Indigenous Astronomy. Enter "snaring the sun" in the search box to find Learning Resources. Once there, click on Indigenous Astronomy.

- **https://www.greenkidcrafts.com/diy-magnifying-glass/**
DIY Magnifying Glass—Green Kid Crafts: Make your own magnifying glass using just water and a recycled soft drink bottle.

- **www.indigenouspeople.net/chipewyn.htm**
Dene—Creation of Seasons: A creation story from the Dene people.

Videos

- **https://www.youtube.com/watch?v=ok_b46A9hvE/**
"FNX Animation: "Grandmother Spider Brings the Sun"." FNX Native Television (10:00).

- **https://www.youtube.com/watch?v=yMMcFSBi2hg**
"Inuit Culture, Lighting the Qulliq." Ottawa Inuit Children's Centre (7:33).

- **https://www.youtube.com/watch?v=3g0oDBRTWes**
"Light, Shadows, and Reflections (Transparent, Opaque and Translucent Objects)." CBSE science class 6—Teach Learn Web (2:11).

- **https://www.youtube.com/watch?v=fVsONlc3OUY**
"Night of the Northern Lights." Maciej Winiarczyk (2:22).

- **https://www.youtube.com/watch?v=fVMgnmi2D1w**
"NASA: Stunning Aurora Borealis from Space." NASA TV UHD (4:36).

- **https://www.youtube.com/watch?v=rjjxUE6XSdQ**
"Qulliq (Oil Lamp)." kellengreffe (10:21).

- **https://www.youtube.com/watch?v=I64YwNl1wr0**
"Earth's Rotation & Revolution: Crash Course Kids 8.1." Crash Course Kids (4:00).

- **https://www.youtube.com/watch?v=EXasopxAFoM**
"Science Video for Kids: Earth's Revolution & Rotation." Turtlediary (8:15)

Sound

Books

Goldsaito, Katrina. *The Sound of Silence*. Little, Brown Books for Young Readers, 2016.

Martin, Bill Jr. and Eric Carle. *Polar Bear, Polar Bear, What Do You Hear?* New York: Holt, 2010.

*Rumbolt, Paula Ikuutaq. *The Legend of Lightning and Thunder*. Iqaluit, NU: Inhabit Media, 2013.

▶

Portage & Main Press, 2018 · Hands-On Science for British Columbia · Properties of Energy for Grades K–2 · ISBN: 978-1-55379-798-2

*Schilling, Vincent. *Great Musicians From Our First Nations*. Toronto: Second Story Press, 2010.

Websites

- **www.landfillharmonicmovie.com**
  Information about the film, *Landfill Harmonic*. Students form an orchestra with instruments made from recycled landfill materials.

- **publications.gc.ca/site/eng/9.614394/ publication.html**
  First Nations Music in Canada—Information about a variety of Indigenous instruments, and how they were made and used.

- **https://www.exploratorium.edu/snacks/ sound-sandwich**
  Sound Sandwich—Science Snacks—Exploratorium: Students construct their own device and manipulate its components to see the effect on sound produced.

- **www.native-drums.ca**
  Native Drums: First Nations culture and music in Canada, featuring interviews, games, videos, images, and teacher resources.

- **https://www.partnersinrhyme.com/ soundfx/Ambience.shtml**
  (Free) Nature Sound Effects and Royalty Free Nature Sounds—Partners in Rhyme.

- **naturesoundsfor.me**
  Nature Sounds for Me—Sound Mixer: A free tool for playing nature sounds.

- **https://acousticalsociety.org/**
  Some Interesting Sounds—Acoustical Society of America: Recordings of insects, underwater sounds, music, and more.

- **eng.universal-soundbank.com/index.htm**
  Universal Soundbank: Free sound effects, samples and loops.

Videos

- **https://www.youtube.com/ watch?v=BZtIL5k2gPM**
  "The Metis Fiddle With Trent Freeman and Ry Moran." learnmichif (9:59).

- **https://www.youtube.com/ watch?v=iArcG-S3_QM**
  "Pow Wow Women's Jingle Dress Dance High Quality." Willis Petti, (2:47).

- **https://www.youtube.com/ watch?v=KNb2ZDjeiU4**
  "Tanya Tagaq- The sounds of throat singing." musicisayer, (3:07).

- **https://www.youtube.com/ watch?v=U7tPwg3af5M**
  "SESQUI 2017 – Throat Singers." SESQUI2017, (2:31)..

- **https://www.youtube.com/ watch?v=vaRsVAKg37M**
  "Benjamin Wawatie (Algonquin Anishnabe Ancinabe) – Native flute inspiration." Kunturumy Eagle & Condor travel, (2:31).

- **https://www.youtube.com/ watch?v=aJffugOR4XE**
  "Buffy Sainte-Marie | Starwalker (Live)." CBC Music, (3:24).

- **https://www.youtube.com/ watch?v=ORIDAmGf_yQ**
  "Invention Of Morse Code | The Dr. Binocs Show | Best Learning Video for Kids | Preschool Learning" Peekaboo Kidz (4:24).

Forces

Books

Dwyer, Mindy. *Aurora: A Tale of the Northern Lights*. Portland, OR: Alaska Northwest Books, 2001.

Portage & Main Press, 2018 · *Hands-On Science for British Columbia · Properties of Energy for Grades K–2* · ISBN: 978-1-55379-798-2

▶

Galimberti, Gabriele. *Toy Stories: Photos of Children from Around the World and Their Favorite Things*. New York: Abrams Image, 2014.

Ives, Rob. *Fun Experiments with Forces and Motion: Hovercrafts, Rockets, and More*. Minneapolis, MN: Learner Publications, 2018.

*Kusugak, Michael. *Northern Lights: The Soccer Trails*. Toronto: Annick Press, 1993.

*Miller, Bruce. *Our Original Games: A Look at Aboriginal Sport in Canada*. Owen Sound, ON: Ningwakwe Learning Press, 2002.

*Rumbolt, Paula Ikuutaq. *The Legend of Lightning and Thunder*. Iqaluit, NU: Inhabit Media, 2013.

*Waboose, Jan Bourdeau. *SkySisters*. Toronto: Kids Can Press, 2002.

Websites

- **www.science.org.au/curious/earth-environment/noise-pollution-and-environment**
  Australian Academy of Science—Noise pollution and the environment: Learn about the harmful effects of noise pollution.

- **lightning.nsstc.nasa.gov/**
  Global Hydrology Resource Center and NASA—Lightning and Atmospheric Electricity Research: An introduction to lightning.

- **https://www.billnye.com/**
  Bill Nye—The Official Website for Bill Nye the Science Guy.

- **www.storyjumper.com/book/index/11697072/Force-and-Motion**
  Story Jumper—Force and Motion: Create your own book to explain force and motion using the tools on this website.

- **www.internet4classrooms.com/science_elem_magnets.htm**
  Internet4Classrooms—Magnets for Elementary Science: A long list of useful resources for teachers on this topic.

- **www.nasa.gov/offices/education/about/index.html**
  NASA STEM Engagement: Find numerous short videos related to electromagnets, static electricity, and lightning.

- **iroquoisnationals.org/the-iroquois/the-story-of-lacrosse/**
  Iroquois Nationals—The Story of Lacrosse: This article captures the oral traditions of the Haudenosaunee people as they relate to lacrosse.

Videos

- **https://www.youtube.com/watch?v=5C-RM4fh5Xg**
  "Magnets for Kids." The Science Bucket (3:00).

- **https://www.youtube.com/watch?v=eYSG5aeTy-Y**
  "Magnets & Magnetism for kids. " makemegenius (5:03).

- **https://www.youtube.com/watch?v=NZlfxWMr7nc**
  "Relax Music & Stunning Aurora Borealis-Northern Polar Lights – 2 Hours." BaLu: Relaxing Nature (1:57:10).

- **https://www.youtube.com/watch?v=5TAIUCYMIIQ**
  "The Sticky Balloon Trick! | Physics for Kids." SciShow Kids (3:11).

- **https://www.youtube.com/watch?v=V7soAsGyfWQ**
  "6 Static Electricity Balloon Experiments You can do at home Easy Kid Science – STEM." JoJo's Science Show - Kid Science (5:57).

Portage & Main Press, 2018 · *Hands-On Science for British Columbia · Properties of Energy for Grades K–2* · ISBN: 978-1-55379-798-2

Initiating Event: What Do We Observe, Think, and Wonder About How Things Move in Nature?

1

Information for Teachers

In this lesson, students will participate in place-based learning to explore motion in a local natural environment. The focus is on forms of energy that make things move (e.g., solar energy, wind energy, muscular energy).

Plan ahead to select a location for place-based learning. Encourage students to suggest natural areas in your local region. Although it is important to introduce students to new areas for place-based learning, also consider using the same location(s) visited in other modules to build strong connections to the land.

If possible, invite a local Elder or Knowledge Keeper to participate in this learning experience. They may be able to share relevant stories, as well as knowledge of the land and its features, and the forms of energy observable there. This connects to the First Peoples Principles of Learning, particularly as they relate to recognizing the role of story and Indigenous knowledge in learning.

NOTE: See Indigenous Perspectives and Knowledge, page 9, for guidelines for inviting Elders and Knowledge Keepers to speak to students.

Materials

- bean bags
- small fans (or paper folded into fans)
- toy cars or trucks
- pencil sharpeners
- pencils
- books
- windup toys
- chart paper
- printer access
- markers
- digital cameras

- place-based journals and supplies (see About this Module, page 60)
- Learning-Centre Task Card: How Can I Sort Photographs of Motion in Nature? (3.1.1)

Engage

Display a variety of objects (e.g., paper fans, toy cars, bean bags, books, windup toys, pencils with pencil sharpeners) at centres around the classroom. Organize the class into working groups and send each group to one of the centres to investigate the objects.

Have students sit in a circle. As a group, do several tasks that show forms of energy making things move, such as:

- throwing a bean bag to a friend
- folding a piece of paper, then using it as a fan
- pushing a toy car or truck across the floor
- bouncing a ball
- rolling on the carpet
- sliding a book across a desk
- sharpening a pencil with a pencil sharpener
- lifting a book
- jumping on the spot
- winding up a toy, and letting it move across the floor

When all of the tasks have been completed, ask students:

- How were all of these activities the same? (all involved movement)

NOTE: Introduce students to the terms *motion* and *movement*, which are synonymous terms. Use them interchangeably throughout the module, and encourage students to use the terms as well.

Demonstrate each task again. Ask students:

- What is happening while I am doing this task?

▶

Portage & Main Press, 2018 · *Hands-On Science for British Columbia · Properties of Energy for Grades K–2* · ISBN: 978-1-55379-798-2

Portage & Main Press, 2018 · Hands-On Science for British Columbia · Properties of Energy for Grades K–2 · ISBN: 978-1-55379-798-2

■ What is moving?

■ What made it move?

Have students share their ideas.

Title a sheet of chart paper "Energy," and create the following table:

Energy	
Things That Move	**How They Move**

Begin with the examples that were demonstrated. Have students identify each item. Record the item on the first column. Then, have students explain what makes the object move (e.g., muscles, electricity, gas, wind), and record this in the second column.

Have students brainstorm a list of other things that move (e.g., humans, cars, clouds, swings, birds, bicycles). Add these to the chart, along with what makes each object move.

Introduce the guided inquiry question: **What do we observe, think, and wonder about how things move in nature?**

Explore Part One

Explain to students that they will be exploring a natural environment through a nature walk.

Discuss the location for this place-based learning. Ask:

■ Who has been to this place before?

■ How did you get there?

■ What is it like there?

■ What do you think we will see there? Smell? Hear? Feel?

■ What kinds of living things might we see?

■ What kinds of nonliving things might we see?

■ What kinds of motion might we see?

Have students share their background knowledge, predictions, inferences, and ideas about the natural environment they will visit, and the objects they might investigate there. Record their ideas on chart paper. Later, students can refer back to their ideas to see how their thinking changes.

Have students share with a partner what they are most excited about in visiting this location.

To help students develop a stronger image of their community and surrounding area, use a map of the local area to identify where the place-based learning location is in relation to the school. This is an excellent opportunity to identify the importance of place.

Identify on whose traditional territory the school is located, the traditional territory of the location for the place-based learning (if different), as well as the traditional names for both locations. The following map, "First Nations in British Columbia," from Indigenous Services Canada can be used for this purpose: <www.aadnc-aandc.gc.ca/DAM/ DAM-INTER-BC/ STAGING/texte-text/ inacmp_1100100021016_eng.pdf>.

This ties into the First Peoples Principles of Learning related to sense of place. Incorporate land acknowledgment when students have learned on whose territory the school and place-based learning location are located. The following example can be used for guidance:

■ We would like to acknowledge that we are gathered today on the traditional, ancestral, and unceded territory of the _____ people, in the place traditionally known as _____.

NOTE: Many school districts have established protocols for land acknowledgment. Check with colleagues who support Indigenous education to see if there are specific protocols to follow.

►

Review any other protocols for field trips, providing students with opportunities to ask questions and clarify expectations.

⚠️ **SAFETY NOTE:** Remind students never to taste anything without permission. Review other safety considerations such as plants that may cause skin irritations and bodies of water that may be present at the place-based learning location. Also be aware of students' allergies during the activity.

Discuss with students the importance of respecting nature. Have them brainstorm ways in which they can demonstrate this. Create an anchor chart on chart paper to display in the classroom. This can be reviewed each time students go outside to visit a natural environment. For example:

- Be respectful of all living things.
- Never break off branches from trees or pick wildflowers.
- Collect only a few objects to take back to the classroom.
- Always clean up after ourselves.

Explore Part Two

When the class has arrived at the place-based learning location, provide time for students to explore the area freely (under adult supervision). As students explore, pose questions for them to ponder. For example:

- What are you examining?
- Why is it interesting to you?
- What can you tell me about it?
- What do you wonder about it?
- Are you seeing any examples of motion?

Encourage students to share their observations, thinking, and questions with you, their peers, and other supervisors.

Regroup to discuss this initial exploration. Have students share their observations, ideas, and questions with the class.

Explore Part Three

As a group, review with students what they learned about motion in the Engage activity. Explain to them that they are going to take photographs of examples of motion they see around them. Ask:

- What kinds of things might we photograph?

Brainstorm examples they might look for, and model the process by using a digital camera to photograph nearby examples of motion, such as:

- things moved by wind (e.g., rustling leaves and seeds, rippling water)
- things moved by muscle (e.g., birds flying, squirrels climbing trees, fish swimming, people walking)

Organize the class into working groups, and provide each group with a digital camera.

NOTE: This task may work best if a supervisor/adult is with each group.

Have groups choose one area of mutual interest to explore and photograph examples of motion. Encourage students to share within their group their observations, ideas, and questions as they conduct deeper exploration.

Explore Part Four

Back in the classroom, discuss this group exploration. Have each group print and share their photographs with the rest of the class, and then share their observations, ideas, and questions. Focus on specific examples of motion as each group shares their photographs. For example, ask:

▶

Portage & Main Press, 2018 · Hands-On Science for British Columbia · Properties of Energy for Grades K-2 · ISBN: 978-1-55379-798-2

- Which objects in your photograph were moving?
- Were there living things moving?
- Were there nonliving things moving?
- What do you think caused them to move?
- What sounds did you hear when you took the photographs?
- Where was the light coming from that helped us see?
- How else does light from the Sun help us?
- How does it help other animals?
- How does it help plants?

Have students share their ideas and background knowledge.

Conclude the discussion with the Observe, Think, Wonder format:

- What did you observe about movement in nature?
- What did you think about movement in nature?
- What did you wonder about movement in nature?

Encourage students to share their observations, ideas, and questions.

Expand

Prepare students for journaling by completing a journal entry as a class. This will require a portable whiteboard and markers, or chart paper with a sturdy backboard.

As a class, choose a place to sit and journal. Brainstorm journaling ideas with students. For example, at the kindergarten to grade-two level, students may wish to:

- sketch or colour objects in the natural environment that show movement
- sketch flowers or leaves
- identify emotions and record feelings about this natural environment (students may use

happy faces, emojis, or their own designs for emotions)
- make rubbings of natural artifacts (e.g., leaves, bark, shells)
- record the sounds in the natural environment using pictures and words
- record movement in the natural environment using pictures and words
- take a photograph that shows movement and sketch it
- draw and label diagrams showing examples of motion
- record the weather conditions in pictures
- draw a map of the local area or journaling location
- lie back and observe the sky, then sketch things that are moving
- draw a moving object, using all five senses to describe it
- find a tree buddy, rock, or special place, sketch it, and give it a name

Work through a few journaling activities together. Then, distribute place-based journals and supplies to each student. Have them choose a place where they would like to sit and journal and one journaling strategy to use.

While students journal, take photographs of the area to display in the classroom and at the learning centre.

Formative Assessment

Photograph students as they journal to collect evidence of learning activities. Be sure to document students' thinking after journaling. For example, meet with students individually to have them share their thoughts about their observations of how things move in nature, the journaling experience, and what they recorded in their journal. Use the photographs taken as they journaled to inspire reflection. Focus on students' ability to express and reflect on personal experiences of place. Use the

▶

Portage & Main Press, 2018 · Hands-On Science for British Columbia · Properties of Energy for Grades K–2 · ISBN: 978-1-55379-798-2

INDIVIDUAL STUDENT OBSERVATIONS template on page 51 to record interview highlights. Provide descriptive feedback to students about how they describe observations of nature, and express and reflect on personal experiences of place.

Learning Centre

At the learning centre, provide a collection of printed photographs taken during the place-based learning activity, as well as a copy of the Learning-Centre Task Card: How Can I Sort Photographs of Motion in Nature? (3.1.1):

Learning Centre

How Can I Sort Photographs of Motion in Nature?

1. With your group, look at each photograph from our nature walk.
2. Describe the photograph.
   - If you were right there, what would you see, hear, smell, and touch? (no tasting!)
3. Describe examples of motion you see in the photograph.
4. Sort all of the photographs into groups.
5. Describe your sorting rules to others.

3.1.1

Download this template at <www.portageandmainpress.com/product/HOSEnergyK2>.

Have students work in groups to examine the photographs and describe them to peers. Then have students sort and classify the photographs according to their own rules.

Exploration of these photographs at the learning centre may also inspire further inquiry. Encourage students to ask questions and find ways to answer those questions, either at the learning centre or as personalized learning experiences.

Embed Part One: Talking Circle

NOTE: See Talking Circles, page 16, for more information.

Revisit the guided inquiry question: **What do we observe, think, and wonder about how things move in nature?** Have students share their experiences and knowledge, provide examples, and ask further inquiry questions.

Embed Part Two

- Focus on students' use of the Core Competencies. Have students reflect on how they used one of the Core Competencies (Thinking, Communicating, or Personal and Social Skills) during the various lesson activities. Project one of the CORE COMPETENCY DISCUSSION PROMPTS templates (pages 38-42), and use it to inspire group reflection. Referring to the template, choose one or two "I Can" statements on which to focus. Students then use the "I Can" statements to provide evidence of how they demonstrated that competency. Ask questions directly related to that competency to inspire discussion. For example:
  - Where did you get your ideas for your place-based journal entry today? (Creative Thinking)

Have students reflect orally, encouraging participation, questions, and the sharing of evidence. (See page 29 for more information on these templates.)

Portage & Main Press, 2018 · Hands-On Science for British Columbia · Properties of Energy for Grades K–2 · ISBN: 978-1-55379-798-2

Portage & Main Press, 2018 · Hands-On Science for British Columbia · Properties of Energy for Grades K–2 · ISBN: 978-1-55379-798-2

As part of this process, students can also set goals. For example, ask:

- What would you do differently next time and why?
- How will you know if you are successful in meeting your goal?

- To encourage self-reflection, provide prompts that students can use to cite examples of how they have used the Core Competencies in their learning. For this purpose, the CORE COMPETENCY SELF-REFLECTION FRAMES (pages 43-47) can be used throughout the learning process. There are five frames provided to address the Core Competencies: Communication, Creative Thinking, Critical Thinking, Positive Personal and Cultural Identity, and Personal Awareness and Responsibility. Teachers can conference individually with students to support self-reflection, or students may complete prompts using words and pictures.

Again, have students set goals by considering what they might do differently on future tasks and how they will know if they are successful in meeting their goal.

NOTE: Use the same prompts from these sheets over time to see how thinking changes with different activities.

Enhance

- **Family Connection**: Provide students with the following sentence starter:
  - When we go for a walk outside, we see things move, such as _____.

Have students complete the sentence starter at home. Family members can help students draw and write about this topic. Have students share their sentences with the rest of the class.

- Follow up the place-based learning activity with a class discussion about the experience. Construct an Observe, Think, Wonder chart as in the example below:

Observe	Think	Wonder
		?

Record students' ideas in the appropriate columns. Also have students compare observations to predictions discussed prior to the place-based learning experience.

What Can We Learn About Motion Through Storytelling?

2

Information for Teachers

Storytelling makes learning more meaningful and engaging for students by connecting science concepts to real life and to other subjects, as well as providing a connection to the First Peoples Principles of Learning related to knowledge embedded in story. In this lesson, students will participate in a variety of storytelling experiences related to motion.

This lesson also provides an opportunity to introduce students to new books with a book walk (see Engage). Use picture books related to motion to help students build background, enhance interest, generate questions, make predictions, examine visuals, learn new concepts, and share their growing knowledge with others.

Energy is a broad theme that can include a wide range of fiction and nonfiction stories related to the use of energy and motion in everyday life. Stories can be shared about:

- learning to ride a bicycle
- learning to skate
- favourite activities using muscles (e.g., sports, dance, hiking, archery)
- fishing in a boat
- favourite road trips
- sailing
- flying a kite

Plan ahead to invite guest storytellers. Also encourage students to offer suggestions for storytellers from your local area, including family and community members.

If possible, invite a local Elder or Knowledge Keeper to participate in this learning experience. They may be able to share relevant stories about motion related to:

- how animals move (e.g., fly, walk, run, hop, swim, crawl)
- outdoor activities (e.g., hiking, playing games, canoeing)
- hunting and fishing
- weather events

NOTE: See Indigenous Perspectives and Knowledge, page 9, for guidelines for inviting Elders and Knowledge Keepers to speak to students.

Materials

- *Brave Irene* by William Steig
- variety of fiction and nonfiction picture books about motion, light, sound, magnetism, and static electricity; include books by Indigenous authors and other books reflective of the community's cultural makeup (one book for each pair; see Resources for Students, page 68)
- chart paper
- markers
- Template: Sharing Stories Interview Guide (3.2.1)
- Learning-Centre Task Card: What Can I Learn About Energy and Movement? (3.2.2)
- drawing paper
- art supplies

Engage

Model a book walk with *Brave Irene*, by William Steig, or another book with a focus on motion. Use the following steps:

1. Show students the cover of the picture book.
2. Discuss the cover illustration.
3. Point out and discuss the various features of the cover, including the title, author, and illustrator.

▶

Portage & Main Press, 2018 · *Hands-On Science for British Columbia · Properties of Energy for Grades K-2* · ISBN: 978-1-55379-798-2

Portage & Main Press, 2018 · Hands-On Science for British Columbia · Properties of Energy for Grades K–2 · ISBN: 978-1-55379-798-2

4. Have students predict what the book is going to be about, based on their observations of the book's cover.

5. Walk through the pages, discussing the pictures but not reading the text. Ask questions about the illustrations. Have students share what they think is happening on each page.

6. Discuss the final illustrations, and have students predict how the story ends.

7. Discuss the sequence of events in the story.

8. Have students share how the book makes them feel, as well as what they wonder about.

9. Have students share stories and experiences related to what they saw in the book.

After students have shared their ideas and experiences, read the book to the class.

Discuss examples of motion in the book. Have students use complete sentences to share their observations of how things moved in the story. Record their ideas on chart paper. For example:

- Irene was pushed by the wind.
- Irene moved by walking.
- The snow moved because it was blown by the wind.
- Irene pulled on her boots.
- Irene ran through the snow.
- Irene fell in the snow.

Introduce the guided inquiry question: **What can we learn about motion through storytelling?**

Explore Part One

Organize the class into pairs and have each pair choose one of the picture books about motion. Have students do a book walk with their partner.

When students have completed the book walk, have each pair introduce their book to the class, presenting the pictures and their ideas about the content of the book. For each book, have students share observations of how things move or other examples of motion.

In the days to follow, read the books from this activity to the class, immersing them in both fiction and nonfiction. Focus on motion, as depicted in the books.

Explore Part Two

Provide an opportunity for students to benefit from the tradition of oral storytelling to learn about motion. Many cultures pass down knowledge and history through the telling of stories.

Invite a local Elder or Knowledge Keeper to share stories with the class. Also consider inviting presenters from other cultures, reflective of your local community, to share their oral traditions with the class.

NOTE: See Indigenous Perspectives and Knowledge, page 9, for guidelines for inviting Elders and Knowledge Keepers to speak to students.

Following presentations by Elders, Knowledge Keepers, or other storytellers, follow up to explore what students learned. Using gradual release of responsibility will help students be successful in subsequent interview tasks (I Do, We Do, You Do model). For example:

- Do a shared writing piece with students about what they learned.
- Use the Template: Sharing Stories Interview Guide (3.2.1):

▶

2

Date: _____   Name: _____

Interview Guide: Sharing Stories About Motion

1. Storyteller _____

2. Draw a picture of their story.

[drawing box]

3. What did you learn about motion?

_____

_____

4. What else would you like to learn about motion?

_____

_____

☐ Permission given by storyteller to share this story.

3.2.1

Download this template at <www.portageandmainpress.com/product/HOSEnergyK2> .

Use the Optimal Learning Model (I Do, We Do, You Do). Model the completion of this template after the first guest has visited the class (I Do). For the second guest, complete the template as a group (We Do). Students will then complete the template for themselves in Explore Part Three (You Do).

Explore Part Three

Have students interview family or community members and ask them to share stories about motion. Make sure students know to clearly ask permission to share the stories publicly. Review with students that one of the First Peoples Principles of Learning recognizes that some knowledge is sacred and only shared with permission and/or in certain situations. If possible, invite an Elder or Knowledge Keeper

to explain this concept to students and provide examples (see First Peoples Principles of Learning, page 12). Topics of stories might include:

- different modes of transportation (e.g., driving cars, riding bicycles, taking a train, walking, running, sailing, canoeing, flying)
- special trips
- favorite activities and sports
- special skills (e.g., sewing, beading, quilting, fishing, hunting, cooking)

Students may use the Template: Sharing Stories Interview Guide (3.2.1) to record this experience (You Do). Family members may help in completing the sheet.

Students may also use other formats for recording these stories, including audio recordings, illustrations, photographs, or using the traditional oral sharing technique themselves to retell the family story.

As students complete this task at home, have them share stories with the class. During discussion, have students do the following:

- Tell the class about the person they interviewed.
- Provide a summary of the story.
- Explain how they know the story was about motion.

NOTE: Based on these interviews, students may be interested in inviting guests to share other stories about motion. Family members, Elders and Knowledge Keepers, school staff, and staff of local organizations who work with energy may be accessed to share stories and skills.

Expand

Provide students with an opportunity to explore storytelling about motion further by posing their own questions for individualized inquiry. They may wish to:

▶

Portage & Main Press, 2018 · Hands-On Science for British Columbia · Properties of Energy for Grades K-2 · ISBN: 978-1-55379-798-2

Portage & Main Press, 2018 · Hands-On Science for British Columbia · Properties of Energy for Grades K–2 · ISBN: 978-1-55379-798-2

■ Initiate a project at the Makerspace (see page 19), such as designing and creating models or puppets of characters from stories they have heard.

■ Explore Loose Parts bins related to motion with collections of objects that spin (e.g., tops) or roll (e.g., marbles). Display a provocation for students:

  ■ What can you learn about motion from our Loose Parts?

NOTE: Ensure the Loose Parts bins contain objects not related to motion, so students use classifying and reasoning skills as they explore and deepen their learning.

■ Use the Loose Parts to build/create a story about motion.

■ Respond to one of the picture books through art (e.g., paint, Plasticine, oil pastels, collage).

■ Create their own oral stories about motion to share with the class.

■ Create a puppet theatre and recreate a story they have heard or created themselves.

■ Conduct an investigation or experiment based on their own inquiry questions.

As students explore and select ideas to expand learning, provide support and guidance as needed, and offer access to materials and resources that will enable students to conduct their chosen investigations.

Learning Centre

NOTE: In preparation for this learning centre, conduct a whole-class lesson where everyone does the activity together to support student success. As a class, explore and discuss questions such as:

■ How do we read pictures?

■ How do we find answers to our inquiry questions when we cannot read all the words in a book?

At the learning centre, set up an Energy and Movement Library with a variety of fiction and nonfiction picture books related to motion, light, sound, magnetism, and static electricity. Also, provide drawing paper and art supplies, as well as a copy of the Learning-Centre Task Card: What Can I Learn About Energy and Movement? (3.2.2):

Download this template at <www.portageandmainpress.com/product/HOSEnergyK2>.

Have students choose anything they want to read from the library. Encourage them to do book walks, examine and discuss illustrations in the books, and share their ideas with peers. Students can then draw a picture reflective of their ideas.

2

Portage & Main Press, 2018 · Hands-On Science for British Columbia · Properties of Energy for Grades K–2 · ISBN: 978-1-55379-798-2

NOTE: Depending on literacy skills, students may choose to print the title and author of a book and recreate an illustration.

Display students' work at the learning centre for everyone to enjoy.

To extend learning, students may also choose to respond to what they learned in other ways, such as telling a story orally, acting it out dramatically, or demonstrating it with puppets. They may even want to take items from the Loose Parts bins or Makerspace to explore their learnings from the books.

Embed Part One: Talking Circle

Revisit the guided inquiry question: **What can we learn about motion through storytelling?** Have students share their experiences and knowledge, provide examples, and ask further inquiry questions.

Embed Part Two

- Focus on students' use of the Core Competencies. Have students reflect on how they used one of the Core Competencies (Thinking, Communicating, or Personal and Social Skills) during the various lesson activities. Project one of the CORE COMPETENCY DISCUSSION PROMPTS templates (pages 38-42), and use it to inspire group reflection. Referring to the template, choose one or two "I Can" statements on which to focus. Students then use the "I Can" statements to provide evidence of how they demonstrated that competency. Ask questions directly related to that competency to inspire discussion. For example:
  - How did you share your learning today? (Communication)

Have students reflect orally, encouraging participation, questions, and the sharing of

evidence. (See page 29 for more information on these templates.)

As part of this process, students can also set goals. For example, ask:
- What would you do differently next time and why?
- How will you know if you are successful in meeting your goal?

- To encourage self-reflection, provide prompts that students can use to cite examples of how they have used the Core Competencies in their learning. For this purpose, the CORE COMPETENCY SELF-REFLECTION FRAMES (pages 43-47) can be used throughout the learning process. There are five frames provided to address the Core Competencies: Communication, Creative Thinking, Critical Thinking, Positive Personal and Cultural Identity, and Personal Awareness and Responsibility. Teachers can conference individually with students to support self-reflection, or students may complete prompts using words and pictures.

Again, have students set goals by considering what they might do differently on future tasks and how they will know if they are successful in meeting their goal.

NOTE: Use the same prompts from these sheets over time to see how thinking changes with different activities.

Enhance

- **Family Connection**: Provide students with the following sentence starters, and have them choose one:
  - When I learned to ride a bicycle _____.
  - When I learned to skate _____.
  - Some of my family's favourite activities using muscles are _____.

▶

Portage & Main Press, 2018 · Hands-On Science for British Columbia · Properties of Energy for Grades K–2 · ISBN: 978-1-55379-798-2

2

- When my family went fishing in a boat _____.
- My family's favourite road trip was _____.
- When my family went sailing _____.
- When I learned to fly a kite _____.

Have students complete the sentence starter at home. Family members can help students draw and write about this topic. These stories can be sent back to school and made into a class book, "Our Stories About Motion."

- Have students draw pictures of different items that move in their homes. Family members can help with this task. Beside each item, have students describe what moves and what makes the object move.

- Learn the lyrics to *The Marvelous Toy*, a song by Fred Penner, to further examine how objects move.

3 | What Do We Know About Motion?

Information for Teachers

In this lesson, students will participate in place-based learning to explore motion in a local natural environment.

Plan ahead to select a location. Encourage students to suggest natural areas in your local region. Although it is important to introduce students to new areas for place-based learning, also consider using the same location(s) visited in previous lessons or modules to build strong connections to the land.

If possible, invite a local Elder or Knowledge Keeper to participate in this learning experience. They may be able to share relevant stories, as well as knowledge of the land and its features, and motion observable there.

NOTE: See Indigenous Perspectives and Knowledge, page 9, for guidelines for inviting Elders and Knowledge Keepers to speak to students.

Materials

- variety of objects to experiment with motion (e.g., pencils, paper, erasers, feathers, wooden blocks, paper clips) (one of each for each student)
- sticky notes (three different colours)
- chart paper
- markers
- digital cameras (or clipboards, drawing paper, and pencils)
- Learning-Centre Task Card: Making a Parachute (3.3.1)
- small plastic figurines
- plastic garbage bags
- tape
- string
- scissors
- centimetre rulers
- access to printer
- interlocking cubes
- materials to experiment with parachute designs (e.g., tissue paper, newsprint, cheesecloth, thick wool, thread, dental floss)

Engage

Provide each student with a sticky note of the same colour. Have students record on the sticky note one thing they know about motion, using pictures or text.

Conduct a Think, Pair, Share activity. Have students share their ideas with a partner. Next, for class sharing, have each student role-play or mime one thing they know about energy. Model this for the class using your own ideas. For example, act out a demonstration of archery or kayaking to show muscular energy, or flying a kite to show wind energy. Challenge the class to guess what you are doing, then have students take turns role-playing while their classmates guess. On chart paper, create a large pyramid graphic organizer to represent ideas, as in the following example:

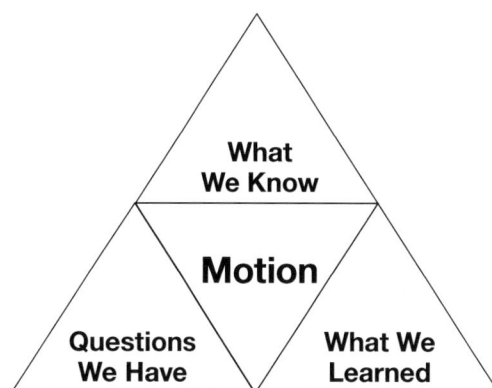

As students role-play and answer, have them add their sticky notes to the top triangle of the pyramid.

Ask:

- What questions do you have about motion?
- What would you like to learn about motion?

▶

Portage & Main Press, 2018 · Hands-On Science for British Columbia · Properties of Energy for Grades K–2 · ISBN: 978-1-55379-798-2

Portage & Main Press, 2018 · Hands-On Science for British Columbia · Properties of Energy for Grades K–2 · ISBN: 978-1-55379-798-2

- What are you most excited to learn about motion?

Record students' questions on a second colour of sticky note, and attach the notes to the pyramid, in the bottom left triangle.

Refer to the pyramid throughout the module. Add answers to students' questions to the bottom right triangle of the pyramid with a third colour of sticky note, as students gather new information and acquire new knowledge. As students generate more inquiry questions, add these to the pyramid as well.

Introduce the term *energy*, discussing that energy is about moving things and doing work. Ask:

- Can you think of an example of energy?

Have students share their ideas.

Introduce the guided inquiry question: **What do we know about motion?**

Explore Part One

Explain to students that they will explore pushes and pulls in a natural environment. Before beginning this activity, have students share with a partner what they are most excited about in visiting this location.

NOTE: Remind students to be respectful of nature and to do no harm. Review the anchor chart created in lesson 1, and add any other ideas that students share about considering the environmental consequences of their actions.

This connects to the First Peoples Principles of Learning as students learn to care for their local environment and take responsibility for the consequences of their actions. To expand on this concept, brainstorm as a class ideas for how students could contribute to the well-being of the place-based learning location. Then implement one of their ideas.

Go out into the school playground or to a local park or nature area. Visit a new place, or consider going back to the place visited in lesson 1 to help students build a stronger connection to place.

As with all place-based learning activities (see page 74 in lesson 1 for more information):

- Identify the importance of place. Use a map of the local area to identify where the location is in relation to the school.
- Identify on whose traditional territory the school is located, as well as the traditional territory of the location for the place-based learning, if different.
- Incorporate land acknowledgment using local protocols.

During this investigation, have digital cameras on hand to capture students' investigations. These photographs will be used in Explore Part Three.

Have students each collect one natural object (e.g., rock, twig, stick, leaf, pine cone).

Then, have students sit in a circle and place their object in front of them. Ask:

- How can the object be moved closer to you?

When students have responded, have them demonstrate by using their hand to pull the object toward them.

Now, ask students:

- How can the object be moved away from you?

Again, when students have responded, have them demonstrate by using their hand to push the object away.

Next, have them stand and hold the object with two hands at chest height. Ask:

- What will happen if you let go of the object?

▶

3

Have students provide predictions, and then demonstrate. Ask:

- Why did the object fall down?
- Would other objects fall in the same way?

Have students select another object and repeat the same task. Compare how different objects (e.g., a leaf and a rock) might fall differently.

Organize the class into pairs, and have each pair select another object. Have them investigate different ways that they can make the object move (e.g., roll a stone, blow on a leaf, push a pine cone with a twig).

⚠ **SAFETY NOTE:** Stress that objects such as twigs and rocks should not be thrown in any way that might harm anyone.

Discuss, and have students look for evidence of, how objects are moved in the place-based learning location (e.g., wind moving leaves, a pine cone falling from a tree, a squirrel carrying acorns).

Explore Part Two

Back in the classroom, provide an opportunity for students to express and reflect on the place-based learning experience, by sharing their personal experiences of place. Encourage them to consider and share how the experience made them feel, think, and wonder.

Print the photographs taken in Explore Part Two and display them around the classroom (e.g., on tables, walls). Organize the class into small groups, and conduct a gallery walk. Encourage students to discuss with their group how the photographs show examples of how things move.

When all groups have viewed all photo displays, meet as a class to debrief. Have students share their ideas and questions from the gallery walk.

Explore Part Three

As a class, brainstorm different terms related to the investigation of motion (e.g., *motion, move, movement, moving, moved, pull, push, roll, throw, fly, float, fall, drop*).

Begin a word wall to display new terms introduced throughout the module, as well as illustrations, photographs, and examples. When possible, add terminology in languages other than English on the word wall, including Indigenous languages. This is a way of acknowledging and respecting students' cultural backgrounds, while enhancing learning for all students.

Words in English and languages other than English can be recorded in the first column, as in the following example:

Word	Picture	Example
Sun hlo<u>k</u>s (Nisga'a language)		The Sun gives us light and heat.
Move		I can move a tin can by rolling it.

NOTE: A variety of online dictionaries may be used as a source for translations. For example:
- <www.firstvoices.com>
- <www.freelang.net/online/haida.php>

Online dictionaries are also available for other languages that may be reflective of the class cultural makeup.

Discuss important words students have been using and learning about (e.g., Sun). Record one of these terms on the word wall. Have students illustrate the term on a large sticky note, and label the parts of their drawing. Add their drawings to the centre column of the word

▶

Portage & Main Press, 2018 · Hands-On Science for British Columbia · Properties of Energy for Grades K–2 · ISBN: 978-1-55379-798-2

Portage & Main Press, 2018 · Hands-On Science for British Columbia · Properties of Energy for Grades K–2 · ISBN: 978-1-55379-798-2

3

wall, along with photographs and other pictures collected throughout the module.

Expand

Provide students with an opportunity to explore motion further by posing their own questions for individualized inquiry. They may wish to:

■ Initiate a project at the Makerspace, such as building a model of a device that can move a load (e.g., crane, truck).

■ Explore Loose Parts bins related to motion. Include collections of objects that spin (e.g., tops) or roll (e.g., marbles). Also include objects that do not spin or roll, so students can identify similarities and differences. Continue the provocation:

■ What can I learn about motion from Loose Parts?

■ Make and display a collection of objects that move (e.g., spinning tops, balls, cars).

■ Build a structure that demonstrates motion.

■ Build a model of an object that uses muscular energy to move (e.g., bicycle, kayak, bow and arrow).

■ Conduct an investigation or experiment based on their own inquiry questions.

As students explore and select ideas to expand learning, provide support and guidance as needed, and offer access to materials and resources that will enable students to conduct their chosen investigations.

Learning Centre

At the learning centre, provide string, plastic garbage bags, scissors, tape, centimetre rulers, interlocking cubes, and small plastic figurines, as well as materials students can use later to experiment with their parachute designs (e.g., tissue paper, newsprint, cheesecloth, thick wool, thread, dental floss). Also provide a copy of the

Learning-Centre Task Card: Making a Parachute (3.3.1):

Making a Parachute

1. Cut a square piece of plastic from a garbage bag (about 30 cm² or 12 cubes square).
2. Measure and cut four pieces of string, each 30 cm or 12 cubes long.
3. Tape one piece of string to each corner of the plastic.
4. Tape or tie the four pieces of string to a small plastic figurine.
5. Stand up, spread out the parachute, and drop it. Try to make it float to the ground.
6. Try dropping the parachute from different heights to see how it moves toward the ground.
7. Experiment with other designs by making parachutes of different materials and shapes. Also, try using different lengths of string and different objects tied to the string.
8. Compare how the different parachutes fall.

Download this template at <www.portageandmainpress.com/product/HOSEnergyK2>.

To further investigate how objects move when dropped, and the effects of air on falling objects, have students design, construct, and test parachutes by following the instructions on the Learning-Centre Task Card (3.3.1).

NOTE: The Learning-Centre Task Card includes instruction for students to measure the parts of the parachute in standard units (centimetres) and nonstandard units (interlocking cubes). If students are using nonstandard units, cut the plastic and strings ahead of time according to the measurements provided on the card.

▶

Embed Part One: Talking Circle

Revisit the guided inquiry question: **What do we know about motion?** Have students share their experiences and knowledge, provide examples, and ask further inquiry questions.

Embed Part Two

- Add to the pyramid chart as students learn new concepts, answer some of their own inquiry questions, and ask new inquiry questions.

- Add new terms and illustrations to the word wall. Include the words in languages other than English, such as Indigenous languages, as appropriate.

- Focus on students' use of the Core Competencies. Have students reflect on how they used one of the Core Competencies (Thinking, Communicating, or Personal and Social Skills) during the various lesson activities. Project one of the CORE COMPETENCY DISCUSSION PROMPTS templates (pages 38-42), and use it to inspire group reflection. Referring to the template, choose one or two "I Can" statements on which to focus. Students then use the "I Can" statements to provide evidence of how they demonstrated that competency. Ask questions directly related to that competency to inspire discussion. For example:

  - How did you decide which questions to ask today? (Critical Thinking)

Have students reflect orally, encouraging participation, questions, and the sharing of evidence. (See page 29 for more information on these templates.)

As part of this process, students can also set goals. For example, ask:

  - What would you do differently next time and why?

  - How will you know if you are successful in meeting your goal?

- To encourage self-reflection, provide prompts that students can use to cite examples of how they have used the Core Competencies in their learning. For this purpose, the CORE COMPETENCY SELF-REFLECTION FRAMES (pages 43-47) can be used throughout the learning process. There are five frames provided to address the Core Competencies: Communication, Creative Thinking, Critical Thinking, Positive Personal and Cultural Identity, and Personal Awareness and Responsibility. Teachers can conference individually with students to support self-reflection, or students may complete prompts using words and pictures.

Again, have students set goals by considering what they might do differently on future tasks and how they will know if they are successful in meeting their goal.

NOTE: Use the same prompts from these sheets over time to see how thinking changes with different activities.

Enhance 🌲 📦 🍃

- **Family Connection**: Provide students with the following sentence starter:

  - Examples of motion in our home are _____.

  Have students take home the sentence starter to complete. Family members can help students draw and write about this topic. Have students share their sentences with the class.

- Use the parachute experiment from the learning centre to introduce single-variable science experiments. Ask:

  - What might happen if we make just one change to our parachutes, and keep everything else the same?

▶

Portage & Main Press, 2018 · Hands-On Science for British Columbia · Properties of Energy for Grades K-2 · ISBN: 978-1-55379-798-2

Portage & Main Press, 2018 · Hands-On Science for British Columbia · Properties of Energy for Grades K–2 · ISBN: 978-1-55379-798-2

■ What does this change tell us?

Students might experiment with the type of fabric, the shape of the parachute, or the object attached to it, to see how objects and materials affect the function of the parachute.

■ Have students brainstorm and implement a project to care for the natural environment(s) visited for the place-based learning activity (e.g., clean up garbage, organize a small fundraiser to support conservation or participate in one already taking place, invite a guest speaker to talk about issues affecting that area, make posters about the issues to spread awareness). This activity connects to the First Peoples Principles of Learning as students support the well-being of their learning environment through a reciprocal relationship.

■ Have students brainstorm and implement a project or activity to care for the natural environment(s) visited for the place-based learning activity (e.g., garbage cleanup, small fundraiser to support conservation, invite a guest speaker to talk about issues affecting that area and making posters about the issues to spread awareness).

■ Provide several containers of small objects (e.g., yo-yos, balls, pencils, erasers, packs of chewing gum, acorns, stones), along with paper plates and index cards. Encourage students to sort the objects on paper plates according to their own rules, and record their sorting rules on the index cards. Have additional index cards with various sorting rules already printed on them, particularly rules that students do not regularly use (e.g., pointed/not pointed, curved/straight edge), and have students use these rules to sort some of the objects onto paper plates. Include picture clues on the index cards, so students do not have to rely on reading alone.

To further extend this activity, make pictographs of students' sorting. On sticky notes, have students draw small pictures of each object in each set. Use the sticky notes on the pictograph to represent sorting data. (See page 24 for information on pictographs.)

4 | How Do Living and Nonliving Things Move?

Materials

- Template: "The Elephant," by Hap Palmer (copy onto chart paper) (3.4.1)
- Template: Elephant Fact Cards (3.4.2)
- *Where Are You?* by Sarah Williamson
- access to school gym or another large space
- computer/tablet with internet access
- markers
- chart paper
- Hula-Hoops (one for each student)
- beanbags (one for each student)
- stopwatch
- pencil crayons
- markers
- access to outdoor playground equipment (e.g., swings, teeter-totters, slides, turn-around structures)*
- pencils with erasers
- straight pins
- scissors
- Learning-Centre Task Card: How Does Air Make Objects Move? (3.4.3)
- Template: Pinwheel (3.4.4)
- pyramid chart (from lesson 3)

---

*NOTE: Although not all playground equipment is necessary, different types of equipment will help to illustrate the concepts in this lesson.

Engage 🖥️1️⃣

Display and read to students the words from the Template: "The Elephant," by Hap Palmer (3.4.1):

The Elephant
by Hap Palmer

The elephant moves very slowly
Oh, so very slowly
He doesn't like to move too fast
Because he is so big and heavy

But should he see a tiger
Or spy a mean old hunter
He will start to run and shake the ground
And make them all fall down

Rumble, rumble, rumble
Hear the jungle rumble
Rumble, rumble, rumble
Hear the jungle rumble

Trees shake and sway
As the birdies fly away
Lions run and hide
With their babies by their side

Rumble, rumble, rumble
Hear the jungle rumble
Rumble, rumble, rumble
Hear the jungle rumble
(repeat)

The elephant moves very slowly
Oh, so very slowly
He doesn't like to move too fast
Because he is so big and heavy

Words and Music by Hap Palmer © Hap-Pal Music.
From the CD *Early Childhood Classics*

3.4.1

Download this template at <www.portageandmainpress.com/product/HOSEnergyK2>.

Next, show students the related video, "The Elephant – by Hap Palmer," at: <https://www.youtube.com/watch?v=xSsDbneWFJ8>. In the video, the song is accompanied by footage of elephants, as well as children role-playing jungle themes.

Play the song (from the video) again. This time have students pretend they are elephants. Hap Palmer suggests the following actions to accompany the song:

1. Bend forward from the waist, and let your arms hang down.
2. Clasp your hands together to form the elephant's trunk.
3. Swing your trunk from side to side as you travel with slow, heavy steps.

▶

Portage & Main Press, 2018 · Hands-On Science for British Columbia · Properties of Energy for Grades K–2 · ISBN: 978-1-55379-798-2

4. When the song mentions the elephant moving faster, run with quick, heavy steps.

Hap Palmer provides the following facts about elephants on his website (see <www.happalmer.com>) that may help to add some variety to students' movements for this activity. Cut out and display the fact cards from the Template: Elephant Fact Cards (3.4.2):

Date: _____   Name: _____

Elephant Fact Cards

An elephant walks and runs with a shuffling step, barely lifting its feet from the ground. With its padded feet, an elephant moves with surprisingly little noise.	An elephant sniffs the air and the ground almost constantly with its trunk. It frequently waves its trunk high in the air to catch the scent of food or enemies.
An elephant's huge ears pick up sounds of other animals from as far as 3 km away. When an elephant is curious about a sound, its ears stand straight out.	An angry or frightened elephant can run more than 40 km/h.
A sudden, strange noise can cause a herd of elephants to panic. The animals may charge at the source of the noise or stampede away from it.	When frightened or angry, elephants sometimes use their trunks to make a loud, shrill cry called trumpeting.
Elephants are excellent swimmers.	An elephant gives itself a shower by shooting a stream of water through its trunk.

3.4.2

Download this template at <www.portageandmainpress.com/product/HOSEnergyK2>.

Read aloud each fact, one at a time. Have students move their bodies to demonstrate the elephant movements.

Encourage students to discuss their movements and compare how they role-played the facts.

Introduce the guided inquiry question: **How do living and nonliving things move?**

Explore Part One

Explore position and motion as related to the elephant song. Ask students:

- When you were pretending you were elephants, what were some of the different movements you made? (walked with slow, heavy steps; sometimes ran with quick, heavy steps; bent forward, let arms hang down; clasped hands together to form trunk; swung trunk from side to side)
- How do trees in the song move? (shake and sway)
- How do the birds move?

Have students identify the names of local animals, and describe how they move. Encourage them to role-play how these animals move in their natural environments.

Focus on position, and encourage students to use positional words to answer the following questions. Ask:

- Where are the birds in the story?
- Where do you think the tiger is?
- Where do you think the hunter is?

As students use positional words to describe relative location, record these on chart paper.

Now, read the book, *Where are You?*, by Sarah Williamson. Have students use the words on the chart paper to describe location of the worm. Record additional positional language words identified while reading the book.

Explore Part Two

Have the class conduct this activity in the school gym or other large space. Give a Hula-Hoop to each student. Explain to students that they are now going to put objects into motion. Ask:

- What does the term *motion* mean?

▶

Have students share their ideas, and record these on chart paper.

Now, explain to students they will use force to put the Hula-Hoops in motion. Ask students:

■ What is a *force*?

Have students share their ideas, and record these on chart paper. Discuss that a *force* is a push or a pull. Tell students they will be applying a force when they move the Hula-Hoops. Ask:

■ How many different ways you can put your Hula-Hoop into motion? Show me.
■ Can you make your hoop go in some of the directions about which we have been talking?

Students will be able to roll their Hula-Hoops forward, backward, to the left and to the right, and rotate them around their waist and their arms. They will also be able to raise the Hula-Hoops up over their head. If they then drop the Hula-Hoops (from above their head), the hoops will fall down to the floor. As students do each activity, discuss motion and position for both the Hula-Hoop and the student.

Now, have students place their Hula-Hoops side by side (with a bit of space in between each hoop) along a line on the gym floor (if needed, use masking tape to create a line). Have students stand a short distance away from their hoops, and then challenge them to throw a beanbag into their Hula-Hoops. Talk about how their position (where they are standing), in relation to the position of the hoop, affects their ability to hit the target. Ask:

■ From what distance is the target easy to hit?
■ What happens if you move farther back?
■ What happens when you stand with your back to the Hula-Hoop and try to hit the target?

Have students share their ideas and experiences.

Extend the discussion to focus on movement of living and nonliving things. Ask:

■ Are beanbags living or nonliving?
■ How did the beanbags move during this activity? What made them move?
■ Are Hula-Hoops living or nonliving?
■ How did the Hula-Hoops move during this activity? What made them move?
■ Are you living or nonliving?
■ How did you move during the activity? What made you move?

Have students share their ideas and experiences.

Explore Part Three

Take students to either the school playground or another local playground with some playground equipment with moving parts, and gather around the playground equipment. Bring a stopwatch.

Have students look at the playground equipment (e.g., swings, teeter-totter, slide, turn-around structures). In pairs, have them discuss what they feel, think, and wonder about the playground. This is an opportunity to express and reflect on personal experiences of place. Ask:

■ What is the position of the object compared to where you are standing?
■ Is everyone's description similar or different? Why?
■ Is any playground object moving right now?
■ What can we do to set it in motion?

Now, encourage students to try to set the objects in motion. Have them take a closer look at the swing. Ask:

■ What part of the swing always remains still?
■ What parts of the swing move?

▶

Portage & Main Press, 2018 · *Hands-On Science for British Columbia · Properties of Energy for Grades K–2* · ISBN: 978-1-55379-798-2

Portage & Main Press, 2018 · Hands-On Science for British Columbia · Properties of Energy for Grades K–2 · ISBN: 978-1-55379-798-2

Have a few students sit still on the swings, and ask other students to make the swings move. Then, have the students in the swings use a pumping action with their legs to keep the swings going. Ask:

■ What happens when you stop pumping your legs?

■ How long do you think the swing will move on its own?

Have students use a stopwatch to measure the time it takes for the swing to change from full motion to no motion. Students can then compare the time to their estimates.

Investigate each piece of playground equipment, examining the moving parts and discussing how each part moves. Explore spinning or moving structures. Ask:

■ How does it move?

■ To get it to spin, what do you have to do?

■ If you want to stop it, what do you need to do?

At the slide, ask:

■ Does the slide move?

■ How do you move when you are on the slide?

■ What would happen if the slide were flat? Would you still move?

While students are on the playground equipment, have them explore their own position in relation to the equipment (e.g., swing, slide, spinning structures). Ask:

■ Are you on the slide/swing/spinning structure, behind it, over it, under it?

When students are in motion, ask:

■ Which words can you use to describe how you are moving? (e.g., around, spinning, up and down, back and forth)

■ What do you see from the top of the slide?

■ How is this different from what you see when you are at the bottom of the slide?

Explore Part Four

Back in the classroom, discuss and record different kinds of motion observed in the playground. Ask:

■ Which objects moved?

■ In which ways did you move when you were on the playground equipment?

Discuss other objects that move. On chart paper, make a two-column chart, and title the columns "Moving Object" and "How It Moves." Have students brainstorm a list of moving objects. Record their ideas on the chart. Include objects in the classroom, school, home, and community.

Now, discuss the various ways that each object moves (e.g., swings, spins, turns), and record these on the chart.

Challenge students to collect some of these objects (e.g., manual eggbeaters, tape recorders, CD players, turntables, drills, toy cars) for further study. Encourage them to record their ideas and experiences through drawing and words. Have students use the SCIENCE JOURNAL template on page 37.

Expand

Provide students with an opportunity to further explore how living and nonliving things move by posing their own questions for individualized inquiry. They may wish to:

■ Initiate a project at the Makerspace, such as designing and constructing a model of a living thing that moves, and researching its features that enable movement (e.g., eagle, fox, salmon).

▶

- Explore Loose Parts related to movement with provide collections of toy cars, spinning tops, gears, and pulleys. Consider including provocations such as:
  - How do these objects move?
  - Can you make two objects move together?

- Create their own graphic organizer to sort and display living and nonliving things in terms of how they move (e.g., fly, swim, crawl, walk, float, spin, twirl). Stickers or images from magazines can be pasted onto the graphic organizer.

- Explore items collected in Explore Part Four. Do a compare/contrast between different objects that move.

- Write a picture book about how animals move.

- Research the movement of nonliving things (e.g., bicycles, motorcycles, or wind turbines) (see Inquiry Through Research, page 26).

- Explore how natural (e.g., limbs) and constructed levers (e.g., seesaw, pliers, scissors) move similarly or differently.

- Conduct an investigation or experiment based on their own inquiry questions.

As students explore and select ideas to expand learning, provide support and guidance as needed, and offer access to materials and resources that will enable students to conduct their chosen investigations.

Learning Centre

At the learning centre, provide pencil crayons, pencils with erasers, straight pins, scissors, a copy of the Learning-Centre Task Card: How Does Air Make Objects Move? (3.4.3), and several copies of the Template: Pinwheel (3.4.4):

Learning Centre

How Does Air Make Objects Move?

1. Cut out the pinwheel along the dotted lines.
2. Poke a pencil tip through the five dots—four at the corners of the pinwheel and one in the centre—to make five holes.
3. Fold the corners into the centre.
4. Push a pin through the centre hole (it should also go through the four folded corner holes) and into the pencil eraser.
5. Check to make sure the pinwheel spins freely.
6. Describe the movement you see.

3.4.3

Pinwheel

3.4.4

Portage & Main Press, 2018 · Hands-On Science for British Columbia · Properties of Energy for Grades K-2 · ISBN: 978-1-55379-798-2

Portage & Main Press, 2018 · Hands-On Science for British Columbia · Properties of Energy for Grades K–2 · ISBN: 978-1-55379-798-2

Download these templates at <www.portageandmainpress.com/product/HOSEnergyK2>.

Have students make pinwheels to demonstrate movement caused by wind energy. Students can decorate their templates, cut out the pinwheel along the dotted lines, and then use a pencil tip to prick through the five dots at the four corners of the template and in the centre, making five holes. Next, have students fold the corners into the centre, and push a pin through the centre hole (and, subsequently, all other holes) into the pencil eraser. Tell students to make sure the pinwheel is able to spin freely.

When students have made their pinwheels, take the class outdoors on a breezy day to investigate wind energy. Ask students to describe the movement of the pinwheel blades in terms of direction and speed. Introduce the terms *clockwise* and *counterclockwise*, as well as *to the right* and *to the left*. Have students experiment with making the blades move in both directions.

Embed Part One: Talking Circle

Revisit the guided inquiry question: **How do living and nonliving things move?** Have students share their experiences and knowledge, provide examples, and ask further inquiry questions.

Embed Part Two

- Add to the pyramid chart as students learn new concepts, answer some of their own inquiry questions, and ask new inquiry questions.

- Add new terms and illustrations to the word wall. Include the words in languages other than English, such as Indigenous languages, as appropriate.

- Focus on students' use of the Core Competencies. Have students reflect on how they used one of the Core Competencies (Thinking, Communicating, or Personal and Social Skills) during the various lesson activities. Project one of the CORE COMPETENCY DISCUSSION PROMPTS templates (pages 38–42), and use it to inspire group reflection. Referring to the template, choose one or two "I Can" statements on which to focus. Students then use the "I Can" statements to provide evidence of how they demonstrated that competency. Ask questions directly related to that competency to inspire discussion. For example:
  - What are you proud of in your learning today? (Personal Awareness and Responsibility)

  Have students reflect orally, encouraging participation, questions, and the sharing of evidence. (See page 29 for more information on these templates.)

  As part of this process, students can also set goals. For example, ask:
  - What would you do differently next time and why?
  - How will you know if you are successful in meeting your goal?

- To encourage self-reflection, provide prompts that students can use to cite examples of how they have used the Core Competencies

▶

in their learning. For this purpose, the CORE COMPETENCY SELF-REFLECTION FRAMES (pages 43-47) can be used throughout the learning process. There are five frames provided to address the Core Competencies: Communication, Creative Thinking, Critical Thinking, Positive Personal and Cultural Identity, and Personal Awareness and Responsibility. Teachers can conference individually with students to support self-reflection, or students may complete prompts using words and pictures.

Again, have students set goals by considering what they might do differently on future tasks and how they will know if they are successful in meeting their goal.

NOTE: Use the same prompts from these sheets over time to see how thinking changes with different activities.

Enhance 🖥

- **Family Connection**: Provide students with the following sentence starters:
  - Some living things that move in our home are _____.
  - Some nonliving things that move in our home are _____.

  Have students complete the sentence starters at home. Family members can help students draw and write about this topic. Have students share their sentences with the rest of the class.

- Connect the learning-centre activity to a discussion about wind farms in your local area. Visit a wind farm, or view a video about wind turbines. Have students describe the movement of the turbine blades.

- Have students bring in toys that move in different ways (e.g., rolling, spinning, bouncing, vibrating) to explore.

Portage & Main Press, 2018 · Hands-On Science for British Columbia · Properties of Energy for Grades K–2 · ISBN: 978-1-55379-798-2

5 | How Do Balls Move?

Materials

- large sticky notes
- chart paper
- markers
- computer/tablet with internet access
- washable markers (optional)
- interlocking cubes (optional)
- paper clips (optional)
- metre sticks (one for each working group)
- masking tape
- sets of three balls (e.g., golf ball, hard rubber ball, tennis ball) (one set for each working group)
- sets of three 60-cm² pieces of various surfaces (e.g., wood, foam, carpet) on which to bounce balls (one set for each working group)
- digital cameras (one for each working group)
- lacrosse sticks
- lacrosse balls
- pyramid chart (from lesson 3)

Engage

Organize the class into pairs of students, and conduct a Turn and Talk activity. Tell students they have one minute to name and describe different types of balls to their partner.

When the minute has passed, as a class, compile a list on chart paper of different types of balls identified by students.

Provide each student with a large sticky note. Ask:

- How could you draw a ball to show it is in motion?

Have students share their ideas, and add their sticky notes to the chart.

Explain to students they will be performing experiments that involve different kinds of balls.

Introduce the guided inquiry question: **How do balls move?**

Explore Part One 🔳1

NOTE: If possible, for the activities in Explore Part One and Explore Part Two, have one student from each group (or an adult supervisor/older student) use a digital camera to video record the group's ball-bouncing experiments. These videos will be used in an Enhance activity toward the end of the lesson. Apps (e.g., Shadow Puppets, Doceri) are also a great way to have students show learning in different ways.

Organize the class into working groups, and provide each group with a metre stick and a set of three balls (e.g., golf ball, hard rubber ball, tennis ball). Have students examine the balls. Ask:

- How are your three balls the same?
- How are your three balls different?
- Are the balls moving right now?
- How do balls move? (e.g., roll, bounce, move through the air)
- Do you think all of the balls will bounce in the same way?

To discuss the importance of fair testing, ask:

- If you want to see how high each ball will bounce, do you think you should bounce them all from the same height or from different heights? Why?
- Do you think it is important to make sure science experiments are done fairly? Why?
- If you were to do an experiment to find out how each ball bounces, how could you make it a fair test?

NOTE: Discuss the concept of variables in general terms with students, focusing on fairness. Throughout the module, continue to ask students if their investigations are fair, and how they know this.

▶

Portage & Main Press, 2018 · Hands-On Science for British Columbia · Properties of Energy for Grades K–2 · ISBN: 978-1-55379-798-2

5

Tell students they will now test the bounciness of their balls by dropping them from a specific height to watch and measure how high each ball bounces back up again after hitting the floor.

NOTE: If students are not using standard measure, this activity can be easily modified by having students mark measurements on the metre stick using a washable marker, and then use interlocking cube trains or paper clip chains to measure.

Have students design and construct a way to record the data from their experiment. For example:

Ball	Height of Drop	Height of Bounce	
		Prediction	Result

If students are working with comparative measures, they might use a checklist chart like the following:

Ball	Prediction			Result		
	Highest Bounce	Middle Bounce	Lowest Bounce	Highest Bounce	Middle Bounce	Lowest Bounce

Have one student in each group hold the group's metre stick vertically, ensuring the 0-cm end is touching the floor and the 100-cm end is at the top. Have students hold one of their three balls at a height of 50 cm (mark this measurement on the metre sticks with masking tape to identify it easily for students). Ask:

- What do you think will happen when you drop the ball?
- How high do you think the ball will bounce?

Have students share their predictions and then test them by dropping the ball. Ask:

- How high did the ball bounce?
- Did it bounce back up to the height from which you dropped it?

Next, have students hold the same ball 1 m above the floor and then drop it. Have them observe and measure how high the ball bounces this time after hitting the floor. Ask:

- Did the ball bounce the same way both times it hit the floor?
- How has its position changed?
- What measurements tell us that its position changed?
- From which measurement did the ball bounce higher—when you dropped it from 50 cm or when you dropped it from 1 m?
- Why do you think this happened?

Challenge students to compare the way the three balls bounced on the floor.

Explore Part Two 🔲

Distribute to each group a set of three 60-cm² pieces of various surfaces (e.g., wood, foam, carpet). Have students examine the three surfaces. Ask:

- How are each of the surfaces the same?
- How are they different?
- Do you think a ball will bounce the same way on each surface? Why or why not?

Now, challenge students to investigate how one ball bounces on each of the three different surfaces. Instruct them to start at 1 m above the floor for each ball, so the test is fair.

Have students design and construct a way to record the data from their experiment. For example:

Portage & Main Press, 2018 · Hands-On Science for British Columbia · Properties of Energy for Grades K–2 · ISBN: 978-1-55379-798-2

Surface	Height of Drop	Height of Bounce	
		Prediction	Result

If students are working with comparative measures, they might use a checklist chart like the following:

Surface	Prediction			Result		
	Highest Bounce	Middle Bounce	Lowest Bounce	Highest Bounce	Middle Bounce	Lowest Bounce

Explore Part Three

Following the investigations, have students present their results and discuss their findings. Ask:

- Were you able to make the experiment fair? How?
- What did you learn from doing this experiment?

Have students share their ideas and responses. Ask:

- Which ball bounced the highest?
- Which ball bounced the lowest?
- Which surface made balls bounce higher?
- Which surface made balls bounce lower?

Have students order the balls from lowest to highest bounce. Order the surfaces as well. Ask:

- If you were to do this experiment again, what other kinds of balls would you test? Why?
- What other surfaces would you test? Why?

Student Self-Assessment ⒸC

Have students complete the COOPERATIVE SKILLS SELF-ASSESSMENT template, on page 49, to reflect on their own work as part of a group. Have students focus on how they shared observations and ideas with others.

Formative Assessment ⒸC

As students conduct the ball-bouncing investigations, use the COOPERATIVE SKILLS TEACHER ASSESSMENT template, on page 52, to record their ability to work together. Focus on how students shared observations and ideas with others. Provide descriptive feedback to students about how they collaborate with others.

Explore Part Four 🖳

Indigenous peoples invented many games that involve balls. The Haudenosaunee are known for inventing lacrosse, while others invented ball games such as shinnie and a version of volleyball.

Consider inviting a local Elder, Knowledge Keeper, or another Indigenous community member with experience in these games to visit the class to share information and demonstrate or teach games.

NOTE: See Indigenous Perspectives and Knowledge, page 9, for guidelines for inviting Elders and Knowledge Keepers to speak to the class.

Display the lacrosse sticks and balls for students to examine. Ask:

- What are these?
- For what are they used?
- What do you know about the game of lacrosse?
- Do you know who invented the game and the equipment?

Have students visit the Iroquois Nationals' website to read "The Story of Lacrosse," a Haudenosaunee story about the creation of lacrosse: <https://iroquoisnationals.org/the-iroquois/the-story-of-lacrosse/>. Have students

▶

Portage & Main Press, 2018 · Hands-On Science for British Columbia · Properties of Energy for Grades K–2 · ISBN: 978-1-55379-798-2

use the *Indigenous Peoples' Atlas of Canada* or a similar resource to identify the traditional territory of the Haudenosaunee.

Then, have students watch videos to learn about the history of lacrosse, such as:

■ "THE STICKMAKER – Alf Jaques "UNSTRUNG" Handmakes Wood Lacrosse Sticks" <https://www.youtube.com/watch?v=iSoR9oGGpOc>

Also, watch a video that talks about the forces involved in lacrosse:

■ "Physics of a Lacrosse Shot" <https://www.youtube.com/watch?v=Bhfw5R2U5mE>

After watching the videos, take students outside or to the gym to practise the lacrosse shot, and discuss the forces used. For a local connection, have students research lacrosse players and teams from British Columbia, as well as in their region.

As an alternative, as a class, research Indigenous games using balls. Some valuable resources for researching this topic are:

■ *Our Original Games: A Look at Aboriginal Sport in Canada* by Bruce Miller

■ "Games From the Aboriginal People of North America" <aboriginalperspectives.uregina.ca/games/>

Provide an opportunity for students to play the games. Debrief after playing the games. Be sure to use the debrief as an opportunity to reinforce the concepts in the module by encouraging students to use vocabulary (e.g., *push, pull, motion*) to discuss the forces used.

Expand

Provide students with an opportunity to explore how balls move further by posing their own questions for individualized inquiry. They may wish to:

■ Initiate a project at the Makerspace, such as designing and constructing a catapult to throw balls.

■ Explore Loose Parts bins of various ball collections (also include some Loose Parts that are not balls). Include a provocation, such as:

■ Can you conduct an experiment using different kinds of balls and surfaces?

■ Build a marble run out of recycled materials. Challenge students to ensure that the marble changes direction and does a drop.

■ Research the production of a specific ball (see Inquiry Through Research, page 26).

■ Choose a specific game or sport to learn about and demonstrate.

■ Take apart a golf ball, tennis ball, or basketball to see how it is made.

■ Learn and demonstrate basketball tricks (look up Harlem Globetrotter videos for examples).

■ Explore the movement of different-sized balls made of the same materials (i.e., only variable changed is the size).

■ Conduct an investigation or experiment based on their own inquiry questions.

As students explore and select ideas to expand learning, provide support and guidance as needed, and offer access to materials and resources that will enable students to conduct their chosen investigations.

Embed Part One: Talking Circle

Revisit the guided inquiry question: **How do balls move?** Have students share their experiences and knowledge, provide examples, and ask further inquiry questions.

Portage & Main Press, 2018 · Hands-On Science for British Columbia · Properties of Energy for Grades K–2 · ISBN: 978-1-55379-798-2

▶

Portage & Main Press, 2018 · Hands-On Science for British Columbia · Properties of Energy for Grades K–2 · ISBN: 978-1-55379-798-2

5

Embed Part Two

- Add to the pyramid chart as students learn new concepts, answer some of their own inquiry questions, and ask new inquiry questions.

- Add new terms and illustrations to the word wall. Include the words in languages other than English, such as Indigenous languages, as appropriate.

- Focus on students' use of the Core Competencies. Have students reflect on how they used one of the Core Competencies (Thinking, Communicating, or Personal and Social Skills) during the various lesson activities. Project one of the CORE COMPETENCY DISCUSSION PROMPTS templates (pages 38-42), and use it to inspire group reflection. Referring to the template, choose one or two "I Can" statements on which to focus. Students then use the "I Can" statements to provide evidence of how they demonstrated that competency. Ask questions directly related to that competency to inspire discussion. For example:
  - Today, we learned about fair tests. How do you play fair with others? (Personal Awareness and Responsibility)

  Have students reflect orally, encouraging participation, questions, and the sharing of evidence. (See page 29 for more information on these templates.)

  As part of this process, students can also set goals. For example, ask:
  - What would you do differently next time and why?
  - How will you know if you are successful in meeting your goal?

- To encourage self-reflection, provide prompts that students can use to cite examples of how they have used the Core Competencies in their learning. For this purpose, the CORE COMPETENCY SELF-REFLECTION FRAMES (pages 43-47) can be used throughout the learning process. There are five frames provided to address the Core Competencies: Communication, Creative Thinking, Critical Thinking, Positive Personal and Cultural Identity, and Personal Awareness and Responsibility. Teachers can conference individually with students to support self-reflection, or students may complete prompts using words and pictures.

  Again, have students set goals by considering what they might do differently on future tasks and how they will know if they are successful in meeting their goal.

NOTE: Use the same prompts from these sheets over time to see how thinking changes with different activities.

Enhance 🖥️ 🌲

- **Family Connection**: Provide students with the following sentence starter:
  - Our favourite games with balls are
    _____.

  Have students complete the sentence starter at home. Family members can help students draw and write about this topic. Have students share their sentences with the rest of the class.

- Have students collect a variety of balls for display purposes.

- Have students research how balls are made and used in various cultures.

- Have students experiment with dropping spherical items (e.g., marble, Styrofoam ball, tennis ball) into different substances such as:
  - a container of water (half full)
  - a container of cooking oil (half full)
  - a container of honey or syrup (half full)

▶

5

- Have students repeat the above experiment, using objects that are pointed (e.g., a small pencil).

- Add a variety of balls and containers to the water table for further exploration.

- Add a variety of balls and digging tools to the sand table for further exploration.

- Investigate and research to find out how balls can be made from recycled materials.

- Use the video recording from the ball-bouncing activities from Explore Part One and Explore Part Two to check the accuracy of their hand-recorded bounce heights, by pausing the video when the ball is at its highest point.

- Encourage inquiry with the Ping-Pong ball and golf ball drop. Conduct the demonstration and challenge students to figure out why the system behaves the way it does. The investigation is demonstrated in the video "Dropping a Ping Pong Ball With a Golf Ball" at: <https://www.youtube.com/watch?v=zpfo55a6YPk>.

Portage & Main Press, 2018 · Hands-On Science for British Columbia · Properties of Energy for Grades K-2 · ISBN: 978-1-55379-798-2

6 | How Can We Move an Object?

Information for Teachers

Simple machines are machines that have been developed to do work for us.

Materials

- baskets of small objects (e.g., paper clips, elastic bands, craft sticks, stir sticks, rulers, pieces of string, drinking straws, wooden dowels, pencils) (one basket for each working group)
- surfaces to test movement (e.g., wax paper, carpet swatches, sandpaper)
- video cameras (optional)
- recycled paper (one sheet for each working group)
- wooden blocks (one for each working group)
- chart paper
- markers
- Image Bank: Movement in Daily Life (see Appendix, page 177)
- computer/tablet with internet access
- drawing paper
- sand table
- variety of toy construction vehicles
- digging tools (e.g., shovels, cups, spoons)
- several identical clear containers
- several identical weights (e.g., large washers or nuts, marbles, gram weights)
- nonfiction books related to construction
- toy bow and arrow
- canoe paddles
- Learning-Centre Task Card: Caution—Construction Zone! (3.6.1)
- pyramid chart (from lesson 3)

Engage

Review with students the ball-bouncing experiment from lesson 5, emphasizing the results, conclusion, and application of the experiment.

Organize the class into working groups. Ask:

- In our previous lesson, how did the balls move in the experiment? (They bounced, then rolled.)
- Why can a ball move with little help from us? (It is spherical/round and can roll.)

Show students a wooden block. Ask:

- Do you think this can move as easily as a ball can? (No.)
- Why not? (It is not round.)
- How could you make the wooden block move?

Display one basket of small objects (e.g., paper clips, elastic bands, craft sticks, stir sticks, rulers, pieces of string, drinking straws, wooden dowels, pencils). Ask:

- Can you use any of the objects in the basket to help you move the wooden block?

Introduce the guided inquiry question: **How can we move an object?**

Explore Part One

NOTE: If possible, have one student from each group (or an adult supervisor/older student) video record the following two activities. The videos can be used for an Enhance activity toward the end of the lesson.

Distribute to each group a basket of small objects (e.g., paper clips, elastic bands, craft sticks, ruler, piece of string, drinking straws, wooden dowels, pencils, stir sticks), a sheet of recycled paper, and a wooden block. Tell students to place the wooden block in the centre of their paper. Challenge students to find a variety of ways to use the objects in the basket to move the wooden block off the piece of paper. Tell them they must find a way to move the block with both a pulling motion and a pushing motion, but without touching the block directly with their hands. Explain that they can attach items

▶

Portage & Main Press, 2018 · *Hands-On Science for British Columbia · Properties of Energy for Grades K–2* · ISBN: 978-1-55379-798-2

6

(e.g., string, elastic bands) to the block. Their strategies for moving the block may include actions such as:

- pull it with a string
- use a ruler as a slide for the block
- place wooden dowels or pencils under it, and roll it
- lift it with bent paper clips

Give students plenty of time to explore and discuss their strategies and to try new ideas. Then have each group explain to the class one or two of their strategies. Encourage them to use vocabulary that explains how the block was moved (e.g., *push, pull, lift, drag, slide*). Allow students to use the materials to demonstrate.

On chart paper, record students' strategies for moving the block. Also record the number of groups who discovered the same strategy.

Explore Part Two 🖥️

Repeat the above activity with the same materials, except instead of recycled paper, have students place their block on other surfaces (e.g., wax paper, carpet swatches, sandpaper). Provide time for students to examine the various materials and make predictions as to how the block will move on each surface.

Then, have students explore the effects of different surfaces on the movement of the block.

After they have completed the investigation, meet to debrief. Ask:

- Did the block move more easily on any of the surfaces?
- On which surface was it easiest to move the block?
- On which surface was it hardest to move the block?
- Why do you think that some surfaces were more difficult to move the block on than others?

- How are the surfaces different?

Introduce students to the term *friction* and co-construct a definition as class. This discussion provides an opportunity to make real-life connections to movement and friction. For example, discuss the use of sand on icy roads to make them safer.

Explore Part Three 🖥️

Explore how Indigenous peoples use pushes and pulls to move objects. Invite a local Elder or Knowledge Keeper to discuss and demonstrate useful objects that use pushes and pulls (e.g., fire starter, bone needle, tomahawk, spear, ulu, bow and arrow, paddle).

Demonstrate the use of a bow and arrow or watch videos such as:

- "Comanche Archery 101: Aiming and Shooting" <https://www.youtube.com/watch?v=RezOCzxcvmM>
- "Native American Bow Hunting" <https://www.youtube.com/watch?v=5mgivuYJ_TM>

Have students observe and discuss the forces and motion involved. Focus on the pulling back of the bow and the forward motion of the arrow. Encourage students to use positional language, as well as vocabulary terms (e.g., push, pull, force, motion).

⚠️ **SAFETY NOTE:** If demonstrating, use a toy bow and arrow without a sharp point, or cover the pointed end of the arrow with a Styrofoam ball for safety purposes.

Next, demonstrate how a paddle is used in a canoe. Sit on a chair, pretending to be seated in a canoe, and demonstrate how the paddle is used. Have students try the same demonstration. Focus on the pulling back of the paddle and the forward motion of the canoe. Again, encourage students to use related

▶

Portage & Main Press, 2018 · Hands-On Science for British Columbia · Properties of Energy for Grades K–2 · ISBN: 978-1-55379-798-2

Portage & Main Press, 2018 · Hands-On Science for British Columbia · Properties of Energy for Grades K–2 · ISBN: 978-1-55379-798-2

6

positional language, as well as vocabulary terms (e.g., *push, pull, force, motion*).

Also watch videos of paddling a canoe, such as:

■ "TRIBAL CANOE JOURNEY – NW COAST FIRST NATION CULTURES" <https://www.youtube.com/watch?v=dhp_MFa6o6c>

Have students use drawing paper to create labelled diagrams of these two demonstrations, or create demonstration videos on how to use a bow and arrow or how to paddle a canoe.

Display the Image Bank: Movement in Daily Life. Have students describe the various objects and infer what their uses are. Discuss the forces acting on these objects as they are used (pushes and pulls).

Expand

Provide students with an opportunity to further explore how to move objects by posing their own questions for individualized inquiry. They may wish to:

■ Initiate a project at the Makerspace, such as designing and constructing a model of a pyramid to demonstrate how they were built.

■ Explore Loose Parts bins of pulley parts (e.g., wheels, rope, hooks, small pails). Also include some bins of objects that can be lifted with pulleys. Consider including a provocation, such as:

■ Can you make a pulley to lift an object?

■ Research and model the process of moving a house (see Inquiry Through Research, page 26).

■ Explore the effects of moving the block over other surfaces (e.g., sand, gravel, a cookie sheet filled with ice, snow, or water).

■ Conduct an investigation or experiment based on their own inquiry questions.

As students explore and select ideas to expand learning, provide support and guidance as needed, and offer access to materials and resources that will enable students to conduct their chosen investigations.

Learning Centre

At the learning centre, provide a sand table, a variety of toy construction vehicles, digging tools (e.g., shovels, cups, spoons), as well as several identical clear containers and weights (any identical items that will fit into the containers can be used, such as large washers or nuts, marbles, gram weights). Also display a variety of nonfiction books related to construction, and a copy of the Learning-Centre Task Card: Caution—Construction Zone! (3.6.1):

Learning Centre

Caution—Construction Zone!

1. Look at the books to learn about construction sites.
   - What kinds of machines are used?
   - How are large objects moved?
   - What parts of the machines enable a large object to be moved?
2. Take some time to play with the construction vehicles in the sand. How do they move? What kinds of jobs do they do?
3. Fill three containers with different numbers of weights.
4. Count the weights in each container and record the number on the lid of the container. Close the lids.
   - Which container is lightest?
   - Which container is heaviest?
5. Find ways to move the containers around the construction site. Use different machines and objects to move the containers.
   - What have you learned about how heavy objects are moved around a construction site?

3.6.1

Download this template at <www.portageandmainpress.com/product/HOSEnergyK2>.

Students will explore how large objects are moved on a construction site, and model these processes at the sand table. Allow students to explore and recreate construction sites with various ways to move objects.

Embed Part One: Talking Circle

Revisit the guided inquiry question: **How can we move an object?** Have students share their experiences and knowledge, provide examples, and ask further inquiry questions.

Embed Part Two

- Add to the pyramid chart as students learn new concepts, answer some of their own inquiry questions, and ask new inquiry questions.
- Add new terms and illustrations to the word wall. Include the words in languages other than English, such as Indigenous languages, as appropriate.
- Focus on students' use of the Core Competencies. Have students reflect on how they used one of the Core Competencies (Thinking, Communicating, or Personal and Social Skills) during the various lesson activities. Project one of the CORE COMPETENCY DISCUSSION PROMPTS templates (pages 38-42), and use it to inspire group reflection. Referring to the template, choose one or two "I Can" statements on which to focus. Students then use the "I Can" statements to provide evidence of how they demonstrated that competency. Ask questions directly related to that competency to inspire discussion. For example:
  - How did you take care of yourself and others today by working safely with materials? (Personal Awareness and Responsibility)

Have students reflect orally, encouraging participation, questions, and the sharing of evidence. (See page 29 for more information on these templates.)

As part of this process, students can also set goals. For example, ask:
- What would you do differently next time and why?
- How will you know if you are successful in meeting your goal?

- To encourage self-reflection, provide prompts that students can use to cite examples of how they have used the Core Competencies in their learning. For this purpose, the CORE COMPETENCY SELF-REFLECTION FRAMES (pages 43-47) can be used throughout the learning process. There are five frames provided to address the Core Competencies: Communication, Creative Thinking, Critical Thinking, Positive Personal and Cultural Identity, and Personal Awareness and Responsibility. Teachers can conference individually with students to support self-reflection, or students may complete prompts using words and pictures.

Again, have students set goals by considering what they might do differently on future tasks and how they will know if they are successful in meeting their goal.

NOTE: Use the same prompts from these sheets over time to see how thinking changes with different activities.

Enhance 🖥️

- **Family Connection**: Have students take home a wooden block to test on different surfaces at home. Provide students with the following sentence starter:
  - We can move the block on _____ by _____.

▶

Portage & Main Press, 2018 · Hands-On Science for British Columbia · Properties of Energy for Grades K–2 · ISBN: 978-1-55379-798-2

Portage & Main Press, 2018 · Hands-On Science for British Columbia · Properties of Energy for Grades K–2 · ISBN: 978-1-55379-798-2

6

Have students complete the sentence starter at home. Family members can help students draw and write about this topic. Have students share their sentences with the rest of the class.

- If students have video recorded their strategies for moving the wooden block in Explore Part One, play back each group's video clip, and have students give either an oral or a written description of the strategies they used, using the terms *push* and *pull*.

- Show students photos and video footage of the moving of large structures from the show *Monster Moves* found on the National Geographic UK site. Go to: <natgeotv.com/uk/monster-moves>. Ask students what questions they have about such moves, and have them conduct research to answer their questions.

7 | How Can We Move Loads More Easily?

Information for Teachers

Round objects (e.g., rollers, wheels and axles) can be used to move heavy loads and reduce work. Sliding objects have more contact on surfaces than rolling objects do, so there is less friction when using rollers.

Rollers were used more than 6,000 years ago, long before the development of the wheel. Rollers are really like a long wheel without an axle. They were used along with inclined planes/ramps to transport very heavy loads, such as large sections of the pyramids in Egypt.

Wheels and axles can be either fixed or moving. By examining several toy cars, it becomes apparent that when the axle is fixed to the chassis (the base frame of the car) and does not move, the wheels spin freely. In other designs, the wheels are fixed to the axle, but the axle spins freely. The following diagrams show examples of a fixed axle and of a fixed wheel.

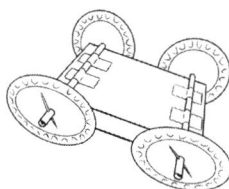
fixed axle

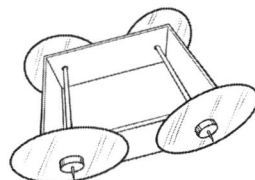
fixed wheel

Materials

- large bin of books (have additional books on hand to add to the bin)
- Image Bank: Travois (see Appendix, page 177)
- sharp pencils
- scissors
- sturdy, cylindrical-shaped tubes (e.g., wooden dowels, PVC piping, tubes from carpet rolls)
- shoeboxes without lids (one for each pair of students)
- wooden blocks, rocks, or other heavy materials
- string
- tape
- metre sticks
- Template: "My New Bike" by David A. Robertson (3.7.1) (copied onto chart paper)
- bicycle
- collection of toys with wheels (including some students can take apart)
- boards or other materials suitable for ramps
- materials to adjust the height of the ramps (e.g., books)
- projection device (optional)
- chart paper
- markers
- natural and recycled materials for constructing model travois
- toy figurines
- Plasticine
- drawing paper
- writing paper
- audio-recording device
- Learning-Centre Task Card: Sing a Song of Bicycles! (3.7.2)
- pyramid chart (from lesson 3)

Engage

Have the students sit in a circle on the floor. Place the large bin of books in the centre of the circle. Ask:

- Do you think you can lift the bin of books?

Have students share their predictions and then test them by having a few volunteers try to lift the bin (one at a time). Ask:

- Do you think you can lift the bin if you have help from a classmate?

Have students share their predictions and then test them by having a few partner volunteers try to lift the bin.

▶

Portage & Main Press, 2018 · *Hands-On Science for British Columbia · Properties of Energy for Grades K–2* · ISBN: 978-1-55379-798-2

Now, add several more books to the bin. Ask:

- If you had to deliver this bin of books to the library, how would you do it?
- What would you use to help you?

Have students share their ideas and role-play the process.

Introduce the guided inquiry question: **How can we move loads more easily?**

Student Self-Assessment (PC)

Using the SCIENCE JOURNAL template on page 37, have students write about and/or draw an experience when they (or their family/friends) had to move a heavy load. Encourage students to reflect on the strategies and tools they used to move the load. Focus on their ability to record observations.

NOTE: To foster family connections, have the students take this sheet home to discuss with family members.

Explore Part One

Organize the class into pairs. Provide each pair with a shoebox, a sharp pencil, string, scissors, a metre stick (or nonstandard measuring devices—see below), and tape. Explain that they are going to build a wagon that will make it easier to carry a load.

Have students use a sharp pencil to poke a hole in the centre of one end of the shoebox. Now, have them use a metre stick or non-standard units (e.g., nine toe-to-toe footsteps, three notebooks) to measure and cut 1 m of string. Tell students to feed the string through the hole in the shoebox, and tie a big knot on the end inside the box. Then have them tape the knot to the inside of the box, so the string is secure and cannot be easily pulled back out through the hole.

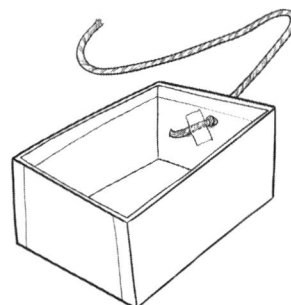

Have students pull their empty wagon along the floor, noting how easily the wagon slides. Ask:

- Is the wagon easy to pull?
- What do you think will happen if you put objects in the wagon?
- Will it be easy or hard to pull?

Have students put some blocks, rocks, or other weight inside their wagons. Ask them to pull their wagons again. They will notice the wagon is harder to pull now than it was when it was empty. Ask:

- Why is it harder to pull now? (The weight prevents it from sliding easily.)

Provide an opportunity for students to investigate the effects of pulling the wagon on different surfaces in the classroom and outdoors (e.g., carpet, flooring, concrete, grass). Discuss how the surfaces cause varying degrees of *friction* that make it easier or more difficult to move the wagon.

Give each pair of students several sturdy, cylindrical-shaped tubes (e.g., wooden dowels, PVC piping, tubes from carpet rolls). Ask:

- How could you use the tubes to make it easier to pull the wagon?

Have students use the tubes as rollers to move their loads, experimenting with the position and number of rollers used. Encourage students to

▶

Portage & Main Press, 2018 · Hands-On Science for British Columbia · Properties of Energy for Grades K–2 · ISBN: 978-1-55379-798-2

7

take turns: while one student pulls the box along on the tubes, the other student places rollers in front of the box to keep it going. Students may notice the cardboard tubes are not strong enough to carry heavier loads.

Explore Part Two

Display the Image Bank: Travois. Record the term *travois* on chart paper. Explain to students that this is the term used for the frame structures in the Image Bank. The term *travois* comes from the French word, *travail*, which means "difficult work." It is also sometimes called a *drag sled*. Travois are used primarily by Indigenous peoples of the plains, but they are used in British Columbia by peoples such as the Kootenay in the southeast of the province. Use a map to help students identify the traditional territory of the Kootenay.

Have students examine and discuss the images. Ask:

- For what do you think the travois structure was used?
- Of what is it made?
- How is it designed?
- How do you think the branches are fastened together?
- How would the travois help move loads more easily?

As students share their ideas, record these on chart paper.

Now challenge them to design and construct a model travois using natural materials as much as possible (and recycled materials when necessary). The travois should be able to carry a load determined by the class (e.g., a wooden block, rock, weight). Have students work in groups, pairs, or individually.

NOTE: In their model, students should also include a horse, human, or other animal to pull the travois. The figurine may be a toy or handmade (e.g., from Plasticine). Select a figurine before designing the travois, in order to create an accurately sized model.

As a class, co-construct criteria for the project. For example:

- uses natural materials (e.g., twigs, branches, grass)
- includes a figurine to "pull" the travois
- carries a load
- sturdy when pulled

Have students draw blueprints of their designs on drawing paper, list materials needed to construct the model, and identify steps in the process. This can be done using text and pictures.

When students have completed their model travois, have them test their models by carrying and pulling the load.

Discuss the various designs and materials used by different groups. Compare their success in meeting the project criteria. Encourage students to discuss how they might change the design of the model travois to better move the load.

Explore Part Three

Read aloud the poem from the Template: "My New Bike" by David A. Robertson (3.7.1) and display the lyrics on chart paper. Engage students in a discussion that gives them opportunities to discuss their own experiences with bicycles (e.g., riding up or down a hill, getting a flat tire).

▶

Portage & Main Press, 2018 · Hands-On Science for British Columbia · Properties of Energy for Grades K-2 · ISBN: 978-1-55379-798-2

Portage & Main Press, 2018 · Hands-On Science for British Columbia · Properties of Energy for Grades K–2 · ISBN: 978-1-55379-798-2

7

My New Bike
by David A. Robertson

Mom got me some streamers
To put on my handlebars
And Dad got me reflectors
To keep me safe near cars.

At the store we found a basket
To put all my things inside
Because, according to my mom
I need two arms to ride.

My brother put some cards
On the spokes of my front tire.
He says Pokemon and hockey
Look good on metal wires.

Grandma got my helmet
Says it'll save my noggin'
When I bike to get some treats
Or decide to do hot doggin'.

And, boy, do I bike fast!
People say, "Wow, look at her!"
I bet nobody's ever seen
Such a stylish blur.

3.7.1

Download this template at <www.portageandmainpress.com/product/HOSEnergyK2>.

Connect this activity with the storytelling activity from lesson 2, if any students explored learning to ride a bicycle. If so, have them share their story with the class.

Display a bicycle for students to examine. Have them manipulate the parts and discuss how the bicycle works. Ask:

- Does a bicycle move on its own?
- What do you have to do to make the bicycle move?
- How can you make the bicycle go fast?
- How can you make the bicycle go slowly?
- What happens when you ride a bicycle down a hill?
- What happens when you ride a bicycle up a hill?

- What part of the bicycle makes it stop?
- What part of the bicycle makes it change direction?
- What happens when you ride a bicycle on a bumpy, gravel road?
- How is riding a bicycle on a bumpy, gravel road different from riding a bicycle on a smooth, paved road?
- What would happen if the wheels on the bicycle were square?
- What would it feel like if there were no tires on the bicycle, just metal rims? Would it be easy or hard to ride?

Provide an opportunity for students to demonstrate and describe the way in which the wheels on the bicycle move. For example, ask:

- Can you show the wheels turning clockwise? Counterclockwise?
- Can you make the wheel spin slowly? Quickly?
- Can you move the wheel with a push? A pull?

Have students share their ideas.

Finally, if there is a local bicycle shop in your community or a community member who is an avid cyclist, invite them to speak to the class about the parts of a bicycle, and how to care for a bicycle to ensure safety and good riding.

Explore Part Four

Next, invite students to explore toys with wheels. Encourage them to take a toy apart to see how the wheels are attached.

Introduce the term *axle*. As a class, co-construct a definition for the term (e.g., the rod on which a wheel turns), and encourage students to use the term as they discuss the toys. Also encourage students to talk about the kinds of motion or movement the toys can perform. Ask:

- How does this one move?

▶

- What happens when you change the amount of force you apply to make it move?
- Can it turn?
- Can it go backwards? Sideways?
- Does it have an axle?

Use a board and a pile of books (or another support) to make a ramp. Have students test various toys on the ramp to see how each toy moves. Encourage them to change the height of the ramp and investigate the motion of the toys.

Follow with a discussion about the importance of wheels and the structure of a wheel-and-axle mechanism. Ask:

- How are wheels important to these toys?
- How are the wheels attached?
- What does the axle do?

Also discuss how movement would be affected if the toy had wheels but no axle, or if the toy had an axle but no wheels.

Expand

Provide students with an opportunity to explore how to move loads farther by posing their own questions for individualized inquiry. They may wish to:

- Initiate a project at the Makerspace, such as designing a vehicle that uses rollers or wheels to move objects.
- Explore Loose Parts bins with objects related to wheels and rollers (e.g., toy cars, wheels, rollers, dowels, wooden blocks). Consider adding a provocation such as:
  - How can you move a load?
- Use their shoebox wagons to investigate how to measure the force needed to move loads with rollers. They can use spring scales and measure the force needed to lift various loads in their wagons.

- Investigate what happens when they pull their wagon up an inclined plane, and test their wagon on inclined planes of various heights, using different rollers.
- Look for and research practical examples of rollers and wheels in use (e.g., boat ramps, moving houses on rollers, strollers, roller blades, skateboards) (see Inquiry Through Research, page 26).
- Design and construct their own trucks and cars, and then test their movement on different surfaces (e.g., boards covered with burlap, sandpaper, aluminum foil, corrugated cardboard). Students can then compare how the toys move on the various surfaces in terms of friction caused by the wheels on the ramp surface.
- Conduct an investigation or experiment based on their own inquiry questions.

As students explore and select ideas to expand learning, provide support and guidance as needed, and offer access to materials and resources that will enable students to conduct their chosen investigations.

Learning Centre

At the learning centre, provide writing paper, an audio-recording device, and a copy of the Learning-Centre Task Card: Sing a Song of Bicycles! (3.7.2):

▶

Portage & Main Press, 2018 · Hands-On Science for British Columbia · Properties of Energy for Grades K–2 · ISBN: 978-1-55379-798-2

Portage & Main Press, 2018 · Hands-On Science for British Columbia · Properties of Energy for Grades K–2 · ISBN: 978-1-55379-798-2

Learning Centre

Sing a Song of Bicycles!

With a partner or by yourself, write a song about how wheels help you in your everyday life.

You can use the melody of one of the songs listed below, or you can use another tune of your choice.

The Farmer in the Dell

Pop Goes the Weasel

London Bridge Is Falling Down

Row, Row, Row Your Boat

Are You Sleeping?

I'm a Little Teapot

Here We Go 'Round the Mulberry Bush

If You're Happy and You Know It

Twinkle, Twinkle Little Star

Mary Had a Little Lamb

Jingle Bells

The Muffin Man

She'll Be Coming 'Round the Mountain

3.7.2

Download this template at <www.portageandmainpress.com/product/HOSEnergyK2>.

Included on the task card (3.7.2) is a list of melodies that easily lend themselves to transitions and the teaching of elementary concepts. Review the songs on the card with students to remind them of how they are sung.

Using the melody from one of the songs in the list, have each student write and a song about how wheels help us in everyday life. Have students audio record their song and share it with the class.

NOTE: Adult or older peer support may be helpful for students as they compose and sing their own songs about bicycles.

Embed Part One: Talking Circle

Revisit the guided inquiry question: **How can we move loads more easily?** Have students share their experiences and knowledge, provide examples, and ask further inquiry questions.

Embed Part Two

■ Add to the pyramid chart as students learn new concepts, answer some of their own inquiry questions, and ask new inquiry questions.

■ Add new terms and illustrations to the word wall. Include the words in languages other than English, such as Indigenous languages, as appropriate.

■ Focus on students' use of the Core Competencies. Have students reflect on how they used one of the Core Competencies (Thinking, Communicating, or Personal and Social Skills) during the various lesson activities. Project one of the CORE COMPETENCY DISCUSSION PROMPTS templates (pages 38–42), and use it to inspire group reflection. Referring to the template, choose one or two "I Can" statements on which to focus. Students then use the "I Can" statements to provide evidence of how they demonstrated that competency. Ask questions directly related to that competency to inspire discussion. For example:

  ■ How did you take care of yourself and others today by working safely with materials? (Personal Awareness and Responsibility)

Have students reflect orally, encouraging participation, questions, and the sharing of evidence. (See page 29 for more information on these templates.)

▶

7

As part of this process, students can also set goals. For example, ask:

- What would you do differently next time and why?
- How will you know if you are successful in meeting your goal?

■ To encourage self-reflection, provide prompts that students can use to cite examples of how they have used the Core Competencies in their learning. For this purpose, the CORE COMPETENCY SELF-REFLECTION FRAMES (pages 43-47) can be used throughout the learning process. There are five frames provided to address the Core Competencies: Communication, Creative Thinking, Critical Thinking, Positive Personal and Cultural Identity, and Personal Awareness and Responsibility. Teachers can conference individually with students to support self-reflection, or students may complete prompts using words and pictures.

Again, have students set goals by considering what they might do differently on future tasks and how they will know if they are successful in meeting their goal.

NOTE: Use the same prompts from these sheets over time to see how thinking changes with different activities.

Enhance

- **Family Connection**: Provide students with the following sentence starter:
  - We use wheels at home to move objects such as _____.

  Have students complete the sentence starter at home. Family members can help students draw and write about this topic. Have students share their sentences with the rest of the class.

Portage & Main Press, 2018 · Hands-On Science for British Columbia · Properties of Energy for Grades K-2 · ISBN: 978-1-55379-798-2

How Can We Design and Build Devices That Move Using Energy From Wind or Air?

8

Materials

- chart paper
- markers
- resources with device projects and designs
- computers/tablets with internet access
- materials identified by students for project designs
- stories by Indigenous authors about wind
- Template: Air Moves Objects! (3.8.1)
- Learning-Centre Task Card: Blow It Away! (3.8.2)
- drinking straws
- writing paper
- drawing paper
- masking tape
- small, light objects (e.g., tissues, pom poms, cotton balls, coins, cubes)
- nonstandard devices for measuring length (e.g., paper clips, interlocking cubes)
- pyramid chart (from lesson 3)

Engage

Review with students that all kinds of things use energy to perform a variety of tasks. Have students think about different devices they have explored during the module and identify the forms of energy these devices use. Record their answers on chart paper.

Introduce the guided inquiry question: **How can we design and build devices that move using energy from wind or air?**

Explore Part One

Discuss previous place-based learning experiences. Review examples of motion caused by wind (e.g., leaves blowing, water rippling, clouds moving).

NOTE: Observe changes in the local wind conditions, and take students outdoors to observe these conditions. Discuss the changes in the local natural environment and community when the wind is calm or strong.

Discuss students' background knowledge of how air moves objects. Ask:

- Can air make things move? How?
- What examples can you give that prove air moves?

Focus on objects such as fans, hair dryers, swaying trees, flying kites, flags, clothes on a clothesline, and leaf blowers.

Now, have students take a deep breath and observe one another while doing so. Ask:

- When you take a deep breath, what do you notice about your chest?
- Why does your chest expand, or get bigger, when you take a breath?
- What is inside your lungs when you breathe in or inhale?
- Using the air in your lungs, can you make things move?

Have students use the air in their lungs to make things move (e.g., blow on a pinwheel, blow on a piece of paper).

Now tell students they are going to design and construct a device that moves using wind or air. Brainstorm a list of possible devices such as:

- kite
- pinwheel
- tabletop game (e.g., mini-soccer, using straws and Ping-Pong balls)
- wind-powered toy

Have students conduct background research by exploring resources to access ideas for their projects and designs (see Inquiry Through Research, page 26). They may work individually or in pairs, depending on interests and project ideas.

Portage & Main Press, 2018 · Hands-On Science for British Columbia · Properties of Energy for Grades K–2 · ISBN: 978-1-55379-798-2

As a class, identify criteria for the design project. For example:

- creates labelled design first
- moves using air
- uses recycled materials
- provides demonstration

Record the criteria on chart paper for students to reference throughout the project.

Provide students with writing and drawing paper to record the design process. For example, they can draw labelled diagrams of their designs, list materials needed, and record observations of how the device works. Or use the Template: Air Moves Objects! (3.8.1).

Date: _____   Name: _____

Air Moves Objects!

1. Record the criteria for the project:
_____
_____
_____
_____

2. What are you going to build?
_____
_____

3. Draw a labelled diagram of your plan.

[ ]

3.8.1

Date: _____   Name: _____

Air Moves Objects! (continued)

4. List the materials you will need to build your project.
_____   _____
_____   _____
_____   _____

5. Build and test your design.

6. How does your project meet the criteria?
_____
_____
_____

7. Draw a labelled diagram of an interesting project done by someone else in the class.

[ ]

8. What questions do you still have about energy?
_____
_____
_____
_____

3.8.1

Download this template at <www.portageandmainpress.com/product/HOSEnergyK2>.

When projects are complete, have students present them to the class.

Formative Assessment (C)

Use the RUBRIC, on page 53, to record the criteria and results as students present their projects for demonstration purposes. Focus on their ability to share observations and ideas orally and through written language and drawing. Provide descriptive feedback to students about how they designed and built an object that moves and about how they shared their ideas.

Portage & Main Press, 2018 · *Hands-On Science for British Columbia · Properties of Energy for Grades K-2* · ISBN: 978-1-55379-798-2

8

Student Self-Assessment (AI)

Have students complete the STUDENT SELF-ASSESSMENT template, on page 35, to reflect on their inquiry project and their overall learning about energy. Students should focus on how they transfer and apply learning to new situations.

Explore Part Two

Explore Indigenous perspectives related to wind. Invite a local Elder or Knowledge Keeper to the class to share knowledge and stories related to wind. Stories by Indigenous authors can also be shared, such as:

- *The Wish Wind* by Peter Eyvindson
- "The First Tornado" from *How We Saw the World* by C. J. Taylor
- *The Blizzard's Robe* by Robert Sabuda

Expand

Provide students with an opportunity to explore wind energy further by posing their own questions for individualized inquiry. They may wish to:

- Initiate a project at the Makerspace, such as designing and constructing a weather vane.
- Explore Loose Parts bins with objects related to air and wind energy (e.g., feathers, leaves, seeds, bubble makers). Considering including a provocation such as:
  - How can you make objects move using air and wind?
- Research the environmental advantages and disadvantages of wind power (see Inquiry Through Research, page 26).
- Learn about how wind power is being harnessed to create electrical energy.

- Use place-based journaling to record observations about air and wind.
- Record local wind conditions and make a video as a weather person.
- Research what wind/air can do in nature. Create a "tornado in a bottle."
- Conduct an investigation or experiment based on their own inquiry questions.

As students explore and select ideas to expand learning, provide support and guidance as needed, and offer access to materials and resources that will enable students to conduct their chosen investigations.

Learning Centre

NOTE: Prior to having students visit the learning centre, discuss the idea of a fair test. For the activity at the learning centre, a fair test would include: objects start on the starting line, the same person blows on the straw, and the student holds the straw the same distance away from each object.

At the learning centre, provide drinking straws, masking tape, several small objects that can be moved a short distance by blowing at them through a drinking straw (e.g., tissues, pom poms, cotton balls, coins, cubes), and nonstandard devices for measuring length (e.g., paper clips, interlocking cubes).

Also provide writing paper for recording estimations and results, as well as a copy of the Learning-Centre Task Card: Blow It Away! (3.8.2):

▶

Portage & Main Press, 2018 · Hands-On Science for British Columbia · Properties of Energy for Grades K–2 · ISBN: 978-1-55379-798-2

Learning Centre

Blow It Away!

1. Look at the objects at the centre.
   - Do you think you can move them by blowing on each one through a straw?
   - Which ones do you think will move farthest?
   - Which ones do you think might not move at all?
2. Place one of the objects at the starting line. On paper, record how far you think the object will move when you blow on it through a straw.
3. Test your prediction by blowing on the object through a straw.
   - What do you need to do to make sure it is a fair test?
4. Measure how many units it moved.
5. Repeat this for other objects at the centre.

STARTING LINE

3.8.2

Download this template at
<www.portageandmainpress.com/product/HOSEnergyK2>.

On the tabletop, create a starting line for this investigation using a marked strip of masking tape.

Have students use nonstandard measurement to estimate and measure their ability to move different objects using their own air energy.

⚠ **SAFETY NOTE:** Students should not share straws.

Student Self-Assessment (AI)

Have students take home a copy of the FAMILY AND COMMUNITY CONNECTIONS: ASSESSING TOGETHER template on page 57. Have them complete the sheet with a family or community member (with permission) to reflect on their learning about how objects move. The focus here is on taking part in caring for self and family through personal approaches.

Embed Part One: Talking Circle

Revisit the guided inquiry question: **How can we design and build devices that move using energy from wind or air?** Have students share their knowledge, provide examples, and ask further inquiry questions.

Embed Part Two

- Add to the pyramid chart as students learn new concepts, answer some of their own inquiry questions, and ask new inquiry questions.

- Add new terms and illustrations to the word wall. Include the words in languages other than English, such as Indigenous languages, as appropriate.

- Focus on students' use of the Core Competencies. Have students reflect on how they used one of the Core Competencies (Thinking, Communicating, or Personal and Social Skills) during the various lesson activities. Project one of the CORE COMPETENCY DISCUSSION PROMPTS templates (pages 38-42), and use it to inspire group reflection. Referring to the template, choose one or two "I Can" statements on which to focus. Students then use the "I Can" statements to provide evidence of how they demonstrated that competency. Ask questions directly related to that competency to inspire discussion. For example:

  - How did you get new ideas as you learned today? (Creative Thinking)

Have students reflect orally, encouraging participation, questions, and the sharing of evidence. (See page 29 for more information on these templates.)

As part of this process, students can also set goals. For example, ask:

▶

Portage & Main Press, 2018 · Hands-On Science for British Columbia · Properties of Energy for Grades K-2 · ISBN: 978-1-55379-798-2

Portage & Main Press, 2018 · Hands-On Science for British Columbia · Properties of Energy for Grades K–2 · ISBN: 978-1-55379-798-2

8

- What would you do differently next time and why?
- How will you know if you are successful in meeting your goal?
- To encourage self-reflection, provide prompts that students can use to cite examples of how they have used the Core Competencies in their learning. For this purpose, the CORE COMPETENCY SELF-REFLECTION FRAMES (pages 43–47) can be used throughout the learning process. There are five frames provided to address the Core Competencies: Communication, Creative Thinking, Critical Thinking, Positive Personal and Cultural Identity, and Personal Awareness and Responsibility. Teachers can conference individually with students to support self-reflection, or students may complete prompts using words and pictures.

  Again, have students set goals by considering what they might do differently on future tasks and how they will know if they are successful in meeting their goal.

NOTE: Use the same prompts from these sheets over time to see how thinking changes with different activities.

Enhance

- **Family Connection**: Have students take home their device to demonstrate for family. Provide students with the following sentence starter:
  - Examples of objects we found that move using energy from wind or air are _____.

  Have students complete the sentence starter at home. Family members can help students draw and write about this topic. Have students share their sentences with the rest of the class.

- Have students design and construct objects that use other kinds of energy. For example,

explore the use of elastics or springs as a form of energy to move toy cars.

- Straw Painting: Paint a picture by placing small amounts of paint on art paper and blowing the paint around the paper with a straw.

SAFETY NOTE: Caution students not to blow too hard through the straws, as this can cause dizziness.

- Bubble Painting: Fill a large baking pan with a mixture of water and paint. Add 250 mL of liquid soap. Give each student a straw and let them blow gently into the water. The bubbles will rise above the top of the pan. Have students gently place art paper on top of the bubbles, then remove it and let it dry. The result will be a painted picture of colourful bubbles.

9 What Do We Know About Sources of Light?

Information for Teachers

Light does not have mass and does not take up space. Thus, it is not matter. Light is a form of energy and, unlike sound, it does not need a medium through which to travel. Light can travel through a vacuum (space that does not contain any matter). For this reason, light from the sun can travel through the vacuum of outer space and reach Earth.

Luminous objects are objects that give off their own light. Sources of *natural light* include the Sun, other stars, fireflies (which flash or glow in the dark), and aurora borealis and aurora australis (dazzling displays of coloured lights that flicker in the sky in the northernmost and southernmost regions of the world).

Humans use technology to create *artificial light* (e.g., oil lamps, electric lights, candles). We can see a non-luminous object when light shines on it, and the light is reflected back to our eyes. When a beam of light is blocked by an opaque object, a shadow is created.

Materials

- several artificial light sources (e.g., flashlights, candles, oil lamp, lantern, electric lamp)
- chart paper
- markers
- sticky notes (three different colours)
- Image Bank: Natural Sources of Light (see Appendix, page 177)
- Learning-Centre Task Card: Take It Apart, Then Turn It On! (3.9.1)
- resources to explore Indigenous perspectives of light and fire (see Explore Part Two)
- bicycle reflectors
- projection device (optional)
- computers/tablets with internet access
- safety vests with reflective tape
- flashlight

Engage

Display the various artificial light sources. Encourage students to examine and manipulate them. When students have had time to investigate each device, for each item, ask:

- What is this called?
- What does it have in common with the other items?
- How does it produce light?
- From where does the energy to produce light come?
- Does it produce both light and heat?
- What are some other sources of light?

Have students brainstorm a list of light sources. Record their ideas on chart paper. Encourage students to include light sources found at school, at home, and in the community. Also, have students describe how light is created by each item (e.g., a house lamp uses electricity, a flashlight uses battery-powered electricity).

Have the students turn on some of the light sources.

> ⚠️ **SAFETY NOTE:** School policy may prohibit the lighting of candles or oil lanterns. Follow division safety regulations.

Compare the way that light is produced by each source. Ask:

- Which device produces the brightest light?
- Which produces the dimmest light?
- Why do you think some devices produce brighter light than others?

Have students examine light bulbs in some of these devices to determine their strength (wattage).

Introduce the guided inquiry question: **What do we know about sources of light?**

▶

Portage & Main Press, 2018 · Hands-On Science for British Columbia · Properties of Energy for Grades K–2 · ISBN: 978-1-55379-798-2

Portage & Main Press, 2018 · Hands-On Science for British Columbia · Properties of Energy for Grades K–2 · ISBN: 978-1-55379-798-2

9

Explore Part One

Give each student one sticky note of the same colour. Ask students to think about what they know about light. Have them record one thing they know, using pictures or text on the sticky note.

Conduct a Think, Pair, Share activity. Have students share their idea (from the sticky note) with a partner. Next, for class sharing, have each student role-play or mime one thing they know about light or a source of light. Model this for the class using your own ideas (e.g., act out turning on a lamp or shining a flashlight). Challenge the class to guess what you are doing, then have students take turns role-playing while their classmates guess. On chart paper, create a large pyramid graphic organizer to represent ideas, as in the following example:

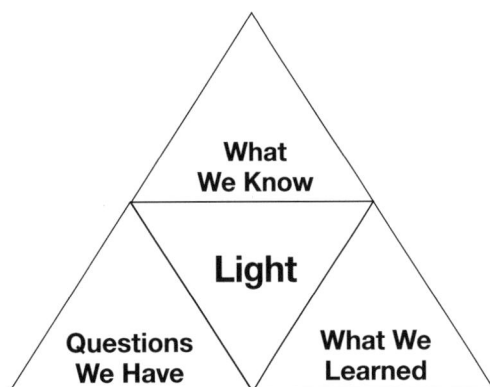

```
              /\
             /  \
            /    \
           / What \
          /   We    \
         /   Know     \
        /--------------\
       /\    Light    /\
      /  \          /   \
     /    \        /     \
    /Questions\  /What We \
   / We Have   \/ Learned  \
  /_____/_____\
```

As students act and answer, have them add their sticky notes to the top triangle of the pyramid.

Ask:

- What questions do you have about light?
- What would you like to learn about light?

Record students' questions on a second colour of sticky note, and attach the notes to the pyramid, in the bottom left triangle.

Refer to the pyramid throughout the module. Answers to students questions may also be added to the bottom right triangle of the pyramid with a third colour of sticky note, as students gather new information and acquire new knowledge. As students generate more inquiry questions, these may be added, as well.

Explore Part Two 🖥️

Explore Indigenous stories related to light. Fire is an essential component of Indigenous life and culture and is related to concepts of light. Invite a local Elder or Knowledge Keeper to share knowledge and stories with the class.

NOTE: See Indigenous Perspectives, page 9, for guidelines for inviting an Elder or Knowledge Keeper to speak to the class.

Use related resources to explore Indigenous perspectives, knowledge, and stories about light. For example:

- *Orphans in the Sky* by Jeanne Bushey
- "Snaring the Sun" <www.virtualmuseum.ca/edu/>. Enter "snaring the sun" in the search box to find Learning Resources. Once there, click on Indigenous Astronomy.
- "Grandmother Spider Brings the Sun" <https://www.youtube.com/watch?v=ok_b46A9hvE>
- "The Raven Steals the Light" <http://www.historymuseum.ca/cmc/exhibitions/aborig/reid/reid14e.shtml>
- *Beaver Steals Fire: A Salish Coyote Story* by Confederated Salish and Kootenai Tribes
- *How We Saw the World: Nine Native Stories of the Way Things Began* by C. J. Taylor

Explore Part Three

Review the recorded list of light sources from the Engage section of the lesson. Ask:

- Which of these sources of light are made by humans?

▶

On a new sheet of chart paper, create a table as follows:

Artificial Light	Natural Light	Reflected Light

Record students' suggestions of sources of artificial light in the first column of the chart. Ask:

■ Do we get light from natural sources, not made by humans?

Focus first on the Sun as an important source of natural light. Ask:

■ What are some other sources of natural light?

Have students share their ideas and record these in the second column of the chart. Display the Image Bank: Natural Sources of Light and discuss each light source. Record new natural light sources in the second column of the chart.

Now, focus on objects that reflect light. Have students examine bicycle reflectors and reflective tape on safety vests. These are designed to reflect the light from car headlights to keep people safe. Have students suggest other uses of reflectors (e.g., on cars, running shoes, street signs). Turn off the classroom lights and shine a flashlight on the reflective materials to demonstrate how they work.

Explore Part Four

Ask:

■ Have you ever experienced a time when the power went out?
■ What do people use for light when electricity is unavailable?
■ What did you use when the power went out? (e.g., fire, torches, sunlight, kerosene lamps, candles, flashlights)

■ Which of these light sources could've been used before electricity and batteries were invented?

As a class, learn about the *qulliq*, an oil lamp used by the Inuit. The qulliq uses seal oil, which is manipulated to provide a gentle consistent light.

Watch videos about the Inuit qulliq, such as:

■ "Inuit Culture, Lighting the Qulliq" <https://www.youtube.com/watch?v=yMMcFSBi2hg>
■ "Qulliq (Oil Lamp)" <https://www.youtube.com/watch?v=rjjxUE6XSdQ>

The book, *The Inuit Thought of It: Amazing Arctic Innovations*, by Alootook Ipellie and David MacDonald, also provides useful information on the invention and development of the qulliq.

Expand

Provide students with an opportunity to explore sources of light further by posing their own questions for individualized inquiry. They may wish to:

■ Initiate a project at the Makerspace, such as designing and constructing a flashlight using recycled parts, or creating a model of a jellyfish or firefly.
■ Explore Loose Parts bins with objects related to sources of light (e.g., batteries, small bulbs, flashlights, reflectors, mirrors). Consider including a provocation such as:
    ■ How can you show what you have learned about sources of light?
■ Research Morse code and record the patterns for different letters of the alphabet. Watch the video: "Invention of Morse Code" at: <https://www.youtube.com/watch?v=ORIDAmGf_yQ.> (see Inquiry Through Research, page 26).

▶

Portage & Main Press, 2018 · Hands-On Science for British Columbia · Properties of Energy for Grades K-2 · ISBN: 978-1-55379-798-2

9

- Create their own graphic organizer to show natural and artificial sources of light, as well as reflectors of light.

- Conduct research on natural sources of light (e.g., meteors falling, northern lights).

- Create a model of a volcano with light produced from lava.

- Conduct an investigation or experiment based on their own inquiry questions.

As students explore and select ideas to expand learning, provide support and guidance as needed, and offer access to materials and resources that will enable students to conduct their chosen investigations.

Learning Centre

At the learning centre, provide a variety of tools and flashlights for a take-apart centre, as well as a copy of the Learning-Centre Task Card: Take It Apart, Then Turn It On! (3.9.1):

Learning Centre

Take It Apart, Then Turn It On!

1. Examine one of the flashlights.
2. Turn it on to produce light.
3. Turn off the flashlight.
4. Take apart the flashlight. Look at all the parts. Think about how the flashlight is put together.
5. Try to put the flashlight back together, so that it produces light again.

3.9.1

Download this template at <www.portageandmainpress.com/product/HOSEnergyK2>.

Challenge students to take apart a flashlight and then reassemble it so it can be turned on again.

Embed Part One: Talking Circle

Revisit the guided inquiry question: **What do we know about sources of light?** Have students share their knowledge, provide examples, and ask further inquiry questions.

Embed Part Two

- Add to the pyramid chart as students learn new concepts, answer some of their own inquiry questions, and ask new inquiry questions.

- Add new terms and illustrations to the word wall. Include the words in languages other than English, such as Indigenous languages, as appropriate.

- Focus on students' use of the Core Competencies. Have students reflect on how they used one of the Core Competencies (Thinking, Communicating, or Personal and Social Skills) during the various lesson activities. Project one of the CORE COMPETENCY DISCUSSION PROMPTS templates (pages 38-42), and use it to inspire group reflection. Referring to the template, choose one or two "I Can" statements on which to focus. Students then use the "I Can" statements to provide evidence of how they demonstrated that competency. Ask questions directly related to that competency to inspire discussion. For example:

  - How did you get new ideas as you learned today? (Creative Thinking)

Have students reflect orally, encouraging participation, questions, and the sharing of

▶

Portage & Main Press, 2018 · Hands-On Science for British Columbia · Properties of Energy for Grades K–2 · ISBN: 978-1-55379-798-2

evidence. (See page 29 for more information on these templates.)

As part of this process, students can also set goals. For example, ask:

- What would you do differently next time and why?
- How will you know if you are successful in meeting your goal?

■ To encourage self-reflection, provide prompts that students can use to cite examples of how they have used the Core Competencies in their learning. For this purpose, the CORE COMPETENCY SELF-REFLECTION FRAMES (pages 43-47) can be used throughout the learning process. There are five frames provided to address the Core Competencies: Communication, Creative Thinking, Critical Thinking, Positive Personal and Cultural Identity, and Personal Awareness and Responsibility. Teachers can conference individually with students to support self-reflection, or students may complete prompts using words and pictures.

Again, have students set goals by considering what they might do differently on future tasks and how they will know if they are successful in meeting their goal.

NOTE: Use the same prompts from these sheets over time to see how thinking changes with different activities.

Enhance

■ **Family Connection**: Provide students with the following sentence starter:

- Sources of light in our home are _____.

Have students complete the sentence starter at home. Family members can help students draw and write about this topic. Have students share their sentences with the rest of the class.

■ On index cards, list several sources of light (e.g., fireflies, fluorescent bulbs, neon lights, lightning, lasers, borealis). Provide a variety of research materials covering a range of reading levels, including reference books, encyclopedias, magazines, and the internet. Have students select a light source to research, then present their research and diagrams on large sheets of art paper; bind the pages together into a class book called "Sources of Light."

■ As a class, make beeswax candles (always under adult supervision) for students to give as gifts or to use at home. Beeswax sheets are available at craft stores; other supplies needed include wicks, hair dryer(s) (to soften the wax before rolling it), and sharp scissors for cutting the wax. When candles are shaped into tapers or pillars, students can decorate them with shapes they cut out from smaller pieces of coloured beeswax.

Portage & Main Press, 2018 · *Hands-On Science for British Columbia · Properties of Energy for Grades K–2* · ISBN: 978-1-55379-798-2

10 | How Do We Know We Get Energy From the Sun?

⚠️ **SAFETY NOTE:** When learning about the Sun, ensure students understand that they should never look directly at the Sun, as it can damage their eyes.

Materials

- lyrics or recording of the song, "Mr. Sun," by Raffi
- chart paper
- markers
- yellow and dark blue construction paper
- clear tape
- chalk
- access to a window that gets lots of sunlight
- ribbon (optional)
- sunscreen products
- digital cameras
- yarn
- scissors
- masking tape
- globe
- flashlight
- *Four Seasons Make a Year* by Anne Rockwell (or another book about living things throughout the seasons)
- computer/tablet with internet access
- picture books, stories, and videos about the Sun by Indigenous authors (see Explore Part Two)
- art paper
- writing paper
- art supplies (e.g., paint, paintbrushes, pastels)
- *Busy, Busy Leaves* by Nadia Higgins (or another book about photosynthesis)
- Learning-Centre Task Card: What If… (3.10.1)
- pyramid chart (from lesson 9)

Engage

Teach students the song "Mr. Sun" by Raffi. Title a sheet of chart paper with the heading "What We Know About the Sun." Have students share what they know about the Sun. Record these ideas on the chart paper.

Introduce the guided inquiry question: **How do we know we get energy from the Sun?**

Explore Part One

Give each student a piece of yellow and a piece of dark blue construction paper. Have students draw a Sun on the yellow construction paper and cut it out. Then have them tape their Sun onto the dark blue construction paper. Explain to students that their Sun pictures will be placed in a window for several days (with the Suns facing outward). Ask:

- Do you think anything will happen to your pictures?
- What do you think might happen? Why?

Tape the pictures to a window that gets a lot of sunlight. Several days later, remove the pictures from the window, and pass them out to students. Have students observe the pictures closely. Ask:

- Has anything changed in your picture?

Have students carefully remove the Suns from the blue construction paper and examine the blue paper. Ask:

- What happened to the blue construction paper?
- What part of the paper is faded?
- Why do you think this happened?
- What role did the Sun play in this?
- What would have happened if the coloured paper had been left in front of the window for a longer period of time?

Discuss with students the fact that energy from the Sun bleached the paper. Have students refer to their pyramid chart on light from lesson 9. Ask:

▶

Portage & Main Press, 2018 · Hands-On Science for British Columbia · Properties of Energy for Grades K–2 · ISBN: 978-1-55379-798-2

- Can you think of something we should add to our pyramid chart, based on today's activity?
- What did the energy from the Sun do to the paper?

Discuss the Sun further. Add more things that students now know about the Sun to the chart started in the Engage part of this lesson. Examples may include:

- The Sun lets us see things.
- The Sun gives us daytime.
- The Sun can cause shadows on the ground.
- The Sun can help dry clothes on a clothesline.
- The Sun can give us a sunburn.
- The Sun can be dangerous to our eyes, so we must not look at it directly.
- The Sun warms the land and water.
- The Sun is a source of light.
- The Sun helps plants grow and makes it possible to grow food.

Reinforce for students that the Sun is the main source of energy on Earth. Without it, living things could not survive. Ask:

- We know that the Sun helps us by giving us light and warmth, but can the Sun also harm us?

Have students share their ideas. Stress the importance of never looking directly at the Sun because it can damage eyes.

Display sunscreen products and pass them around for students to examine. Ask:

- For what are these products used?
- When do you use sunscreen?
- Why is sunscreen important?

Relate this back to the Sun bleaching their pictures. Ask:

- What would the Sun's energy do to our skin?

Focus on the ratings on the sunscreen containers and discuss their meaning in terms of strength and duration of safe use.

Formative Assessment **QP**

Observe students as they discuss what they know about the Sun, examine and describe their Sun pictures, and provide ideas about the Sun as a form of energy. Focus on their ability to make simple predictions about energy. Use the ANECDOTAL RECORD template, on page 50, to record results. Provide descriptive feedback to students about how they described and made predictions about the Sun.

Explore Part Two

Invite a local Elder or Knowledge Keeper to share knowledge and stories about the Sun with the class.

NOTE: See Indigenous Perspectives, page 9, for guidelines for inviting an Elder or Knowledge Keeper to speak to the class.

Share stories, children's books, and videos depicting local Indigenous stories about the Sun. For example:

- "Snaring the Sun" <www.virtualmuseum.ca/edu/>. Entering "snaring the sun" in the search box will take you to Learning Resources. Once there, click on Indigenous Astronomy.
- "The Raven Steals the Light" <www.historymuseum.ca/cmc/exhibitions/aborig/reid/reid14e.shtml>
- "Grandmother Spider Brings the Sun" <https://www.youtube.com/watch?v=ok_b46A9hvE>

Explore Part Three

NOTE: Outdoor shadow activities must be done on sunny days. These activities should begin early in the school day.

▶

Portage & Main Press, 2018 · Hands-On Science for British Columbia · Properties of Energy for Grades K–2 · ISBN: 978-1-55379-798-2

10

As with all place-based learning activities (see page 74 in lesson 1 for more information):

- Identify the importance of place. Using a map of the local area, identify where the location is in relation to the school.
- Identify on whose traditional territory the school is located, as well as the traditional territory of the location for the nature walk, if different.
- Incorporate land acknowledgment using local protocols.

Take students outside to the playground for a shadow walk. Have students use digital cameras to take photographs of the shadows they see around them outside. Ask them to observe the shadows cast by posts, basketball standards, flagpoles, buildings, and classmates. Then have them look at their own shadows. Ask:

- Does your shadow move when you move?
- Can you jump on your own shadow?
- What are the biggest and smallest shadows you can make with your body?
- Can you make your shadow touch a friend's shadow without touching your bodies together?

Now focus on shadows cast by still objects such as play structures and flagpoles. As you focus on each shadow, ask:

- What is the shape of the shadow?
- What causes a shadow?
- Where is the light coming from that makes the shadow?
- Does the shadow always touch the ground?
- Do you think the shadow will change during the day?

Organize the class into working pairs and provide each group with yarn, chalk, scissors, masking tape, and a marker. Have each student mark an X with chalk on the pavement, print their name under the X, and then stand on that spot.

Have the students trace the shape of one another's shadows with chalk. Then, have them use yarn to measure the length of the shadow, then cut the piece of yarn to that length. Have them put a small piece of masking tape around their piece of yarn and record their name. Ask:

- Do you think that the shadow will change if we come back to look at it later in the day? How?
- In which direction does your shadow point?

Using the compass, mark N, S, E, and W on the pavement with chalk, so students can see the direction their shadow is pointing. Go back to the classroom and have students note the time of day. You do not have to use standard time measure. You can record times using intervals of the school day; for example, the beginning of the day, before recess, before lunch, after lunch, and before home time.

Provide each group with a sheet of chart paper. Have them tape their piece of yarn onto the paper and record the time that the shadow was measured.

Go outside several times during the day to observe the shadows and the position of the Sun. Each time, have the groups trace the new shadows with chalk and measure the length of the shadows with yarn.

NOTE: Ensure students are consistent in where they measure (such as from toe to top of head).

Ask:

- How have the shadows changed?
- Are the shadows in different places?
- Are the shadows shorter or longer?
- Are the shadows bigger or smaller?
- Why do you think the shadows have changed?

After each observation, return to the classroom. Have the groups tape their yarn onto a piece of chart paper and record the time of day. At the

▶

Portage & Main Press, 2018 · Hands-On Science for British Columbia · Properties of Energy for Grades K–2 · ISBN: 978-1-55379-798-2

end of the day, have the groups title their chart and present it to the class. During presentations, focus on their understanding of shadows. Ask:

- What creates shadows?
- Why do they change during the day?
- When is your shadow the shortest? Why?
- Do you think you would see shadows clearly on a cloudy day?

Record student ideas on chart paper.

Formative Assessment (PA)

Observe each group as they present their findings about shadows. Focus on their ability to respond to the questions above. Use the ANECDOTAL RECORD template on page 50 to record results. The focus here is on discussing observations about energy from the Sun. Provide descriptive feedback to students about how they share their observations about energy from the Sun.

Record students' ideas on chart paper.

Explore Part Four

Read the story, *Four Seasons Make a Year*, by Anne Rockwell, or another book about living things throughout the seasons. Discuss the events and ideas in the book. Ask:

- What do you know about seasons?
- What season is it now?
- What are the names of the four seasons?
- What is the order of the four seasons?
- What happens to plants in spring?
- What happens to plants in summer?
- What happens to plants in fall?
- What happens to plants in winter?
- Why do you think the seasons change?
- How does the weather change during the seasons?
- Why do you think the weather changes during the seasons?
- What is the temperature like in each of the seasons?

Use a globe and flashlight to introduce the idea of Earth's rotation and its orbit around the Sun. This will help the students to understand how Earth's position changes, causing the day/night cycle and the seasonal cycle. Also, watch videos such as

- Earth's Rotation & Revolution <https://www.youtube.com/watch?v=I64YwNl1wr0> or
- Science Video for Kids: Earth's Revolution & Rotation <https://www.youtube.com/watch?v=EXasopxAFoM>

NOTE: The rotation of the Earth causes day and night. In 24 hours, the world turns round once. When we are facing the Sun it is day. When we face away it is night. The changing seasons are due to the way the Earth spins on a tilted axis. When part of the Earth is leaning toward the Sun, summer will occur in that hemisphere. The part of the Earth leaning away from the Sun will have winter.

Take students out to examine a deciduous tree in the school yard or local community. Discuss the appearance of the tree and take a photograph of the tree with a digital camera. If possible, mark the tree with a ribbon, so you can revisit the tree throughout the year to take photographs of how it has changed. Ask the students:

- What are the characteristics of trees in this season?

▶

Portage & Main Press, 2018 · *Hands-On Science for British Columbia · Properties of Energy for Grades K-2* · ISBN: 978-1-55379-798-2

Portage & Main Press, 2018 · Hands-On Science for British Columbia · Properties of Energy for Grades K–2 · ISBN: 978-1-55379-798-2

- What happens to trees during other seasons?
- Do all trees change?
- Which trees do not seem to change from season to season?
- What do you think you could watch for as we study our tree?

Back in the classroom, organize the class into working groups. Give each group a piece of chart paper and assign each group one of the four seasons. Explain that each group will develop a poster about their assigned season. Work with students to co-construct criteria for their posters. For example, the poster must:

- include the name of the season
- have a large labelled diagram of the tree that was observed
- describe and illustrate the weather of the season
- show how the season affects this tree and other living things

Have the students work together to create a poster depicting characteristics of each season, with the tree as a focal point of the image.

Have each group present their poster to the class, and display these throughout the school year. As each season comes, have students compare their posters to the season, the weather, and their tree.

Explore Part Five

NOTE: The following activity also ties into the module *Living Things for Grades K-2*.

Read *Busy, Busy Leaves*, by Nadia Higgins, or another book that introduces students to the role of the Sun in plant life.

Conduct a classroom experiment on the effect of sunlight on the growth of plants. Place one plant in front of a window that gets a lot of sunlight. Water and fertilize it as required. Place a second plant in a cupboard or dark corner of the classroom. Water and fertilize it as required. Have students record the growth of the plants over a period of time. Have students graph the results.

Expand

Provide students with an opportunity to explore the characteristics of the Sun further by posing their own questions for individualized inquiry. They may wish to:

- Initiate a project at the Makerspace, such as making a model of the Sun, Earth, and moon to demonstrate the seasonal or day/night cycle.
- Explore light and shadows using an overhead projector to experiment with various materials (e.g., fabric, foil, tissue, cellophane, Plexiglas) to make shadows.
- Create shadow puppets and a shadow-puppet play. An overhead projector can be used as a light source with a sheet on the wall as a backdrop for the play.
- Write and illustrate a picture book about the Sun.
- Use place-based journaling to express and reflect on personal experiences of place with regard to shadows.
- Create riddles about the Sun.
- Use lists of characteristics of the Sun to create a text-visual using a program such as a Wordle, as in the following example:

►

- Conduct an investigation or experiment based on their own inquiry questions.

As students explore and select ideas to expand learning, provide support and guidance as needed, and offer access to materials and resources that will enable students to conduct their chosen investigations.

Learning Centre

At the learning centre, provide art paper, writing paper, and art supplies (e.g., paint, paintbrushes, pastels), along with a copy of the Learning-Centre Task Card: What If… (3.10.1):

> **Learning Centre**
>
> ## What If…
>
> 1. Think about how the Sun helps all living things on Earth.
>   - What would happen if there were no Sun?
>   - What would happen to plants?
>   - What would happen to animals?
>   - What would happen to humans?
>   - Could humans survive without the Sun?
>   - What does this tell you about the Sun?
> 2. Draw a picture and write about what you think would happen if there were no Sun.
>
> 3.10.1

Download this template at <www.portageandmainpress.com/product/HOSEnergyK2>.

Have students work independently to explore the role of the Sun for life on Earth. They can draw, paint, and/or write their thoughts.

Embed Part One: Talking Circle

Revisit the guided inquiry question: **How do we know we get energy from the Sun?** Have students share their experiences and knowledge, provide examples, and ask further inquiry questions.

Embed Part Two

- Add to the pyramid chart as students learn new concepts, answer some of their own inquiry questions, and ask new inquiry questions.

- Add new terms and illustrations to the word wall. Include the words in languages other than English, such as Indigenous languages, as appropriate.

- Focus on students' use of the Core Competencies. Have students reflect on how they used one of the Core Competencies (Thinking, Communicating, or Personal and Social Skills) during the various lesson activities. Project one of the CORE COMPETENCY DISCUSSION PROMPTS templates (pages 38-42), and use it to inspire group reflection. Referring to the template, choose one or two "I Can" statements on which to focus. Students then use the "I Can" statements to provide evidence of how they demonstrated that competency. Ask questions directly related to that competency to inspire discussion. For example:

  - How did you grow as a learner today? (Positive Personal and Cultural Identity)

Have students reflect orally, encouraging participation, questions, and the sharing of evidence. (See page 29 for more information on these templates.)

As part of this process, students can also set goals. For example, ask:

- What would you do differently next time and why?

▶

Portage & Main Press, 2018 · Hands-On Science for British Columbia · Properties of Energy for Grades K–2 · ISBN: 978-1-55379-798-2

Portage & Main Press, 2018 · Hands-On Science for British Columbia · Properties of Energy for Grades K–2 · ISBN: 978-1-55379-798-2

- How will you know if you are successful in meeting your goal?

- To encourage self-reflection, provide prompts that students can use to cite examples of how they have used the Core Competencies in their learning. For this purpose, the CORE COMPETENCY SELF-REFLECTION FRAMES (pages 43–47) can be used throughout the learning process. There are five frames provided to address the Core Competencies: Communication, Creative Thinking, Critical Thinking, Positive Personal and Cultural Identity, and Personal Awareness and Responsibility. Teachers can conference individually with students to support self-reflection, or students may complete prompts using words and pictures.

  Again, have students set goals by considering what they might do differently on future tasks and how they will know if they are successful in meeting their goal.

NOTE: Use the same prompts from these sheets over time to see how thinking changes with different activities.

Enhance 🔲

- **Family Connection**: Provide students with the following sentence starter:
  - We know that the Sun is important because _____.

  Have students complete the sentence starter at home. Family members can help students draw and write about this topic. Have students share their sentences with the rest of the class.

- Read poems about shadows (e.g., "Shadow Race" and "Shadow Wash" by Shel Silverstein, "My Shadow" by Robert Louis Stevenson). Then have them write their own poems about shadows.

- Have students investigate and compare the different shadows created by different kinds of light bulbs (e.g., incandescent, compact fluorescent, LED). More pronounced shadows will be visible with incandescent light bulbs; shadows created by fluorescent light bulbs will be less pronounced until the object is held close to the light source.

- Have students create shadow plays of familiar stories or books, cutting out characters from cardboard and attaching these to craft sticks. Challenge students to change the shadows cast in relation to the story. For example, for the story *Little Red Riding Hood*, they could make a large, long shadow of the wolf for dramatic effect.

- Solar toys sold at dollar stores provide inexpensive devices that can be used to show energy from the Sun being turned into movement.

- Explore the use of UV Beads. These ultra-violet sensitive beads provide a health connection (Sun safety). Beads can be ordered from the following website: <www.ibeadcanada.com/collections/plastic-3/uv-beads>.

- Place one tray of ice cubes in direct sunlight and another tray of ice cubes in a dark corner of the classroom. Observe which tray of ice cubes melts first. Research and discuss with students how this experiment connects to the greenhouse effect and how they affect the polar ice caps.

- Butterflies in a net: Cut several butterfly shapes from dark paper. Tape the butterflies in a bright sunny window. The Sun should project the shapes onto the floor. Have the students capture (cover) the shadow butterflies with a butterfly net (or stretch a pair of nylons over a bent coat hanger frame and tape the end of the hanger). Leave the net in place on top of the butterflies. Check

▶

on the butterflies later as a class. As the Sun moves, the students will observe the butterflies "escaping" from the net. Ask the students to explain how this happened.

■ Have students make paper-plate sundials. Push a sharp pencil halfway through the centre of an upside-down paper plate. Take the sundial outside and push the pencil into the ground. The pencil will make a shadow on the plate. Students can mark the position of the shadow at this time, and several times during the day.

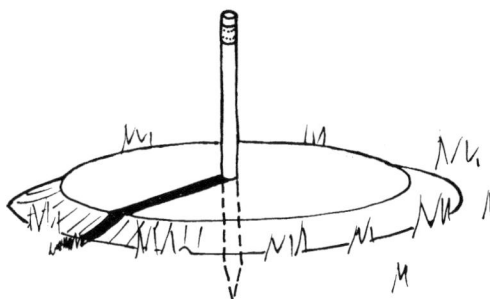

■ Play shadow tag in the morning and afternoon. The object of the game is for students to try to touch one another's shadows. Encourage them to explain how the game changed when they played it at two different times of the day.

■ Research different ways that humans use the Sun to measure time (it varies culturally and historically).

Portage & Main Press, 2018 · *Hands-On Science for British Columbia · Properties of Energy for Grades K–2* · ISBN: 978-1-55379-798-2

11 | How Does Light Help Us See Objects?

Information for Teachers

Reflection occurs when a surface returns light that hits it. White material reflects light, whereas black material absorbs it. That is why, to stay cooler during hot summer months, we wear lighter-coloured clothing.

Luminous objects—such as fire, light bulbs, stars, the Sun, and even hot (molten) metals—make their own light. When you shine light on a *non-luminous* object, you are able to see it because it reflects light back to you.

Other luminous objects in the sky are the *auroras*, which appear when energetic gas particles from the Sun create a solar wind. These particles could be dangerous to us, but we are protected by an invisible shield around our planet. This shield is magnetic (called the *magnetosphere*) and sometimes traps these particles. Auroras are most likely to be found at the poles of the planet because the poles' strong magnetic force attracts the gas particles. When these particles collide with the gases in Earth's atmosphere (mainly oxygen and nitrogen), an aurora's colourful display of light occurs.

Materials

- *Walk With Your Eyes* by Marcia Brown
- a version of *The Ugly Duckling* (optional)
- scissors
- large cardboard box with a lid that can be completely closed
- several smaller cardboard boxes with lids that can be completely closed
- objects with varying abilities to reflect light (e.g., black socks, aluminum foil, plastic balls, safety vests, reflective tape, books, bicycle reflectors, hockey pucks, mirrors)
- access to a room that can be darkened
- various light sources (e.g., flashlights, penlights, book lights, small lamps) (several for each working group)

- mirrors
- aluminum foil
- flashlight
- computer/tablet with internet access
- art supplies (e.g., pastels, pencil crayons, markers)
- a treat for students (e.g., cookies, stickers) (optional)
- Plasticine and play dough
- drawing paper
- pencils
- Learning-Centre Task Card: Mirror, Mirror on the Wall (3.11.1)
- pyramid chart (from lesson 9)

⚠️ **SAFETY NOTE:** Always double-check student allergies before introducing any food into the classroom.

Engage

Read aloud to students the poems in the book, *Walk With Your Eyes,* by Marcia Brown. The book has many vivid pictures for students to examine and discuss, including excellent examples of reflections in nature. Alternatively, read the story, *The Ugly Duckling*. The swan believes it is ugly until it finally sees its own reflection and realizes it has become beautiful.

After reading the selected book, have students close their eyes and visualize what they think is happening to light as you read excerpts from the story.

NOTE: Visualizing is a powerful comprehension strategy that can also help students enhance their understanding of science concepts.

Introduce the guided inquiry question: **How does light help us see objects?**

▶

Portage & Main Press, 2018 · Hands-On Science for British Columbia · Properties of Energy for Grades K–2 · ISBN: 978-1-55379-798-2

11

Explore Part One

Before beginning this activity, make a mystery box. Take a large cardboard box, and cut a small peephole (about 5-cm square) in the top. Push a pencil through the side of the box to create a hole for a light source. Fill the box with an assortment of objects that have varying abilities to reflect light (e.g., black socks, aluminum foil, plastic ball, book, bicycle reflector, hockey puck, pocket mirror). For added excitement, consider including a class treat inside the box.

Darken the classroom (or another room in the school that can be darkened). Close curtains or cover windows, turn off the lights, and display the mystery box for students to examine.

Explain there are a number of mystery objects inside the box. Ask:

- How can you find out what is inside the box without touching it?

Encourage students to work together and brainstorm how to find out what is inside the box.

Have students look through the peephole at the top of the box. Ask:

- Can you see what is inside the box?
- Why is it difficult for you to see what is inside the box?

Discuss how objects cannot be seen when no light is available—objects can only be seen if they create their own light or if light is reflected off them. Turn the lights back on in the room. Ask:

- Is there enough light now for you to see what is inside the box?
- Why is it still difficult for you to see some objects?

Discuss how some objects do not reflect light as well as others, so they are difficult to see when light is blocked. Have students shine a flashlight through the pencil hole on the side of the box and examine the objects inside. Ask:

- Can you name all the objects in the box now?
- Which objects can you see now that you could not see before?
- Why were these objects difficult for you to see earlier?

Remove all the objects from the box, and have students examine them. Ask:

- Why are the objects easier to see now?
- What would happen if we turned off all the lights in the classroom? Would you be able to see all of the objects?

Test students' predictions. Turn off the lights in the room, and have students observe the objects. Ask:

- Can you see these objects in the dark?
- What do you need so you can see the objects better?

Have a student shine a flashlight toward the objects. Ask:

- Can you see all of the objects now?
- What happens to the objects when you shine the light on them?

Have students discuss how the light from the flashlight reflects brightly on certain objects (e.g., reflectors, mirrors). Turn on the lights in the room, and further discuss the various objects. Ask:

- How are these objects important to you in your everyday lives?
- When do you need reflective objects?

Discuss the safety aspects of reflective material for cyclists, drivers, patrols, and pedestrians.

▶

Portage & Main Press, 2018 · Hands-On Science for British Columbia · Properties of Energy for Grades K–2 · ISBN: 978-1-55379-798-2

Explore Part Two

Organize the class into working groups, and have them construct their own mystery boxes. Distribute a smaller cardboard box with a lid to each group, and guide students through the process of using scissors to cut a small peephole in the top of each box. Next, have them push a pencil through the side of the box to create a hole for a light source.

When all groups have constructed their boxes, place several objects inside each box (do not allow students to see what you place in each box). Provide each group with a variety of light sources (e.g., flashlights, lamps, penlights). Have the groups try to identify the objects in their boxes by illuminating the objects with the various instruments.

Explore Part Three

In a dark room, have students set a mirror on a table and shine a flashlight on the mirror. The reflected light should seem almost as bright as the flashlight beam. Then, ask students to try the same task using a piece of aluminum foil instead of the mirror and observe how the light is reflected. Finally, have them repeat the task using a piece of foil crumpled into a ball shape. The crinkles should cause the light to bounce in all directions.

NOTE: The above activity shows that rough surfaces do not reflect light as evenly or as well as smooth surfaces do.

Explore Part Four 🖥️

As a class, explore the auroras. Many videos offer the opportunity to view the northern lights, or aurora borealis. For example:

■ "Night of the Northern Lights" <https://www.youtube.com/watch?v=fVsONlc3OUY>

■ "NASA UHD Video: Stunning Aurora Borealis from Space in Ultra-High Definition (4K)" <https://www.youtube.com/watch?v=fVMgnmi2D1w>

Consider inviting a local Elder or Knowledge Keeper to speak to the class to share knowledge and stories about the northern lights.

NOTE: See Indigenous Perspectives, page 9, for guidelines for inviting Elders and Knowledge Keepers to speak to the class.

As a class, read books by Indigenous author about the aurora borealis, such as:

■ *Warren Whistles at the Sky* by David Alexander Robertson

■ *Painted Skies* by Carolyn Mallory

■ *Aurora: A Tale of the Northern Lights* by Mindy Dwyer

■ *SkySisters* by Jan Bourdeau Waboose

Expand 🖥️

Provide students with an opportunity to explore how light helps us to see objects further by posing their own questions for individualized inquiry. They may wish to:

■ Initiate a project at the Makerspace, such as creating a new design for safety vests or a Halloween costume, using reflective tape; or designing a helmet with reflectors for safe cycling at night.

■ Explore Loose Parts bins related to reflection. Include various reflective materials (e.g., flashlights, tinfoil, mirrors, plastic, glass beads, reflectors), as well as materials that do not reflect light. Consider a provocation, such as:

  ■ How can you reflect light?

■ Research and create paintings or illustrations of the northern lights (see Inquiry Through Research, page 26).

▶

Portage & Main Press, 2018 · Hands-On Science for British Columbia · Properties of Energy for Grades K–2 · ISBN: 978-1-55379-798-2

- Research what would happen if Earth lost its magnetic field (see <https://futurism.com/6-horrible-consequences-earth-losing-magnetic-field/>).
- Create a mystery box at home to test the reflective ability of objects.
- Conduct an investigation or experiment based on their own inquiry questions.

As students explore and select ideas to expand learning, provide support and guidance as needed, and offer access to materials and resources that will enable students to conduct their chosen investigations.

Learning Centre

At the learning centre, provide mirrors, Plasticine or play dough, drawing paper, art supplies (e.g., pastels, pencil crayons, markers), and a copy of the Learning-Centre Task Card: Mirror, Mirror on the Wall (3.11.1):

Learning Centre

Mirror, Mirror on the Wall

1. Look at your face in a mirror. You may stand the mirror up using play dough.
2. Carefully examine each of your features in the mirror.
3. Draw a picture of your face.
4. Under your picture, draw three stars. Describe one of your strengths as a learner next to each star.

3.11.1

Download this template at <www.portageandmainpress.com/product/HOSEnergyK2>.

Have students draw self-portraits by examining themselves in the mirrors. They will then record, in drawings or words, their strengths as a learner.

Embed Part One: Talking Circle

Revisit the guided inquiry question: **How does light help us see objects?** Have students share their experiences and knowledge, provide examples, and ask further inquiry questions.

Embed Part Two

- Add to the pyramid chart as students learn new concepts, answer some of their own inquiry questions, and ask new inquiry questions.
- Add new terms and illustrations to the word wall. Include the words in languages other than English, such as Indigenous languages, as appropriate.
- Focus on students' use of the Core Competencies. Have students reflect on how they used one of the Core Competencies (Thinking, Communicating, or Personal and Social Skills) during the various lesson activities. Project one of the CORE COMPETENCY DISCUSSION PROMPTS templates (pages 38-42), and use it to inspire group reflection. Referring to the template, choose one or two "I Can" statements on which to focus. Students then use the "I Can" statements to provide evidence of how they demonstrated that competency. Ask questions directly related to that competency to inspire discussion. For example:
  - How did you explore materials to learn about how light helps us see objects today? (Critical Thinking)

▶

Portage & Main Press, 2018 · Hands-On Science for British Columbia · Properties of Energy for Grades K-2 · ISBN: 978-1-55379-798-2

Portage & Main Press, 2018 · Hands-On Science for British Columbia · Properties of Energy for Grades K–2 · ISBN: 978-1-55379-798-2

Have students reflect orally, encouraging participation, questions, and the sharing of evidence. (See page 29 for more information on these templates.)

As part of this process, students can also set goals. For example, ask:

- What would you do differently next time and why?
- How will you know if you are successful in meeting your goal?

- To encourage self-reflection, provide prompts that students can use to cite examples of how they have used the Core Competencies in their learning. For this purpose, the CORE COMPETENCY SELF-REFLECTION FRAMES (pages 43-47) can be used throughout the learning process. There are five frames provided to address the Core Competencies: Communication, Creative Thinking, Critical Thinking, Positive Personal and Cultural Identity, and Personal Awareness and Responsibility. Teachers can conference individually with students to support self-reflection, or students may complete prompts using words and pictures.

Again, have students set goals by considering what they might do differently on future tasks and how they will know if they are successful in meeting their goal.

NOTE: Use the same prompts from these sheets over time to see how thinking changes with different activities.

Enhance

- **Family Connection**: Provide students with the following sentence starter:
  - We use mirrors in our house for

    _____.

Have students complete the sentence starter at home. Family members can help students draw and write about this topic. Have students share their sentences with the rest of the class

- Have students use a flashlight to shine light onto a large piece of white paper. Tell them to hold their hands about 30 cm above the paper, so their hands can pick up the light being reflected from the paper. Encourage students to observe how brightly lit their hands are from the reflected light. Now, repeat the same task with a large sheet of black paper. Since black absorbs most of the light, not much light is reflected, and students' hands will not appear very brightly lit.

- Focus on how light and heat work together in reflection and absorption. Paint one large empty soup tin black, and paint one white. Fill them both with water, place a thermometer into each tin, and place the tins in direct sunlight. Observe and record the temperature of the water in each tin. As visible light is absorbed, it gets transformed into heat, so the water temperature will be higher in the black tin than in the white tin.

- Have students research light pollution and its impact on surrounding ecosystems.

- Have students research how mirrors are made.

12 | How Can We See Light's Many Colours?

Information for Teachers

Rainbows consist of several bands of colour. The bands are not distinct but, rather, blend into each other and create various shades. There are seven bands of colour, from the outside to the inside: red, orange, yellow, green, blue, indigo, and violet (ROYGBIV). The order is always the same but some bands may be wider than others.

Rainbows are created by *refraction*. When conditions are right, water droplets in the air can separate the colours in sunlight—the water droplets act like prisms, refracting and reflecting the sunlight and separating the colours. This creates the colours of the rainbow. Sometimes, you will see a rainbow in a fine spray of water (e.g., from a lawn sprinkler or waterfall).

Objects around us appear to be different colours because they reflect some of the colours in light and absorb other colours. A chalkboard appears black because the board absorbs almost all the light and all the colours. It reflects back hardly any light. A red stop sign appears red because it reflects only red light and absorbs all other colours. Snow appears white because it reflects all colours equally.

⚠ **SAFETY NOTE:** Remind students never to look directly at the Sun or at its reflection in a mirror because it can damage their eyes.

Materials

- *The Good Rainbow Road* by Simon J. Ortiz (or another book about rainbows)
- various books and pictures related to rainbows
- clear glasses of water (one for each working group)
- black hockey tape or duct tape
- flashlights (one for each working group)
- white paper
- convex lenses (one for each working group)
- concave lenses (one for each working group)
- stories by Indigenous authors related to rainbows
- prisms (one for each working group)
- Learning-Centre Task Card: What Are the Colours in a Rainbow? (3.12.1)
- art paper
- watercolour paints and supplies (e.g., brushes, water)
- writing paper
- audio-recording device
- video-recording device
- pyramid chart (from lesson 9)

Engage

Read *The Good Rainbow Road,* by Simon J. Ortiz (or another book about rainbows). Discuss the events in the story, especially the characteristics of the rainbow.

Display other books and pictures about rainbows for students to examine. Ask:

- When have you seen a rainbow?
- What colours do you see in a rainbow?
- Are the colours always the same?
- Are they always in the same order?
- How do you think a rainbow is created?

Introduce the guided inquiry question: **How can we see light's many colours?**

Explore Part One

Organize students into working groups, and distribute to each group a flashlight, two pieces of black hockey tape or duct tape, white paper, and a clear glass of water. Tell students to cover the lens of the flashlight with the two pieces of tape, leaving a slit in the middle. Then, have them shine the flashlight through the glass of water onto the piece of paper. A rainbow should appear on the paper (turn off the classroom lights to see it better). Have students experiment

▶

Portage & Main Press, 2018 · Hands-On Science for British Columbia · Properties of Energy for Grades K-2 · ISBN: 978-1-55379-798-2

Portage & Main Press, 2018 · Hands-On Science for British Columbia · Properties of Energy for Grades K–2 · ISBN: 978-1-55379-798-2

with the angle of light shining through the glass to see what produces the most visible rainbow.

NOTE: Shining the light near the top of the glass (by the rim) often works best.

Ask students:

- What did you observe?
- Why do you think a rainbow appeared when you shone the flashlight through the glass of water?

NOTE: The glass of water acts like one large drop of water that bends (or refracts) the light and spreads out the colours, which separate because different wavelengths of light have different angles of refraction. The rainbow that appears in front of the glass, spreading back toward the light source, is light that has been refracted and reflected. This is what happens in nature. Students will be able to see another rainbow behind the glass, made up of light that was refracted but not reflected. Sometimes, a double rainbow is seen in the sky. The light is reflected twice, which creates the double rainbow (a fainter rainbow appears on top of the primary one, with the colours reversed [red at the bottom]).

Now, distribute a convex lens, a concave lens, and a prism to each group. Allow students plenty of time to investigate the colours of light by having them shine the flashlight at each of the three items and observe the results.

NOTE: The following diagram depicts how light reacts when it passes through a prism.

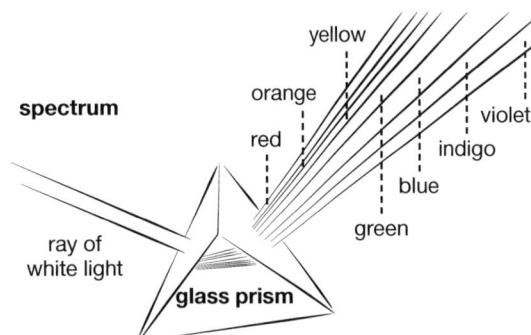

Explore Part Two

Explore stories by Indigenous authors related to rainbows. For example:

- *Rainbow Crow* by David Bouchard
- *Enora and the Black Crane* by Arone Raymond Meeks

While reading these books, have students discuss the connections to rainbows. Also encourage them to pay close attention to the use of colour in the images. Follow up by examining the use of colour in other examples of local Indigenous art.

Expand

Provide students with an opportunity to explore how we see light's colours further by posing their own questions for individualized inquiry. They may wish to:

- Initiate a project at the Makerspace, such as constructing a model rainbow using coloured beads, natural dyes and fabric, tissue paper, crêpe paper, or play dough.
- Explore Loose Parts related to colour (e.g., coloured marker caps, beads, wool, craft sticks, glass beads, plastic jewels). Students may create repeating patterns using the colours of the rainbow. Consider a provocation such as:
  - Can you use these objects to create a rainbow?

NOTE: Be sure to photograph students' creations so you can document their learning before they are disassembled into the Loose Parts bins.

- Research to find out how double rainbows are created (see Inquiry Through Research, page 26).
- Write poems and songs about the order of colours in a rainbow.

- Research and construct a kaleidoscope.
- Conduct an investigation or experiment based on their own inquiry questions.

As students explore and select ideas to expand learning, provide support and guidance as needed, and offer access to materials and resources that will enable students to conduct their chosen investigations.

Learning Centre

At the learning centre, provide art paper, watercolour paints and supplies (e.g., brushes, water), and various pictures and books related to rainbows. Also, provide writing paper, an audio-recording device, a video-recording device, and a copy of the Learning-Centre Task Card: What Are the Colours in a Rainbow? (3.12.1):

Learning Centre

What Are the Colours in a Rainbow?

1. Look at the pictures and books about rainbows.
2. Make a painting of a rainbow.
3. Show your understanding of how a rainbow is created. You may:
   - write a description
   - make an audio recording
   - make a video recording

3.12.1

Download this template at <www.portageandmainpress.com/product/HOSEnergyK2>.

Have students examine the pictures and books and then create a watercolour painting of a rainbow, with the colours accurately sequenced.

When students have completed their paintings, have them show their understanding of how a rainbow is created. They may do this in writing, or they may make a video recording.

Embed Part One: Talking Circle

Revisit the guided inquiry question: **How can we see light's many colours?** Have students share their experiences and knowledge, provide examples, and ask further inquiry questions.

Embed Part Two

- Add to the pyramid chart as students learn new concepts, answer some of their own inquiry questions, and ask new inquiry questions.

- Add new terms and illustrations to the word wall. Include the words in languages other than English, such as Indigenous languages, as appropriate.

- Focus on students' use of the Core Competencies. Have students reflect on how they used one of the Core Competencies (Thinking, Communicating, or Personal and Social Skills) during the various lesson activities. Project one of the CORE COMPETENCY DISCUSSION PROMPTS templates (pages 38-42), and use it to inspire group reflection. Referring to the template, choose one or two "I Can" statements on which to focus. Students then use the "I Can" statements to provide evidence of how they demonstrated that competency. Ask questions directly related to that competency to inspire discussion. For example:

▶

Portage & Main Press, 2018 · Hands-On Science for British Columbia · Properties of Energy for Grades K-2 · ISBN: 978-1-55379-798-2

- How did you show how you can work in a group today? (Communication)

Have students reflect orally, encouraging participation, questions, and the sharing of evidence. (See page 29 for more information on these templates.)

As part of this process, students can also set goals. For example, ask:
- What would you do differently next time and why?
- How will you know if you are successful in meeting your goal?

- To encourage self-reflection, provide prompts that students can use to cite examples of how they have used the Core Competencies in their learning. For this purpose, the CORE COMPETENCY SELF-REFLECTION FRAMES (pages 43-47) can be used throughout the learning process. There are five frames provided to address the Core Competencies: Communication, Creative Thinking, Critical Thinking, Positive Personal and Cultural Identity, and Personal Awareness and Responsibility. Teachers can conference individually with students to support self-reflection, or students may complete prompts using words and pictures.

Again, have students set goals by considering what they might do differently on future tasks and how they will know if they are successful in meeting their goal.

NOTE: Use the same prompts from these sheets over time to see how thinking changes with different activities.

Formative Assessment (AI)

As students conduct investigations in their groups, observe their ability to work together. Use the COOPERATIVE SKILLS TEACHER-ASSESSMENT template, on page 52, to record results. The focus here is on caring for self and others.

Provide descriptive feedback to students about how they demonstrated care for self and others.

Student Self-Assessment (AI)

Have students use the COOPERATIVE SKILLS SELF-ASSESSMENT template, on page 49, to reflect on their own work in a group. The focus here is on caring for self and others.

Enhance 🔲1

- **Family Connection:** Provide students with the following sentence starter:
  - We have seen a rainbow _____.

  Have students complete the sentence starter at home. Family members can help students draw and write about this topic. Have students share their sentences with the rest of the class.

- On a bright, sunny day take students outside, along with a white sheet of paper and a clear glass filled halfway with water. Have students place the glass on the paper and tilt it to and fro. They will see spots of colour form on the paper; challenge them to produce all colours of the rainbow. Ask:
  - What order are the colours in?
  - Are some bands of colour larger than others?

NOTE: Each colour, or wavelength, making up white light is bent, or refracted, a different amount: the shorter wavelengths (those toward the violet end of the spectrum) are bent the most, and the longer wavelengths (those toward the red end of the spectrum) are bent the least.

- Students can use a pan of water and a mirror to conduct a variation of the preceding activity. Have them place the pan of water in direct sunlight and put the mirror in the pan so most of it is underwater. Then, tell them to angle the mirror so reflected sunlight falls onto a white surface (e.g., sheet of paper). The colours of light will appear on the paper.

▶

Portage & Main Press, 2018 · Hands-On Science for British Columbia · Properties of Energy for Grades K–2 · ISBN: 978-1-55379-798-2

12

> **⚠ SAFETY NOTE:** Remind students never to look directly at the Sun or at its reflection in a mirror. Introduce students to the colour wheel, focusing on primary, secondary, and tertiary colours.

- Put out cups with water and food colouring in each of the primary colours (red, yellow, blue). Also provide a variety of clear containers and paper towels. Encourage students to make the secondary colours and experiment with colour mixing.

- Read *Hello, Red Fox,* by Eric Carle. The story focuses on complementary colours and light.

- Have students research to find out how prisms are used in various forms of technology.

Portage & Main Press, 2018 · *Hands-On Science for British Columbia · Properties of Energy for Grades K–2* · ISBN: 978-1-55379-798-2

13 | What Do We Know About Sound?

Information for Teachers

The next few lessons focus on sound energy. A new pyramid chart will be created for these lessons.

Lightning consists of huge static electric sparks that jump from cloud to cloud or from a cloud to Earth. They usually occur during a heavy rainstorm. Turbulence in storm clouds creates static electric charges that build up until they are released as a stream of electrons. This sudden release of electrons (known as electrostatic discharge) creates a bolt of lightning and a shock wave that is the sound of thunder.

Materials

- chart paper
- markers
- *The Legend of Lightning and Thunder* by Paula Ikuutaq Rumbolt
- audio recordings of 10 different sounds made by familiar objects (e.g., ringtones, piano, dog barking, guitar, alarm clock, owl hooting, heart beating, choir singing, water running/ dripping or rain falling, doorbell, drum beating, fire crackling, siren, car horn) (Assign each sound a number.)
- sticky notes (three different colours)
- writing paper
- audio-playing device

Engage Part One

To make the connection between previous lessons on light and subsequent lessons on sound, discuss students' understand of lightning and thunder. Ask:

- Have you ever experienced a thunderstorm?
- What did you see?
- What did you hear?
- How do you think lightning happens?
- What causes thunder?

- How do you feel when you hear thunder or see lightning?

Have students share their ideas.

Read the book, *The Legend of Lightning and Thunder*, by Paula Ikuutaq Rumbolt. This is an Inuit story from the Kivalliq region of Nunavut. Have students examine the images and recount the events in the story.

Engage Part Two

Provide each student with writing paper. Have students listen to the audio recording of each of the 10 different sounds and infer the source of each sound they hear. Tell them to record their inferences on their paper.

Play each sound again. For each one, ask:

- What do you think made that sound?

Have students check their inferences. Discuss the unique features of each sound, encouraging students to use descriptive vocabulary to describe its characteristics (e.g., hum, buzz, loud, quiet, high, low). Also, have them describe how each sound is created (e.g., a guitar sound is created by strumming on the strings; a doorbell rings when someone presses it, and an electrical circuit is completed).

Next, have each student put their hand on their throat and hum. They will feel the vibrations of their vocal chords. Compare this to vibrations on a guitar string or drum skin.

Introduce the guided inquiry question: **What do we know about sound?**

Explore Part One

Provide each student with a sticky note. On the sticky note, have them write down or draw any object or living thing that makes a sound (other than those heard in the Engage audio recordings).

▶

Portage & Main Press, 2018 · Hands-On Science for British Columbia · Properties of Energy for Grades K–2 · ISBN: 978-1-55379-798-2

Collect all of the sticky notes. Have a volunteer select one and try to recreate, for the rest of the class, the sound the object or living thing makes. (Encourage the volunteer not to add any visual clues or actions.) Ask the rest of the students to guess the identity of the object or living thing.

Create a t-chart on chart paper, as in the following example:

Sources of Sounds

Sounds in Nature	Other Sounds

Have students sort their sticky notes on the t-chart to show which sounds are heard in nature and which are not.

Explore Part Two

Go on a walk or visit a local nature preserve, park, or forest.

As with all place-based learning activities (see page 74 in lesson 1 for more information):

- Identify the importance of place. Use a map of the local area to identify where the location is in relation to the school.
- Identify on whose traditional territory the school is located, as well as the traditional territory of the location for the nature walk, if different.
- Incorporate land acknowledgment using local protocols.

When there, have students sit quietly and observe nature using their sense of hearing. Have them close their eyes and listen for an extended period of time. Afterward, have them use digital cameras to photograph the objects or living things that made the sounds they heard. These pictures can be used throughout the remainder of the module.

Have students express and reflect on personal experiences of place using their place-based journals to record their observations of sound in nature (see lesson 1 for more information about place-based journals).

Explore Part Three

Ask students to think about what they know about sound. Provide each student with a sticky note of the same colour, and have them record one thing they know, using pictures or text.

Conduct a Think, Pair, Share activity. Have students share their idea with a partner. Next, for class sharing, have each student role-play or mime one thing they know about sound. Model this for the class using your own ideas (e.g., act out playing a piano or cupping hands to call someone far away). Challenge students to guess what you are doing, then have students take turns role-playing while their classmates guess. On chart paper or mural paper, create a large pyramid graphic organizer to record ideas, as in the following example:

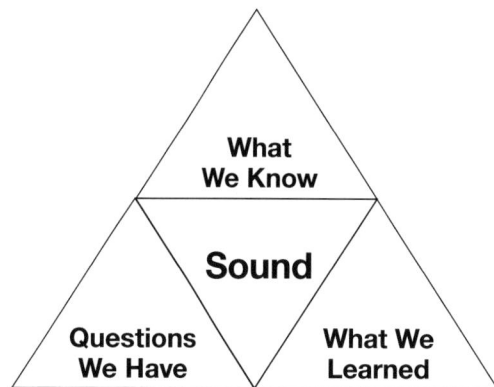

As students act and answer, have them add their sticky notes to the top triangle of the pyramid.

Ask:

- What questions do you have about sound?
- What would you like to learn about sound?

Portage & Main Press, 2018 · Hands-On Science for British Columbia · Properties of Energy for Grades K–2 · ISBN: 978-1-55379-798-2

Portage & Main Press, 2018 · Hands-On Science for British Columbia · Properties of Energy for Grades K–2 · ISBN: 978-1-55379-798-2

Record students' questions on a second colour of sticky note and attach each note to the pyramid, on the bottom left triangle.

Refer to the pyramid throughout the module. Answers to students' questions may also be added to the bottom right triangle of the pyramid with sticky notes, as students gather new information and acquire new knowledge. As students generate more inquiry questions, these may be added, as well.

Expand

Provide students with an opportunity to explore sound further by posing their own questions for individualized inquiry. They may wish to:

- Initiate a project at the Makerspace, such as designing and constructing a noisemaker for a local sports team. As an open-ended exploration, provide a variety of items (e.g., paper plates, beans, rice, paper towel tubes, tin cans, small boxes) to allow for discovery as students create instruments that make sound.

- Explore Loose Parts bins with objects related to sound (e.g., elastic bands, combs, tuning forks, whistles, shakers, bells). Consider a provocation such as:
    - What different sounds can you make?

- Research how specific animals make sounds (see Inquiry Through Research, page 26).

- Research the harmful effects of noise pollution on animals (see <www.science. org.au/curious/earth-environment/noise-pollution-and-environment>).

- Write poems and songs about sounds in nature.

- Create a recording of natural sounds.

- Conduct an investigation or experiment based on their own inquiry questions.

As students explore and select ideas to expand learning, provide support and guidance as needed, and offer access to materials and resources that will enable students to conduct their chosen investigations.

Embed Part One: Talking Circle

Revisit the guided inquiry question: **What do we know about sound?** Have students share their experiences and knowledge, provide examples, and ask further inquiry questions.

Embed Part Two

- Add to the pyramid chart as students learn new concepts, answer some of their own inquiry questions, and ask new inquiry questions.

- Add new terms and illustrations to the word wall. Include the words in languages other than English, such as Indigenous languages, as appropriate.

- Focus on students' use of the Core Competencies. Have students reflect on how they used one of the Core Competencies (Thinking, Communicating, or Personal and Social Skills) during the various lesson activities. Project one of the CORE COMPETENCY DISCUSSION PROMPTS templates (pages 38-42), and use it to inspire group reflection. Referring to the template, choose one or two "I Can" statements on which to focus. Students then use the "I Can" statements to provide evidence of how they demonstrated that competency. Ask questions directly related to that competency to inspire discussion. For example:
    - How do you feel about sounds in nature? (Personal Awareness and Responsibility)

Have students reflect orally, encouraging participation, questions, and the sharing of evidence. (See page 29 for more information on these templates.)

▶

13

As part of this process, students can also set goals. For example, ask:

- What would you do differently next time and why?
- How will you know if you are successful in meeting your goal?

- To encourage self-reflection, provide prompts that students can use to cite examples of how they have used the Core Competencies in their learning. For this purpose, the CORE COMPETENCY SELF-REFLECTION FRAMES (pages 43-47) can be used throughout the learning process. There are five frames provided to address the Core Competencies: Communication, Creative Thinking, Critical Thinking, Positive Personal and Cultural Identity, and Personal Awareness and Responsibility. Teachers can conference individually with students to support self-reflection, or students may complete prompts using words and pictures.

Again, have students set goals by considering what they might do differently on future tasks and how they will know if they are successful in meeting their goal.

NOTE: Use the same prompts from these sheets over time to see how thinking changes with different activities.

Enhance 🖥️

- **Family Connection**: Provide students with the following sentence starter:
  - Sounds we hear at home are _____.

  Have students complete the sentence starter at home. Family members can help students draw and write about this topic. Have students share their sentences with the rest of the class.

- Take a walk around the school neighbourhood, and have students listen to and record the sounds they hear. Back in the classroom, brainstorm a list of outdoor sounds and sound-words (e.g., bark, meow, birds, chipmunks/squirrels, crickets, flies, bees/wasps and other insects, traffic, siren, wind, rain, footsteps, car-door slam). Record these words on a sheet of chart paper, and then have students draw the object or living being that makes each sound.

- Have students brainstorm lists of sounds heard in different locations (e.g., restaurant, forest, farm, amusement park, grocery store, shopping mall, hospital, beach). Students can also make a mural and/or picture book for each location, with titles such as "Sounds in the Forest."

- Have students become Foley artists by making their own sound effects. Foley artists work in recording studios, making many of the sounds heard on radio, television, and in movies. Students can write short stories or plays for presentation, and then create the sounds to go with their stories. Have them either use an audio-recording device to record the sounds beforehand or sound them out during their presentations.

NOTE: There are many YouTube videos of Foley artists at work; simply type "foley artist" into the search bar to bring up a variety of videos.

- To make their stories seem more realistic, comic-book writers often use *onomatopoeia*, words that sound like actual or natural sounds such as *buzz* or *hiss*. Some real and nonsense words writers use to describe sounds include *screeeeeeeech, eerrrrrrrrk,* and *kapowww*. Connect this lesson to language arts by having students review comic books, graphic novels, and comic strips for examples of onomatopoeia and then create their own examples.

▶

Portage & Main Press, 2018 · Hands-On Science for British Columbia · Properties of Energy for Grades K–2 · ISBN: 978-1-55379-798-2

- Encourage students to make their own audio recordings of the sounds various objects and living beings make. Have each student state their name at the beginning of the recording, as well as a number to go with each sound (e.g., L: one: *bzzzzzzz*; two: *hsssssssssss).* Have other students listen to the recordings and infer the identity of the object or living thing that made each sound. Have students check their inferences on an answer key.

Portage & Main Press, 2018 · Hands-On Science for British Columbia · Properties of Energy for Grades K–2 · ISBN: 978-1-55379-798-2

14 | How Is Sound Created?

Information for Teachers

Sound needs matter through which to travel. In outer space, there is not enough matter through which sound can travel in order for the human ear to detect sound.

Sound energy moves in pressure waves through a medium, such as air or water. It even travels through solid objects, such as walls or metal instruments. Sound occurs when particles within the medium vibrate, causing waves. Eventually, when the waves reach your ear, you hear the sound.

Visualize sound using a vibrating tuning fork. When the fork is placed in water, the vibrations cause a ripple because the sound waves are travelling through the water.

Materials

- chart paper
- markers
- uncooked rice
- clear plastic wrap
- empty glass jars (one for each working group)
- elastic bands
- drawing paper
- metal trays (one for each working group)
- spoons (or pencils or drumsticks)
- shallow pan of water
- tuning forks
- pyramid chart (from lesson 13)

Engage

Organize the class into pairs of students and distribute an elastic band to each pair. Have one student in each pair stretch an elastic band between their index fingers while the other student plucks it. (Teachers may wish to define and demonstrate the term *pluck*.) Have students observe the elastic band. Ask:

- What did you notice when the elastic band was plucked?
- What did you hear?
- What did you see?

Introduce the guided inquiry question: **How is sound created?**

Explore Part One

Have students focus on the sound created as the elastic band is plucked, and on the vibrating motion as the sound is heard. Ask:

- How do you think sound is created when you pluck the elastic band?

Have students share their ideas. Record these on chart paper. Introduce the term *vibrate*. Ask:

- What do you think the word *vibrate* means?
- Did you see the elastic band vibrate?
- How do we hear sounds?

Discuss the "back and forth" motion of the elastic band, and the sound created as the elastic vibrates.

Explore Part Two

Display several tuning forks, and give students an opportunity to examine and manipulate them. Ask:

- Do you know what this object is called?
- How does it work?

Have students take a tuning fork and tap the side of it. Ask:

- What do you observe when the tuning fork is tapped?
- Do you hear a sound?
- How is the sound produced?

Have students strike the tuning fork again and then touch it. Ask:

- Do you feel something?

▶

Portage & Main Press, 2018 · *Hands-On Science for British Columbia · Properties of Energy for Grades K–2* · ISBN: 978-1-55379-798-2

Portage & Main Press, 2018 · Hands-On Science for British Columbia · Properties of Energy for Grades K–2 · ISBN: 978-1-55379-798-2

- What happens to the bars on the tuning fork when you strike it?
- What do you think will happen if you strike the tuning fork, and then place it in water?

Set out a shallow pan of water and allow the water to settle. Have students test their predictions by striking the tuning fork and then touching it against the still surface of the water. Ask:

- What happens to the water?
- Why do you think tiny waves or ripples are created in the water?

Discuss how the tuning fork vibrated once it was struck. This movement caused sound.

Have students closely observe the wave pattern created in the water by the tuning fork's vibrations. Encourage them to draw labelled diagrams to represent this motion, as the waves move outward from the fork and become less distinct. This is similar to what happens when a pebble is dropped in water. The waves move outward from the pebble and lessen in strength. This demonstrates how sound waves move, and why sounds become less audible at a distance.

Explore Part Three

Organize the class into working groups, and distribute to each group a glass jar, a piece of plastic wrap, and an elastic band. Have students stretch the piece of plastic wrap tightly over the open end of the jar and secure the wrap with the elastic band. Distribute a few grains of rice to each group, and have students place these on the plastic wrap. Hold up one of the metal trays

and a spoon (or pencil or drumstick) for all to see. Ask:

What do you think will happen if you hold this metal tray near the jar, and then bang it with a spoon (or pencil or drumstick)?

Distribute a tray to each group (if only one is available, pass it around from group to group).

Have students place the metal tray close to the jar, bang the tray with the spoon, and observe what happens. (The sound waves from the tray cause the plastic wrap to vibrate and the grains of rice to move.)

Expand

Provide students with an opportunity to explore how sound is created further by posing their own questions for individualized inquiry. They may wish to:

- Initiate a project at the Makerspace, such as designing and constructing an object that demonstrates sound vibration. Also continue open-ended exploration with a variety of items (e.g., paper plates, beans, rice, paper towel tubes, tin cans, small boxes) to allow for discovery as students create instruments that make sound.
- Explore Loose Parts bins with objects related to sound (e.g., elastic bands, combs, tuning forks, shakers). Consider including the provocation:
  - How can you create different sounds?
- Research to find out how we make sound with our voices (see Inquiry Through Research, page 26).
- Write poems and songs about sounds.
- Conduct an investigation or experiment based on their own inquiry questions.

As students explore and select ideas to expand learning, provide support and guidance as

▶

14

needed, and offer access to materials and resources that will enable students to conduct their chosen investigations.

Embed Part One: Talking Circle

Revisit the guided inquiry question: **How is sound created?** Have students share their experiences and knowledge, provide examples, and ask further inquiry questions.

Embed Part Two

- Add to the pyramid chart as students learn new concepts, answer some of their own inquiry questions, and ask new inquiry questions.

- Add new terms and illustrations to the word wall. Include the words in languages other than English, such as Indigenous languages, as appropriate.

- Focus on students' use of the Core Competencies. Have students reflect on how they used one of the Core Competencies (Thinking, Communicating, or Personal and Social Skills) during the various lesson activities. Project one of the CORE COMPETENCY DISCUSSION PROMPTS templates (pages 38-42), and use it to inspire group reflection. Referring to the template, choose one or two "I Can" statements on which to focus. Students then use the "I Can" statements to provide evidence of how they demonstrated that competency. Ask questions directly related to that competency to inspire discussion. For example:
  - How did you share your learning today? (Communication)

  Have students reflect orally, encouraging participation, questions, and the sharing of evidence. (See page 29 for more information on these templates.)

  As part of this process, students can also set goals. For example, ask:

- What would you do differently next time and why?
- How will you know if you are successful in meeting your goal?

- To encourage self-reflection, provide prompts that students can use to cite examples of how they have used the Core Competencies in their learning. For this purpose, the CORE COMPETENCY SELF-REFLECTION FRAMES (pages 43-47) can be used throughout the learning process. There are five frames provided to address the Core Competencies: Communication, Creative Thinking, Critical Thinking, Positive Personal and Cultural Identity, and Personal Awareness and Responsibility. Teachers can conference individually with students to support self-reflection, or students may complete prompts using words and pictures.

  Again, have students set goals by considering what they might do differently on future tasks and how they will know if they are successful in meeting their goal.

NOTE: Use the same prompts from these sheets over time to see how thinking changes with different activities.

Enhance 🔲

- **Family Connection**: Provide students with the following sentence starter:
  - We can create sounds at home by _____.

  Have students complete the sentence starter at home. Family members can help students draw and write about this topic. Have students share their sentences with the rest of the class.

- Have students gather around a record player. Provide vinyl records for them to examine. Ask:

▶

Portage & Main Press, 2018 · Hands-On Science for British Columbia · Properties of Energy for Grades K-2 · ISBN: 978-1-55379-798-2

Portage & Main Press, 2018 · Hands-On Science for British Columbia · Properties of Energy for Grades K–2 · ISBN: 978-1-55379-798-2

- How do you think sound is made from a record?
- What do you notice about the surface of a record?
- Why do you think there are tiny grooves on the record?

Place a record on the record player, and have students observe the needle as it moves over the groove. Ask:

- Why is sound made when the needle moves over the grooves of the record?

To further demonstrate how sound is created on a record, make a needle for the record player. Push a sewing needle through a cone-shaped paper cup. Turn on the record player, and carefully place the point of the needle on a groove of the record. As the needle comes in contact with the grooves, the sound vibrations will travel up the needle and into the cone. Students will be able to hear the sound from the record clearly.

- Ask a student to place a ruler so that half of it extends over the edge of a tabletop. Tell the student to hold the ruler down where it is resting on the table, bend the extended end down, and then quickly let go of the extended end. The vibrations of the ruler will create sound waves, which travel to the ear, enabling students to hear the sound.

- Have students make kazoos: place a piece of wax paper over the end of a short cardboard tube, and secure it in place by wrapping an elastic band around the tube. Tell students to place their mouths loosely over the open end of the tube, without completely sealing the opening. By humming into the tube, the wax paper will vibrate and create a buzzing kazoo sound. This same effect is possible by covering a comb with tissue paper, placing the mouth against the comb, and humming. A related idea is the Exploratorium's Sound Sandwich; Students can construct

the device, and manipulate some of the components (e.g., size of elastic) to see what effect it has on the sound produced. See instructions at: <www.exploratorium.edu/afterschool/activities/docs/soundsandwich.pdf>.

15 | How Do Musical Instruments Use Sound Energy?

Information for Teachers Musical instruments are classified by how the instrument creates vibrations to produce sound waves. The three major instrument groups are *stringed*, *wind*, and *percussion*.

Stringed instruments cause vibrations when a string is plucked or bowed. A guitar produces sound when the strings are plucked with fingers or a pick. A violin or cello produces sound when a bow is drawn across the strings. *Pitch*, a property of sound that changes with the frequency of vibration, is changed by changing the length of the vibrating string. By pushing down on the string with a finger, the length is shortened, producing a higher-pitched sound. Strings with a larger diameter also produce lower-pitched sounds.

Wind instruments produce sound when air is blown through the instrument. In brass instruments, like the trumpet and trombone, the lips produce the vibration. Pitch is changed by using the valves, or slides, on the instrument. In most woodwind instruments, the reed in the mouthpiece produces the vibrations. In a flute or piccolo, the air itself vibrates in the column of the instrument to produce the sound. In all wind instruments, the length of the air column affects the pitch. A larger instrument (e.g., a saxophone) will have a lower sound than a smaller instrument (e.g., a clarinet).

Percussion instruments, such as bells, cymbals, and drums produce sound when struck. When struck, these instruments vibrate, which causes changes in the air pressure. The air vibrates, and your ears hear these vibrations as sound. Most percussion instruments do not produce a definite pitch, so they are often called *rhythm instruments*. The piano and the xylophone can produce a definite pitch, but they are still classified as percussion instruments because the strings of the piano and the bars of the xylophone are struck.

NOTE: This lesson presents an excellent opportunity to connect to the music curriculum and to request support from the music teacher at your own school or a local secondary school. Consider inviting a member of a local symphony or band to present to the class.

Materials

- chart paper
- markers
- index cards
- sticky notes
- masking tape
- variety of stringed, wind, and percussion instruments
- Image Bank: Indigenous Instruments (see Appendix, page 177)
- pyramid chart (from lesson 13)

Engage Part One

Invite a musician to the class to play for students and share what goes into making music. Consider presentations by students who play instruments, family members, as well as school staff and community members.

Engage Part Two

Have students share their personal experiences with musical instruments. Ask:

- Do any of you play musical instruments?
- Which instrument?
- How did you learn to play it?
- Why did you choose to play this instrument?

After students share their personal stories, expand the topic to include other personal connections to musical instruments. Ask:

- Does someone in your family or a friend play a musical instrument?
- Which instrument?

▶

Portage & Main Press, 2018 · Hands-On Science for British Columbia · Properties of Energy for Grades K–2 · ISBN: 978-1-55379-798-2

15

- Do you know the names of any professional musicians?
- Which instruments do they play?

Encourage discussion of concerts students have attended, as well as traditions such as campfire singsongs (with guitar accompaniment) and holiday performances. Include discussion about Indigenous events such as powwows, and other cultural events involving musical instruments.

Introduce the guided inquiry question: **How do musical instruments use sound energy?**

Explore Part One

⚠️ **SAFETY NOTE:** Students are presented with opportunities to try out some instruments in the following activity. To ensure good hygiene and health for all students, be sure that any instrument with a mouthpiece is thoroughly cleaned after each student uses it.

Display a variety of musical instruments for students to examine and manipulate. Have students identify by name as many of the instruments as they can. Record the names of these instruments on index cards and use tape to affix the cards to chart paper. As students identify each instrument, ask:

- How is sound made from this instrument?
- What does the musician have to do to make music?
- What kinds of sounds does the instrument make?

When you have discussed all the instruments, demonstrate how each one makes music, and have students attempt to create sound from each one. Ask:

- How was the sound created for this instrument?
- Could you see or feel the vibrations?
- Can you change how loud the instrument sounds? How?

Challenge students to sort the instruments in a variety of ways, such as by size, how they make sound (wind, strings, percussion), what materials they are made of, or what kinds of sounds they produce.

As a class, construct a pictograph of students' sorting. Have them draw the instruments on sticky notes, labelling them by name. As a class, make the same number of drawings as there are instruments in each sorted group. The sticky notes can then be used to construct a pictograph to display sorting data (see page 24 for more information about pictographs).

Explore Part Two

As a class, investigate different types of Indigenous instruments. Display the Image Bank: Indigenous Instruments. Have students discuss the features of the various instruments, as well as the materials from which they are made (see information in the image descriptions in the Appendix, page 177).

Drums and other instruments are very important cultural symbols and are central to Indigenous community celebrations and ceremonies. Cultural practices vary among communities, so it is best to refer to individual Nations for their information about instruments. For example, in some Nations, certain people use drums and others use rattles. Due to the importance of drums and other instruments to Indigenous culture, discussions should involve Elders or Knowledge Keepers.

NOTE: See Indigenous Perspectives, page 9, for guidelines for inviting Elders or Knowledge Keepers to speak to the class.

If possible, also invite Indigenous musicians into the classroom to demonstrate the use of various instruments (e.g., drums, rattles, whistles, flutes), and to discuss how these instruments are made.

▶

Portage & Main Press, 2018 · Hands-On Science for British Columbia · Properties of Energy for Grades K–2 · ISBN: 978-1-55379-798-2

It may be possible for this musician to teach the students a local song or drum piece.

Expand 🎲 1️⃣

Provide students with an opportunity to explore how musical instruments use sound energy further by posing their own questions for individualized inquiry. They may wish to:

■ Initiate a project at the Makerspace, such as designing and constructing an original instrument.

■ Research a specific instrument to find out how it is made and played and collect recordings of this instrument (see Inquiry Through Research, page 26).

■ Write poems and songs about music.

■ Research and role-play a favourite musician.

■ Conduct an investigation or experiment based on their own inquiry questions.

As students explore and select ideas to expand learning, provide support and guidance as needed, and offer access to materials and resources that will enable students to conduct their chosen investigations.

Embed Part One: Talking Circle

Revisit the guided inquiry question: **How do musical instruments use sound energy?** Have students share their experiences and knowledge, provide examples, and ask further inquiry questions.

Embed Part Two

■ Add to the pyramid chart as students learn new concepts, answer some of their own inquiry questions, and ask new inquiry questions.

■ Add new terms and illustrations to the word wall. Include the words in languages other than English, such as Indigenous languages, as appropriate.

■ Focus on students' use of the Core Competencies. Have students reflect on how they used one of the Core Competencies (Thinking, Communicating, or Personal and Social Skills) during the various lesson activities. Project one of the CORE COMPETENCY DISCUSSION PROMPTS templates (pages 38-42), and use it to inspire group reflection. Referring to the template, choose one or two "I Can" statements on which to focus. Students then use the "I Can" statements to provide evidence of how they demonstrated that competency. Ask questions directly related to that competency to inspire discussion. For example:

■ How did you decide which questions to ask today? (Critical Thinking)

Have students reflect orally, encouraging participation, questions, and the sharing of evidence. (See page 29 for more information on these templates.)

As part of this process, students can also set goals. For example, ask:

■ What would you do differently next time and why?

■ How will you know if you are successful in meeting your goal?

■ To encourage self-reflection, provide prompts that students can use to cite examples of how they have used the Core Competencies in their learning. For this purpose, the CORE COMPETENCY SELF-REFLECTION FRAMES (pages 43-47) can be used throughout the learning process. There are five frames provided to address the Core Competencies: Communication, Creative Thinking, Critical Thinking, Positive Personal and Cultural Identity, and Personal Awareness and Responsibility. Teachers can conference individually with students to support self-reflection, or students may complete prompts using words and pictures.

▶

Portage & Main Press, 2018 · *Hands-On Science for British Columbia · Properties of Energy for Grades K–2* · ISBN: 978-1-55379-798-2

15

Again, have students set goals by considering what they might do differently on future tasks and how they will know if they are successful in meeting their goal.

NOTE: Use the same prompts from these sheets over time to see how thinking changes with different activities.

Enhance

- **Family Connection**: Provide students with the following sentence starters:
    - People in my family who play musical instruments include _____.
    - Our favourite music to listen to at home is _____.

    Have students complete the sentence starter at home. Family members can help students draw and write about this topic. Have students share their sentences with the rest of the class.

- Make other musical instruments as a class. Some examples include:
    - tambourine: two aluminum pie plates, facing inward, with beans or buttons inside, and secured together with tape
    - drums: milk cartons, cereal boxes, or tissue boxes stuffed with paper or cloth to dampen the sound
    - rattles/maracas/drums: potato-chip tins (with plastic lids) or smaller margarine or yogurt containers filled with dried beans
    - guitars: various lengths of wire, fishing line, or elastic bands strung between nails on a board or across a tissue box
    - xylophone: glass bottles filled with water, in varying amounts
    - steel drums: assorted tin cans and metal bowls, with wooden spoons, pencils, or paint sticks as drumsticks

- Plan a field trip for students to see and hear a local symphony, band, or another musical group in your community.

- Conduct research on local musicians.

- Learn about Indigenous musicians. The book, *Great Musicians from Our First Nations* by Vincent Schilling is a good place to start.

- Have students conduct research projects about a musical instrument of their choice.

Portage & Main Press, 2018 · Hands-On Science for British Columbia · Properties of Energy for Grades K–2 · ISBN: 978-1-55379-798-2

16 | How Can We Use Recycled Materials to Construct Instruments That Make Sound?

Materials

- chart paper
- markers
- thumbtacks
- boards (20–30 cm long; thickness and width are not important)
- small pieces of wood (1 cm x 5 cm x 1–2 cm)
- elastic bands (various thicknesses)
- fishing line
- drinking straws (thicker, milkshake size)
- tape
- scissors
- cardboard-box lids (e.g., shoebox lids)
- cardboard boxes with tops cut off (empty tissue boxes work well)
- wooden dowels
- string
- copper piping (cut to various lengths)
- paint and painting supplies (e.g., water, brushes) (optional)
- glue (optional)
- tissue paper (optional)
- mallet (optional)
- metal coffee tins with plastic lids (Make sure edges are smooth.)
- computer/tablet with internet access
- pyramid chart (from lesson 13)

Engage

Show the video *Landfill Harmonic*. In it, students form an orchestra in which they play instruments they made from recycled materials found at a local landfill. Although the students featured live in extreme poverty, they found a means of making music (see <http://www.landfillharmonicmovie.com/>). Similar videos on the same topic, describing orchestras from various countries, are available online.

After viewing the video, discuss the ways students made instruments and the materials they used for construction.

Introduce the guided inquiry question: **How can we use recycled materials to construct instruments that make sound?**

Explore Part One

Provide students with opportunities to construct several simple homemade musical instruments (wind, stringed, percussion) with the materials provided. This activity can be a prelude to the subsequent activity, in which students are challenged to design and build their own unique instrument.

NOTE: Depending on fine motor skills, some students may benefit from adult support when constructing these instruments.

Some simple instrument construction projects are as follows:

Single Stringed

Provide students with boards, thumbtacks, small pieces of wood, fishing line, and scissors. Have them use the materials to make one-stringed instruments (see illustration below). By pressing a finger against the string at different locations, students will be able to create different pitches.

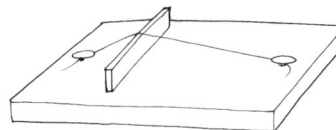

Harp

Students can make simple harps from cardboard-box lids, wooden dowels, and elastic bands. The fixed angle of the wooden dowels determines the length of each string (as pictured below), so students can create various pitches by plucking the different strings.

▶

Portage & Main Press, 2018 · Hands-On Science for British Columbia · Properties of Energy for Grades K-2 · ISBN: 978-1-55379-798-2

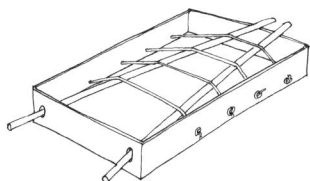

Portage & Main Press, 2018 · *Hands-On Science for British Columbia* · *Properties of Energy for Grades K–2* · ISBN: 978-1-55379-798-2

Xylophone

Students can construct xylophones by using string, scissors, tape, and copper piping cut to various lengths. Have them wind and tape the string around each piece of pipe, as shown in the diagram below (the horizontal parts represent the tubing, while the rest is the string) from shortest to longest in length. When students hold up the constructed xylophone and strike one of the pipes with a mallet, they will hear a note. The different lengths of piping will create various pitches.

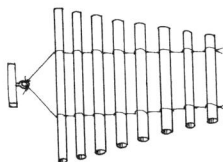

String Thickness

Have students discover how pitch is related to the thickness of strings on an instrument. Provide small cardboard boxes with the tops cut off (empty tissue boxes work well). Also, provide several elastic bands of different thicknesses, but the same length. Have students stretch the elastic bands around the box, so the elastics extend over the open top. When students pluck the bands, they will notice the thick bands create lower pitches, while the thin bands create higher pitches. (Thick bands vibrate more slowly than thin bands, and the slower frequency creates a lower pitch.)

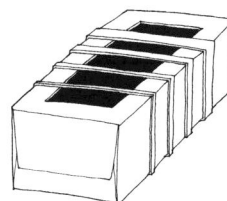

Pan Flute

Have students experiment with sound as it relates to air and open columns. Distribute drinking straws, tape, and scissors. Have students cut the straws to various lengths, flatten one end of each straw, and cut the flat end to a point. By blowing through the other end of the straw, they will create a sound. The short straws will create higher-pitched notes because the frequency of the vibrations is faster. The longer straws will create lower-pitched notes because the frequency of the vibrations is slower. Challenge students to arrange the straws in order from lowest to highest pitch. They can then tape the straws together to make a pan flute.

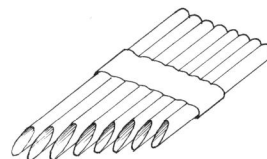

Barrel Drum

Students can make simple barrel drums to experiment with sound created from striking an instrument. Give students round metal coffee tins with plastic lids (make sure edges are smooth), and have them decorate the tins. They can either paint the coffee tins or glue on small tissue-paper shapes. Both the metal bottom and the plastic lid of the decorated drum can be struck with hands or mallets, for different sounds.

▶

16

After building each instrument, have students experiment with the sounds they create. Ask:

- How do you make sound with this instrument?
- How can you make a high-pitched sound?
- How can you make a low-pitched sound?
- How could you change or modify the instrument to create more sounds?

If not all students have made the same instruments, have different students demonstrate the use of each type, and as a class, discuss the various ways sound is produced.

Explore Part Two

Challenge each student to build their own musical instrument. As a class, establish criteria for the task. For example, the instrument should:

- be one the student has not built before
- include recycled materials
- be playable to show different sounds
- include a labelled diagram

Record these criteria on chart paper for students to refer to throughout the process. Provide plenty of time for students to work on their musical instruments, encouraging them to plan/ design their projects first, create blueprints, and make modifications and improvements during the construction process.

⚠ **SAFETY NOTE:** During construction of their instruments, stress the importance of safety to students (e.g., use tools and materials correctly and carefully). Loud noise can also be a

safety concern; students need to be careful not to produce sound at volumes that may be harmful to others.

Have students make their instruments, and identify questions that they should answer as part of their presentations to the class. For example:

- Why did you choose the materials you did to build your musical instrument?
- How does your instrument create sound?
- What does your diagram tell us?
- What would you do differently if you could redesign your instrument?

Formative Assessment Ⓒ

As students present their musical instruments, observe their ability to address the criteria identified by the class. List these criteria on the RUBRIC template, on page 53, and record results during presentations. Focus on students' ability to share observations and ideas orally. Provide descriptive feedback to students about how they met the criteria in the design and construction of a musical instrument that plays sound.

Student Self-Assessment Ⓔ

Have students complete the STUDENT REFLECTIONS template, on page 36, to reflect on their learning while designing and constructing their own musical instrument. Students should focus on reflecting on their ideas and the ideas of others.

Expand

Provide students with an opportunity to explore musical instruments further by posing their own questions for individualized inquiry. They may wish to:

- Initiate a project at the Makerspace, such as making a model of another instrument that produces a variety of different sounds.

▶

Portage & Main Press, 2018 · Hands-On Science for British Columbia · Properties of Energy for Grades K-2 · ISBN: 978-1-55379-798-2

Portage & Main Press, 2018 · Hands-On Science for British Columbia · Properties of Energy for Grades K–2 · ISBN: 978-1-55379-798-2

- Research a specific instrument to find out how it is made and played, and collect recordings of this instrument (see Inquiry Through Research, page 26).
- Write a song and perform it with an instrument accompaniment.
- Research and role-play a favourite musician.
- Conduct an investigation or experiment based on their own inquiry questions.

As students explore and select ideas to expand learning, provide support and guidance as needed, and offer access to materials and resources that will enable students to conduct their chosen investigations.

Embed Part One: Talking Circle

Revisit the guided inquiry question: **How can we use recycled materials to construct instruments that make sound?** Have students share their experiences and knowledge, provide examples, and ask further inquiry questions.

Embed Part Two

- Add to the pyramid chart as students learn new concepts, answer some of their own inquiry questions, and ask new inquiry questions.
- Add new terms and illustrations to the word wall. Include the words in languages other than English, such as Indigenous languages, as appropriate.
- Focus on students' use of the Core Competencies. Have students reflect on how they used one of the Core Competencies (Thinking, Communicating, or Personal and Social Skills) during the various lesson activities. Project one of the CORE COMPETENCY DISCUSSION PROMPTS templates (pages 38-42), and use it to inspire group reflection. Referring to the template, choose one or two "I Can" statements on which

to focus. Students then use the "I Can" statements to provide evidence of how they demonstrated that competency. Ask questions directly related to that competency to inspire discussion. For example:

- How did you grow as a learner today? (Positive Personal and Cultural Identity)

Have students reflect orally, encouraging participation, questions, and the sharing of evidence. (See page 29 for more information on these templates.)

As part of this process, students can also set goals. For example, ask:

- What would you do differently next time and why?
- How will you know if you are successful in meeting your goal?

- To encourage self-reflection, provide prompts that students can use to cite examples of how they have used the Core Competencies in their learning. For this purpose, the CORE COMPETENCY SELF-REFLECTION FRAMES (pages 43-47) can be used throughout the learning process. There are five frames provided to address the Core Competencies: Communication, Creative Thinking, Critical Thinking, Positive Personal and Cultural Identity, and Personal Awareness and Responsibility. Teachers can conference individually with students to support self-reflection, or students may complete prompts using words and pictures.

Again, have students set goals by considering what they might do differently on future tasks and how they will know if they are successful in meeting their goal.

NOTE: Use the same prompts from these sheets over time to see how thinking changes with different activities.

▶

Enhance

- **Family Connection**: Have students take home their designed instruments to demonstrate. Provide students with the following sentence starter:
  - Other instruments we could make at home are _____.

  Have students complete the sentence starter at home. Family members can help students draw and write about this topic. Have students share their sentences with the rest of the class.

- Together with students, make an instrument called "Household Bells." Tie a string between two chairs, so the string is taut. Use small pieces of string or long twist ties to attach utensils and other objects (e.g., metal hanger, spoon, fork, ruler, pencil) to the horizontal string, so it looks like a clothesline. Then, working with a partner or a small group, have one student place their ear against the string while another student uses a metal spoon to tap each different hanging object. The listening student should be able to hear sound from the string and feel vibrations. Have students try hanging other objects (e.g., plastic forks, aluminum pie plates). Ask:
  - Which objects seem to work the best?
  - Which objects produce the most interesting sounds?

- Have students make grass whistles, using the following instructions: Choose a blade of grass about 12–15 cm long. Hold the blade of grass between your thumbs with your hands closed in a prayer position. The edge of the blade should face you. Hold the grass firmly with the ball of your hand below each thumb and the tops of both thumbs. Now, blow steadily through your thumbs onto the vertical edge of the grass. Practise until you get a smooth sound. Adjust the tension of your hand to produce different sounds (with different pitches). Try other varieties of grass to hear if they produce different sounds.

Portage & Main Press, 2018 · Hands-On Science for British Columbia · Properties of Energy for Grades K–2 · ISBN: 978-1-55379-798-2

17 | Which Objects Do Magnets Attract?

Information for Teachers

Earth is a giant magnet, and like all magnets, it has a north pole and a south pole. In fact, Earth's magnetic poles are not in the same geographical position as the North Pole and the South Pole, but the same terms are used.

Long bar magnets usually have the poles marked. If like poles meet, they will repel each other. If unlike poles meet, they will attract each other.

Some metals are attracted to the *magnetic pull* or *magnetic force*. Other metals do not react. Objects made from iron, cobalt, nickel, and some steel are attracted to magnets, while objects made from aluminum, copper, and tin are not affected.

Ensure students use proper scientific vocabulary to describe how objects react when they are near a magnet; verbs such as *attract* and *repel* are correct, but students may be tempted to use verbs like *stick*, which is not proper terminology.

Materials

- chart paper
- markers
- variety of magnets (e.g., bar, horseshoe, cylinder)
- variety of small objects to test magnetism (e.g., coins [nickels, dimes, quarters], buttons, pencils, pens, combs, erasers, paper clips, nails, tacks, steel teaspoons, steel thimbles, screws, rocks, rulers, staples, safety pins)
- glasses of water (one for each working group)
- small pieces of cloth
- plastic wrap
- wax paper
- tissue paper
- computers/tablets with internet access
- projection device (optional)
- aluminum foil
- sticky notes
- Learning-Centre Task Card: Going Fishing (3.17.2)
- Learning Centre Task Card: Treasure Hunt (3.17.3)
- string
- low divider (e.g., piece of cardboard leaning against a chair)
- sand or uncooked rice (or use a sand or water table)
- metre sticks
- two large basins
- digital camera
- writing paper

Engage

Organize the class into working groups of two to three students and provide each group with various magnets (e.g., bar, horseshoe, cylinder). Give students time to examine and discuss the magnets. Ask:

- What are these objects?
- What do you know about magnets?
- What kinds of objects do they attract?
- How are magnets used in everyday life?

Record students' responses on chart paper.

Introduce the guided inquiry question: **Which objects do magnets attract?**

Explore Part One

Have students continue to work in the same groups. Provide each group with several small objects to examine (e.g., coins [nickels, dimes, quarters], buttons, pencils, pens, combs, erasers, paper clips, nails, tacks, rocks, rulers, staples, safety pins). Tell students they will be using the objects to test how each reacts to a magnet. Have them examine each object as a group, passing it around and discussing its characteristics and the materials from which it

▶

Portage & Main Press, 2018 · Hands-On Science for British Columbia · Properties of Energy for Grades K–2 · ISBN: 978-1-55379-798-2

17

is made. Have each group predict whether the object will be attracted to a magnet, then sort the objects according to their predictions.

Next, provide each group with a magnet to test their predictions. Have them first test the objects they did not think would be attracted to a magnet. Then, have the groups test the objects they thought would be attracted to magnets. Have each group sort their objects according to those that were attracted to magnets and those that were not.

Discuss their findings as a class. Ask:

■ Which objects were attracted to magnets?

Record a list of these objects on chart paper. Ask:

■ What was the same about the objects that were attracted to magnets?

As a class, discuss the characteristics and materials of those objects that were attracted to the magnets.

Explore Part Two

Have students work in the same groups, using the same collection of objects that were attracted to a magnet. Ask:

■ Do you think these objects will always be attracted to different kinds of magnets?

Have students test their predictions. Provide the groups with a variety of different magnets (e.g., bar, horseshoe, cylinder) to test.

As a class, discuss the various magnets. Ask:

■ Were the objects attracted to all of the magnets?
■ Was there any difference in how the objects were attracted to the different magnets?
■ Do you think some of the magnets were more powerful or stronger than other?

■ How could we test this idea?

Have students discuss in their groups how to test the strength of different magnets, so they could be ordered from strongest attraction to weakest attraction. For example, students might test to see how many paper clips or nails different magnets can pick up. Have students record their data and then create a graph to compare magnet strength.

Explore Part Three

Have students return to their working groups. Provide each group with a glass of water, a magnet, a safety pin, a paper clip, a staple, and a tack. Have students place the items in their glass of water. Ask:

■ What do you think would happen if you placed the magnet next to the glass?

Have students share their predictions. Now ask students to move a magnet up and down along the outside of the glass. Ask:

■ Are the objects attracted to the magnet at the side of the glass?
■ Do they follow the magnet as you move it up and down the side of the glass?

Discuss students' observations and inferences.

Explore Part Four

Distribute to the groups small pieces of cloth, plastic wrap, aluminum foil, wax paper, and tissue paper. Have students use these materials to wrap around the objects from Explore Part One that were attracted to magnets. Ask:

■ Do you think these objects will still be attracted to the magnets?

Have students test the objects with a magnet to see if they are affected by being wrapped in other materials.

▶

Portage & Main Press, 2018 · Hands-On Science for British Columbia · Properties of Energy for Grades K–2 · ISBN: 978-1-55379-798-2

17

Explore Part Five 🖥

Engage the class in a follow-up discussion, to provide students with ideas of how magnets work, and what materials are attracted to magnets. Ask:

- What characteristics do the objects that were attracted to the magnets have in common?
- What characteristics do the objects that were not attracted to the magnets have in common?
- Why do you think some objects are attracted to the magnets?
- Could you pick up a nickel with the magnets? Why not? (The Canadian nickel is made from an alloy—a combination of metals—so even though the metal nickel is attracted to magnets, there is not enough nickel in the coin for it to be attracted to the magnets.)
- Which part of the magnet attracts the best?

Create a sorting mat on chart paper:

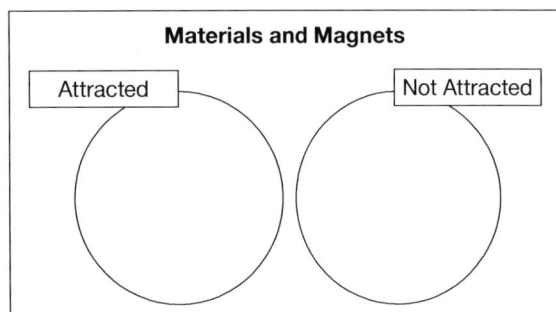

Materials and Magnets

Attracted   Not Attracted

Complete the sorting mat together using examples of objects tested throughout the module. Names of objects can be recorded on sticky notes and attached to the sorting mat.

As a class, co-construct and record a class statement on chart paper that answers the question:

- What kinds of objects do magnets attract?

Follow this discussion by watching videos to enhance understanding of how magnets work, such as "Magnets for Kids" at: <https://www.youtube.com/watch?v=5C-RM4fh5Xg>.

Expand 🎲 🖥

Provide students with an opportunity to explore magnets further by posing their own questions for individualized inquiry. They may wish to:

- Initiate a project at the Makerspace, such as designing and constructing model buildings using magnetic building blocks.
- Explore Loose Parts bins related to magnetism including both objects that are attracted to magnets, as well as those that are not (e.g., buttons, bolts, nuts, marbles, bread ties). Consider a provocation such as:
  - What can you learn about magnetism?
- Make fridge magnets using foam and magnetic tape. Foam can be cut into different shapes and decorated with additional foam. A strip of magnetic tape can be attached to the back of students' creations. Students can then test their fridge magnets on different surfaces to determine to which materials the magnet is attracted.
- Research a specific device that uses magnets (see Inquiry Through Research, page 26).
- Make a display of objects that are attracted to magnets.
- Write a song about magnets and perform it.
- Conduct an investigation or experiment based on their own inquiry questions.

As students explore and select ideas to expand learning, provide support and guidance as needed, and offer access to materials and resources that will enable students to conduct their chosen investigations.

▶

Portage & Main Press, 2018 · Hands-On Science for British Columbia · Properties of Energy for Grades K–2 · ISBN: 978-1-55379-798-2

Learning Centre A

At the learning centre, provide a fishing pond (a large basin filled with a variety of small objects—some that will attract magnets and some that will not) and fishing rods (tie string to metre sticks and then tie a magnet to the end of each string). Also provide a low divider (e.g., a piece of cardboard leaning against a chair), paper clips, a digital camera, writing paper, pencils, and a copy of the Learning-Centre Task Card: Going Fishing (3.17.2) and copies of the Template: Spinner (3.17.3):

Learning Centre

Let's Go Fishing!

1. Work in pairs.
   - One student stands and holds the fishing rod.
   - The other student sits by the fishing pond.
2. The seated student spins the spinner.
   - If the spinner lands on a √, place a magnetic object on the fishing rod and call out, "It's a catch!"
   - If the spinner lands on an X, call out, "No catch!"
3. The fisher gets three tries. Then, switch roles.
4. Once you have "caught" all of the objects possible, sort and display all objects.
5. Take a photograph, and draw your final results.

3.17.2

Download this template at <www.portageandmainpress.com/product/HOSEnergyK2>.

Demonstrate the use of the spinner for students before they visit the centre. Place a paper clip on the centre dot of the spinner and hold it in place

Date: _____   Name: _____

Spinner

3.17.3

with the tip of a pencil. The paper clip will spin freely when flicked.

Have students work in pairs, with one sitting beside the pond and one standing with the fishing rod. Use the divider to make sure the fisher cannot see the pond. The seated student spins the spinner to determine if the fisher will make a catch. If the spinner lands on a checkmark (√), the student guides the fishing rod magnet to an object to catch, then calls out "It's a catch!" If the spinner lands on an X, the student calls out "No catch!"

The fisher gets three tries, and then the students switch roles. Once they have "caught" all of the objects possible, have the students sort and display all objects, take a photograph, and then draw their final results. They may also construct their own sorting mat for this task.

Portage & Main Press, 2018 · Hands-On Science for British Columbia · Properties of Energy for Grades K–2 · ISBN: 978-1-55379-798-2

Learning Centre B

At the learning centre, provide a large basin filled with sand or uncooked rice (or use a sand or water table), as well as at least 20 magnetic items (e.g., nails, paper clips, screws, steel teaspoons, steel thimbles) and several nonmagnetic items hidden in it. Also provide a copy of the Learning-Centre Task Card: Treasure Hunt (3.17.4):

Learning Centre

Treasure Hunt

1. **Work as a group to go on a treasure hunt! Use a magnet to look for the buried treasures at the centre.**

2. **Sort the objects into two groups to show which are attracted to magnets and which are not.**

3. **Can your group find one more object that is attracted to magnets, and one that is not attracted to magnets? Bury your treasures!**

3.17.4

Download this template at <www.portageandmainpress.com/product/HOSEnergyK2>.

Challenge students to find the "buried treasures" using only magnets.

Students can also be challenged to find additional objects to add to the centre.

Formative Assessment

Have students use the sorting mat from Explore Part Five to show which objects from the lesson are attracted to magnets and which are not. Ask students to either write or draw the objects attracted to magnets in the left circle and the objects not attracted to magnets in the right circle. This task focuses on students sorting and classifying using drawings or text. Use the ANECDOTAL RECORD template on page 50 to provide descriptive feedback to students about how they classified objects and explained their sorting rules.

Embed Part One: Talking Circle

Revisit the guided inquiry question: **Which objects do magnets attract?** Have students share their experiences and knowledge, provide examples, and ask further inquiry questions.

Embed Part Two

- Add to the pyramid chart as students learn new concepts, answer some of their own inquiry questions, and ask new inquiry questions.

- Add new terms and illustrations to the word wall. Include the words in languages other than English, such as Indigenous languages, as appropriate.

- Focus on students' use of the Core Competencies. Have students reflect on how they used one of the Core Competencies (Thinking, Communicating, or Personal and Social Skills) during the various lesson activities. Project one of the CORE COMPETENCY DISCUSSION PROMPTS templates (pages 38-42), and use it to inspire group reflection. Referring to the template, choose one or two "I Can" statements on which to focus. Students then use the "I Can" statements to provide evidence of how they demonstrated that competency. Ask

▶

17

questions directly related to that competency to inspire discussion. For example:

- What are you proud of in your learning today? (Personal Awareness and Responsibility)

Have students reflect orally, encouraging participation, questions, and the sharing of evidence. (See page 29 for more information on these templates.)

As part of this process, students can also set goals. For example, ask:

- What would you do differently next time and why?
- How will you know if you are successful in meeting your goal?

- To encourage self-reflection, provide prompts that students can use to cite examples of how they have used the Core Competencies in their learning. For this purpose, the CORE COMPETENCY SELF-REFLECTION FRAMES (pages 43-47) can be used throughout the learning process. There are five frames provided to address the Core Competencies: Communication, Creative Thinking, Critical Thinking, Positive Personal and Cultural Identity, and Personal Awareness and Responsibility. Teachers can conference individually with students to support self-reflection, or students may complete prompts using words and pictures.

Again, have students set goals by considering what they might do differently on future tasks and how they will know if they are successful in meeting their goal.

NOTE: Use the same prompts from these sheets over time to see how thinking changes with different activities.

Enhance

- **Family Connection**: Have students take home a magnet. Provide students with the following sentence starter:
  - Objects in my home that are attracted to magnets are _____.

Have students complete the sentence starter at home. Family members can help students draw and write about this topic. Have students share their sentences with the rest of the class.

Portage & Main Press, 2018 · Hands-On Science for British Columbia · Properties of Energy for Grades K-2 · ISBN: 978-1-55379-798-2

18 What Is Static Electricity, and How Is It Created?

Information for Teachers

All matter is made up of *atoms*. Atoms are made up of smaller particles called *protons*, *electrons*, and *neutrons*. Protons carry positive charge, electrons carry negative charge, and neutrons have no charge.

Static electricity is electricity that builds up on an object due to an imbalance of negative and positive charges. Static electricity can be produced when one object rubs against another. When you rub a cloth against a balloon, some electrons are transferred from the cloth to the balloon, which then becomes negatively charged. As with magnets, negative charges repel negative charges. A negatively charged balloon will attract an uncharged balloon. A charged balloon will repel another similarly charged balloon.

The activities in this lesson work best on cold, dry winter days, when it is easier to produce static electricity. Moisture in the air allows accumulated static electricity to discharge, making it more difficult to achieve good results from the experiments.

Materials

- inflated balloons (one for each pair of students)
- combs (one for each working group)
- wool mittens (one for each working group)
- tissue paper
- paper
- aluminum foil
- various materials to test with static electricity (e.g., copper wire, wax pieces, sawdust, thread, Styrofoam chips)
- scissors (one pair for each student)
- pyramid chart (from lesson 13)

Engage

Ask students if they have ever experienced a shock when they touched something after walking in socks on carpet or if their hair has ever stood up on end after brushing it or wearing a toque. Encourage students to discuss these events and elaborate on other similar incidents. Ask:

- Why do you think this happens?

Have students work in pairs. Provide each pair with a wool mitten and an inflated balloon. Have one student hold the balloon by the tied end, while the other rubs the balloon with the mitten. As a class, count to 20 while the students do this.

Next, have the student holding the balloon hold it near a wall or window. Have students observe as the balloons "stick" to the surface, and infer why this happens.

Introduce the guided inquiry question: **What is static electricity, and how is it created?**

Explore Part One

In small working groups, have students cut or tear up the paper, aluminum foil, and tissue paper into small bits, about the size of a dime. Provide each group with a comb and a wool mitten.

Ask the groups to spread the tissue paper bits onto another sheet of paper. Have one student from each group use the wool mitten to rub the comb briskly, about 10 times, back and forth. This should produce a static electric charge.

Now, have students hold the charged comb near the tissue paper bits without touching either the bits or the sheet of paper the tissue paper bits are on, and observe what occurs. Ask:

- What happened to the pieces of tissue paper?

▶

Portage & Main Press, 2018 · *Hands-On Science for British Columbia · Properties of Energy for Grades K–2* · ISBN: 978-1-55379-798-2

- Why do you think this happened?
- What do you think will happen if you do the same test using small bits of regular paper or aluminum foil, rather than the tissue paper?

Have students test their predictions by rubbing the comb with the wool mitten and observing its effects on the paper and on the aluminum foil.

Explore Part Two 🖥️

Repeat the above activity having students choose and prepare other materials to test (e.g., cut thread into 1-cm lengths, break up wax into pea-size pieces, strip copper wire and cut into 1-cm pieces). Students can test different materials to see how each reacts to the charged comb. Encourage students to make predictions before they test the materials.

Following the investigation, ask:

- How did the different materials react to the charged comb?
- Which materials jumped onto the comb and stayed there?
- Which materials attached themselves to the comb, fell off, and then reattached themselves?
- Did any materials try to attach themselves but could not actually be attracted?
- Why do you think that happened?
- How was the comb like a magnet?
- What do you think caused certain materials to be attracted to the comb?
- What caused the comb to attract materials?
- Do you think that rubbing the comb with the wool mitten did anything to the comb? What?

Have students share their ideas. To further explore static electricity, watch videos such as:

- "The Sticky Balloon Trick! | Physics for Kids" <https://www.youtube.com/watch?v=5TAIUCYMIIQ>

- "6 Static Electricity Balloon Experiments You can do at home Easy Kid Science – STEM" <https://www.youtube.com/watch?v=V7soAsGyfWQ>

Expand 🖥️ 🎲

Provide students with an opportunity to explore static electricity further by posing their own questions for individualized inquiry. They may wish to:

- Initiate a project at the Makerspace, such as designing and constructing an electroscope.
- Test materials other than the wool mitten to see if they cause static charge to build up in a balloon or comb.
- Research lightning to find out how it is related to static electricity (see Inquiry Through Research, page 26).
- Collect video clips of lightning to create a video put to music.
- Conduct an investigation or experiment based on their own inquiry questions.

As students explore and select ideas to expand learning, provide support and guidance as needed, and offer access to materials and resources that will enable students to conduct their chosen investigations.

Embed Part One: Talking Circle

Revisit the guided inquiry question: **What is static electricity, and how is it created?** Have students share their experiences and knowledge, provide examples, and ask further inquiry questions.

Embed Part Two

- Add to the pyramid chart as students learn new concepts, answer some of their own inquiry questions, and ask new inquiry questions.

▶

Portage & Main Press, 2018 · *Hands-On Science for British Columbia · Properties of Energy for Grades K–2* · ISBN: 978-1-55379-798-2

18

- Add new terms and illustrations to the word wall. Include the words in languages other than English, such as Indigenous languages, as appropriate.

- Focus on students' use of the Core Competencies. Have students reflect on how they used one of the Core Competencies (Thinking, Communicating, or Personal and Social skills) during the various lesson activities. Project one of the CORE COMPETENCY DISCUSSION PROMPTS templates (pages 38-42), and use it to inspire group reflection. Referring to the template, choose one or two "I Can" statements on which to focus. Students then use the "I Can" statements to provide evidence of how they demonstrated that competency. Ask questions directly related to that competency to inspire discussion. For example:

  - How did you care for yourself and make safe choices today? (Personal Awareness and Responsibility)

  Have students reflect orally, encouraging participation, questions, and the sharing of evidence. (See page 29 for more information on these templates.)

  As part of this process, students can also set goals. For example, ask:

  - What would you do differently next time and why?

  - How will you know if you are successful in meeting your goal?

- To encourage self-reflection, provide prompts that students can use to cite examples of how they have used the Core Competencies in their learning. For this purpose, the CORE COMPETENCY SELF-REFLECTION FRAMES (pages 43-47) can be used throughout the learning process. There are five frames provided to address the Core Competencies: Communication, Creative Thinking, Critical Thinking, Positive Personal and Cultural Identity, and Personal Awareness and Responsibility. Teachers can conference individually with students to support self-reflection, or students may complete prompts using words and pictures.

  Again, have students set goals by considering what they might do differently on future tasks and how they will know if they are successful in meeting their goal.

NOTE: Use the same prompts from these sheets over time to see how thinking changes with different activities.

Enhance 🖥️1

- **Family Connection**: Provide students with the following sentence starter:

  - Examples of static electricity at home are _____.

  Have students complete the sentence starter at home. Family members can help students draw and write about this topic. Have students share their sentences with the rest of the class.

- Have students experiment with charged balloons. Ask them to spread out small pieces of tissue paper across a table. Tell them to rub the balloon briskly for 10 seconds with the wool mitten. Have them bring the balloon close to the tissue paper pieces and observe the reaction. Then, have students neutralize the balloon by wiping it with a damp cloth (make sure no water remains on the balloon). Now, ask students to test the balloon using materials other than the mitten (e.g., fake fur, a cotton or silk cloth, burlap, hair). Have students record how much tissue paper is attracted each time and create a pictograph of their results.

- Tie this lesson to previous learning about lightning and thunder. Have students research the role of static electricity and

▶

friction in the creation of lightning and thunder.

- Tie threads to two inflated balloons. Have students hold them so the balloons are a few centimetres apart. Charge one of the balloons with the wool mitten or with a plastic bag. Hold the balloons apart again and observe (the balloons will be attracted because one is charged and the other is not). Have students predict what might happen if they rubbed both balloons with the mitten/ bag, and then test their predictions (the balloons will be repelled because both are charged).

Portage & Main Press, 2018 · Hands-On Science for British Columbia · Properties of Energy for Grades K–2 · ISBN: 978-1-55379-798-2

19 Inquiry Project: How Can I Design a Toy or Game That Uses Energy?

Materials

- toys that require muscular force for movement (e.g., toy cars, hockey sticks/pucks)
- toys that store energy to create movement (e.g., jack-in-the-box, elastic band-propelled plane, windup toys, slingshots)
- toys and games that use sound or light (e.g., lightsabers, toy microphones, Operation game)
- toys and games that use magnets (e.g., magnetic building blocks)
- Template: How Can I Design a Toy or Game That Uses Energy? (3.19.1)
- chart paper
- markers
- drawing paper
- building materials as identified by students to create their games or toys (e.g., cardboard boxes, cardboard, poster board, paper, string or yarn, tape, glue, pencil crayons, ball bearings, paper clips, magnets)
- digital camera
- pyramid chart (from lesson 13)

Engage

Have students sit in a circle. In the centre of the circle, display toys and games that use muscular force, store energy, or use sound, light, or magnet. Ask individual students to demonstrate how each toy/game is used (e.g., push a toy car, wind up the windup toy, twist the elastic band on the propeller of the airplane to make it fly, turn on the light on a lightsaber, sing into the microphone). Ask students:

- How did the objects move?
- What did you need to do to make the objects move?

- As a class, sort the toys/games into groups according to how they move (e.g., pushing, winding, twisting). Other games that do not move, but use light or sound, can be sorted into separate groups.

On chart paper, create a chart like the one below:

Energy	Examples
muscles	
light	
sound	
magnets	

Have the class complete the chart using the toys and games on display. Encourage students to brainstorm other examples of toys and games that use these forms of energy.

Explain to students they will be demonstrating their knowledge about energy by designing a game or toy that uses one or more of these kinds of energy.

Introduce the guided inquiry question: **How can I design a toy or game that uses energy?**

Explore Part One

For this activity, students can work individually, in pairs, or in groups to design and create a game or toy that uses at least one of the forms of energy studied. Some examples may include:

- muscular energy: pull toy, catapult, yo-yo, Chinese checkers, ball toss, paper plane contest/game, spear toss, archery game

⚠️ **SAFETY NOTE:** Ensure designs are not made with pointed spear or arrow heads.

Portage & Main Press, 2018 · Hands-On Science for British Columbia · Properties of Energy for Grades K–2 · ISBN: 978-1-55379-798-2

- light energy: lightsaber, coloured play dough, magnifiers, sunglasses
- sound energy: megaphone, musical instrument, bell, buzzer
- magnetic energy: maze, fishing game, car or boat race, magnetic building block model or sculpture

As a class, co-construct criteria for the project. For example:

- includes one or more of the forms of energy learned about
- uses a variety of materials, including recycled items
- includes rules for playing with the game or toy
- includes explanation of how forces, motion, and energy are used in the game or toy

Give students ample time and opportunity to work on creating their games or toys. The specific amount of time can be discussed and decided upon as a class.

Have students create blueprints of their designs on drawing paper before they begin construction. They should include labelled diagrams and lists of required materials. These should be reviewed with the teacher. Have students use drawing paper or the Template: How Can I Design a Toy or Game That Uses Energy (3.19.1):

Date: _____ Name: _____

How Can I Design a Toy or Game That Uses Energy?

Criteria for the Project:
_____
_____
_____
_____

What I am making: _____

Blueprint of my design

Materials Needed:
_____
_____
_____
_____

3.19.1

Download this template at <www.portageandmainpress.com/product/HOSEnergyK2>.

Explore Part Two

Have students and groups present their projects to the rest of the class, demonstrating how it is played or used. Be sure each student or group of students reports about:

- which forms of energy their toy or game uses
- what they learned
- what they would change in their model
- what things worked best
- what was the hardest part of the construction

Have students use digital cameras to take photographs of their completed games and toys. Students can compare these to their original designs to see what changed as they were constructing their game or toy.

▶

Portage & Main Press, 2018 · Hands-On Science for British Columbia · Properties of Energy for Grades K–2 · ISBN: 978-1-55379-798-2

19

Embed Part One: Talking Circle

Revisit the guided inquiry question: **How can I design a toy or game that uses energy?** Have students share their experiences and knowledge and provide examples to consolidate learning.

Embed Part Two

- Add to the pyramid chart as students learn new concepts, answer some of their own inquiry questions, and ask new inquiry questions.

- Add new terms and illustrations to the word wall. Include the words in languages other than English, such as Indigenous languages, as appropriate.

- Focus on students' use of the Core Competencies. Have students reflect on how they used one of the Core Competencies (Thinking, Communicating, or Personal and Social Skills) during the various lesson activities. Project one of the CORE COMPETENCY DISCUSSION PROMPTS templates (pages 38-42), and use it to inspire group reflection. Referring to the template, choose one or two "I Can" statements on which to focus. Students then use the "I Can" statements to provide evidence of how they demonstrated that competency. Ask questions directly related to that competency to inspire discussion. For example:

  - How did you show that you were an active listener today? (Communication)

Have students reflect orally, encouraging participation, questions, and the sharing of evidence. (See page 29 for more information on these templates.)

As part of this process, students can also set goals. For example, ask:

- What would you do differently next time and why?
- How will you know if you are successful in meeting your goal?

- To encourage self-reflection, provide prompts that students can use to cite examples of how they have used the Core Competencies in their learning. For this purpose, the CORE COMPETENCY SELF-REFLECTION FRAMES (pages 43-47) can be used throughout the learning process. There are five frames provided to address the Core Competencies: Communication, Creative Thinking, Critical Thinking, Positive Personal and Cultural Identity, and Personal Awareness and Responsibility. Teachers can conference individually with students to support self-reflection, or students may complete prompts using words and pictures.

Again, have students set goals by considering what they might do differently on future tasks and how they will know if they are successful in meeting their goal.

NOTE: Use the same prompts from these sheets over time to see how thinking changes with different activities.

Enhance

- **Family Connection**: Have students take home their inquiry project to play/demonstrate with family. Provide students with the following sentence starter:

  - Games and toys that use energy that we could make at home are _____.

Have students complete the sentence starter at home. Family members can help students draw and write about this topic. Have students share their sentences with the rest of the class.

Module Assessment Summary

- Consider having a collection of student work gathered in a portfolio, so students can examine and discuss these artifacts of learning during a conference. This collection may include artifacts such as photographs

▶

Portage & Main Press, 2018 · Hands-On Science for British Columbia · Properties of Energy for Grades K–2 · ISBN: 978-1-55379-798-2

19

that they have taken, drawings, and place-based journals. This will allow them to recall specific activities and learning experiences, and to reflect on their use of the Core Competencies throughout the module of study.

■ Have students take home a copy of the FAMILY AND COMMUNITY CONNECTIONS: ASSESSING TOGETHER template (page 57). Have them complete the sheet with a family or community member (with permission) to reflect on their learning about the properties of energy.

■ Have students focus on the CORE COMPETENCIES STUDENT REFLECTIONS MODULE SUMMARY template (page 48) to reflect on their use of the Core Competencies throughout the module. Students' reflections are recorded in the rectangle on the template (using pictures and text). Next, the student considers next steps in learning as related to that particular Core Competency. These reflections are recorded in the arrow in the template, again, using words and drawings.

■ It is beneficial to review all assessment templates completed throughout the module. This includes all documentation for student self-assessment, formative assessment, and summative assessment. This will provide a more comprehensive picture of student progress as related to the Big Ideas, Core Competencies, Curricular Competencies, and Content of the module.

Portage & Main Press, 2018 · Hands-On Science for British Columbia · Properties of Energy for Grades K–2 · ISBN: 978-1-55379-798-2

Appendix: Image Banks

Images appearing in the appendix are thumbnails from the Image Banks referenced in the lessons. Corresponding full-page, high-resolution images can be printed or projected for the related lessons, and are found on the Portage & Main Press website at: <www.portageandmainpress.com/ product/HOSENERGYK2>. Use the password **LIGHTANDSOUND** to access the download for free. This link and password can also be used to access the reproducible templates for this module.

Please follow these steps to retrieve the images and reproducible templates for this book.

1. Go to <www.portageandmainpress.com/ product/HOSENERGYK2>.
2. Type the password **LIGHTANDSOUND** into the password field.
3. Select Add to Cart.
4. Select View Cart.
5. Select Proceed to Checkout. No coupon code is required.
6. Enter your billing information or log in to your existing account using the prompt at the top of the page.
7. Select Place Order.
8. Under Order Details, click the link for your download.
9. Save the file to the desired location on your computer.

NOTE: This is a large file. Download times will vary due to your internet speeds.

Lesson 6: How Can We Move an Object?
Movement in Daily Life

1. Dogsled

2. Sto:lo, Coast Salish Toboggan

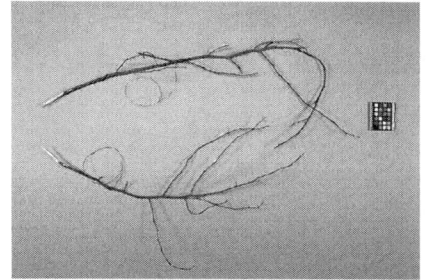
3. Dunne-Za Rabbit Snare

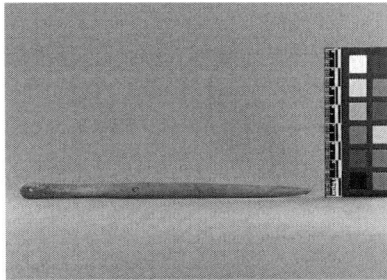
4. Haida Bone Needle

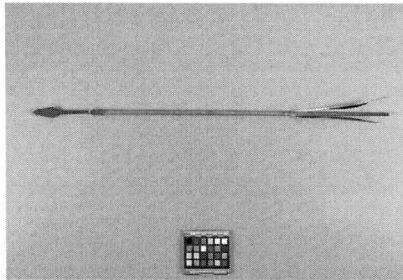
5. Sto:lo, Coast Salish or Kwantlen Arrow

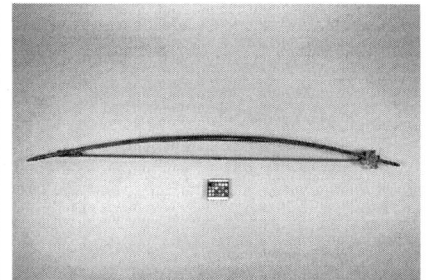
6. Mamalilikala or Kwakwaka'wakw Bow

7. Ktunaxa Sturgeon-Nosed Canoe

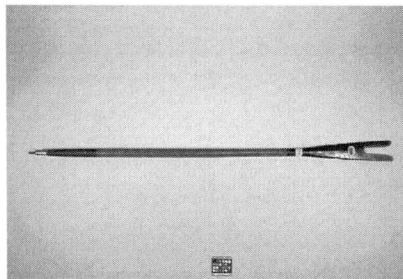
8. Da'naxda'xw, Kwakwaka'wakw Harpoon

9. Kayak

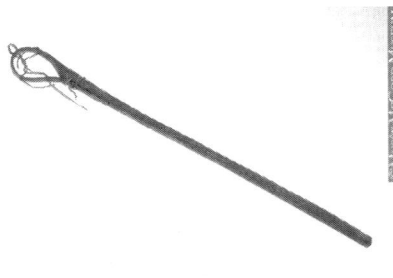
10. Eastern Woodlands Lacrosse Stick

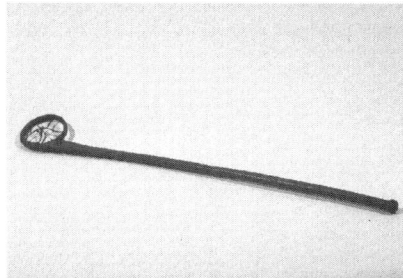
11. Iroquois Lacrosse Stick

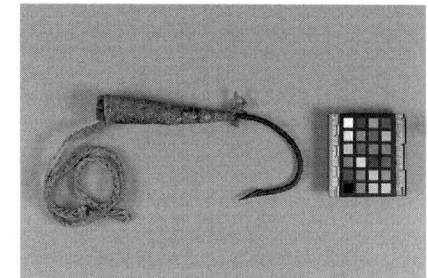
12. Northwest Coast Fish Hook

Portage & Main Press, 2019 · Hands-On Science for British Columbia · Properties of Energy for Grades K–2 · ISBN: 978-1-55379-799-9

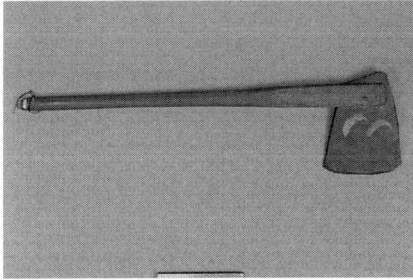

13. Tsimshian Axe

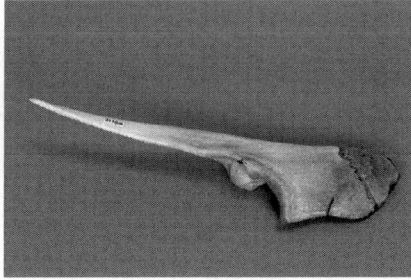

14. Sto:lo, Coast Salish Basket-Making Awl

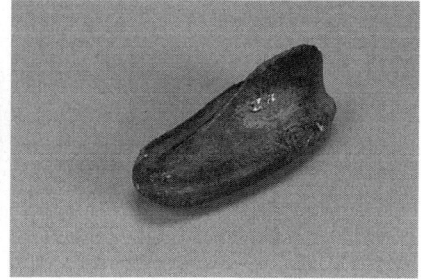

15. Stl'atl'imx, Interior Salish Scraper
Uses: scraping skins, pounding and grinding red ochre

Image Credits:

1 – Winters, Snow, Nature, Mountain, Landscape, Cold, White by 3938030. Used under CC0 licence.

2 – toboggan (Sled) Object ID #A4380, photographed by Derek Tan. Courtesy of UBC Museum of Anthropology, Vancouver, Canada.

3 – Rabbit Snare Object ID #Na722 a-b, photographed by Jessica Bushey. Courtesy of UBC Museum of Anthropology, Vancouver, Canada.

4 – Needle Object ID #A7176, photographed by Jessica Bushey. Courtesy of UBC Museum of Anthropology, Vancouver, Canada.

5 – Arrow Object ID #Nb661, photographed by Kyla Bailey. Courtesy of UBC Museum of Anthropology, Vancouver, Canada.

6 – Bow Object ID #A6530, photographed by Jessica Bushey. Courtesy of UBC Museum of Anthropology, Vancouver, Canada.

7 – yaksumit (Sturgeon Nosed Canoe) Object ID #Nd714, photographed by Kyla Bailey. Courtesy of UBC Museum of Anthropology, Vancouver, Canada.

8 – Harpoon Object ID #A7475, photographed by Rebecca Pasch. Courtesy of UBC Museum of Anthropology, Vancouver, Canada.

9 – Think Outside Photo Contest Fairy Stone State Park by Virginia State Parks. Used under CC by 2.0 licence.

10 – McCord Museum ACC3189

11 – McCord Museum ACC3190

12 – Fish Hook Object ID #A1576, photographed by Jessica Bushey. Courtesy of UBC Museum of Anthropology, Vancouver, Canada.

13 – Axe Object ID #1432/4, photographed by Rebecca Pasch. Courtesy of UBC Museum of Anthropology, Vancouver, Canada.

14 – Awl Object ID #3116/9, photographed by Kyla Bailey. Courtesy of UBC Museum of Anthropology, Vancouver, Canada.

15 – Scraper Object ID #D1.228, photographed by Kyla Bailey. Courtesy of UBC Museum of Anthropology, Vancouver, Canada.

Portage & Main Press, 2019 · Hands-On Science for British Columbia · Properties of Energy for Grades K–2 · ISBN: 978-1-55379-799-9

Lesson 7: How Can We Move Loads More Easily?
Travois

1. Travois Carrying Child (Calgary, AB)

2. Blackfoot Travois (Fort McLeod, AB)

3. Travois (Fort McLeod, AB)

4. Cree Travois Belonging to Kuskita and Kenepequoshes (Calgary, AB)

Image Credits:

1 – McCord Museum MP-0000.2016.2
2 – McCord Museum MP-1986.64.4
3 – McCord Museum MP-1988.74.62
4 – McCord Museum VIEW-1817

Lesson 9: What Do We Know About Sources of Light?
Natural Sources of Light

1. Lightning

2. Lightning

3. Fireflies

4. Firefly Insect or Lightning Bug

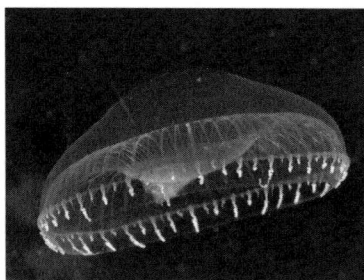
5. Aequorea Victoria Jellyfish

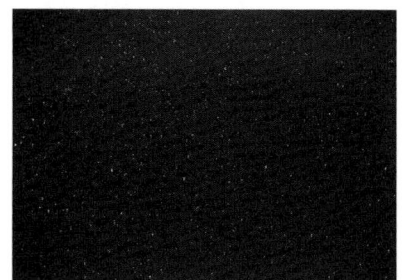
6. Stars

Portage & Main Press, 2019 · Hands-On Science for British Columbia · Properties of Energy for Grades K–2 · ISBN: 978-1-55379-799-9

7. Northern Lights or Aurora Borealis

8. Southern Lights or Aurora Australis

9. Meteor

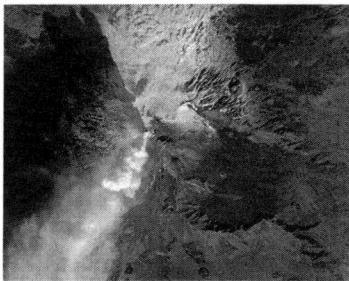

10. Erupting Volcano

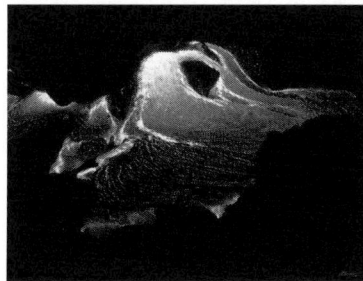

11. Lava Flow

12. Forest Fire

13. Forest Fire

Portage & Main Press, 2019 · Hands-On Science for British Columbia · Properties of Energy for Grades K–2 · ISBN: 978-1-55379-799-9

Lesson 15: How Do Musical Instruments Use Sound Energy?
Indigenous Instruments

1. Haida Drum

Materials: wood, animal skins, cotton fibre, metal

2. Tsimshian Drum

Materials: animal skin, wood, paint, metal

3. Coast Salish Box Drum

Materials: wood, paint, metal

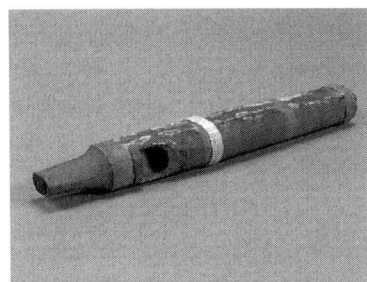

4. Kwikwasut'inuxw, Kwakwaka'wakw Whistle

Materials: wood, resin, twine, pitch

5. Northwest Coast Clappers

Materials: wood, fibre cording

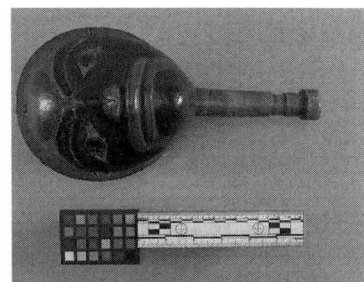

6. Nisga'a Rattle

Materials: wood, stone, bark, paint

Portage & Main Press, 2019 · Hands-On Science for British Columbia · Properties of Energy for Grades K–2 · ISBN: 978-1-55379-799-9

About the Contributors

Jennifer Lawson, PhD, is the originator and senior author of the Hands-On series in all subject areas. Jennifer is a former classroom teacher, resource/special education teacher, consultant, and principal. She continues to develop new Hands-On projects, and also serves as a school trustee for the St. James-Assiniboia School Division in Winnipeg, Manitoba.

Rosalind Poon has been a science teacher and Teacher Consultant for Assessment and Literacy with the Richmond School District for the past 18 years. In her current role, she works with school teams to plan and implement various aspects of the curriculum by collaborating with teams in professional inquiry groups on topics such as descriptive feedback, inquiry, assessment, and differentiation. Her passions include her family, dragon boating, cooking with the Instant Pot and making sure that all students have access to great hands-on science experiences.

Deidre Sagert specializes in early years education, and is currently working as the Early Years Support Teacher for the St. James-Assiniboia School Division. She brings 20 years of experience to her current role where she mentors early years teachers in incorporating play-based learning and inquiry into all subject areas. She is passionate about ensuring all students have access to a stimulating environment where they are engaged in hands on experiences and authentic learning. She enjoys spending time with her family in nature for rejuvenation and inspiration.

Melanie Nelson is from the In-SHUCK-ch and Stó:lō Nations, and has experience teaching kindergarten through grade 12, as well as adults in the Lower Mainland of British Columbia. She has taught in mainstream, adapted, modified, and alternate settings, at the classroom, whole school, and district levels. Trained as an educator in science, Melanie approaches Western science through an Indigenous worldview and with Indigenous ways of knowing. Her Master of Arts thesis explored the experience of Indigenous parents who have a child identified as having special needs in school, and she is currently completing a Doctor of Philosophy in School Psychology at the University of British Columbia.

Lisa Schwartz has been a Teacher Consultant for Assessment and Literacy with the Richmond School District for the past six years. As a consultant, Lisa facilitates professional learning with small groups and school staffs on topics such as the redesigned curriculum, Core Competencies, differentiation, inquiry, and assessment. She also works side by side with teachers co-planning, co-teaching and providing demonstration lessons to highlight quality, research-based instruction that supports all learners. Lisa is passionate about engagement, joyful learning and success for all students.

Portage & Main Press, 2019 · *Hands-On Science for British Columbia · Properties of Energy for Grades K-2* · ISBN: 978-1-55379-799-9